HAMISH

PATHFINDERS

HAMISH

The Memoirs of
Group Captain T.G.Mahaddie
DSO, DFC, AFC, CZMC, CENG, FRAeS

[handwritten inscription, partly illegible]

Signed for Andy an Jenny xxx
me love Baby and Ref. and.
with my Best Wishes — and
to Pathfinder the long
Press-on Regardless.

Hamish
Biggin Hill Bee and his Bod (PFT)
15 Sept. 90.

LONDON

IAN ALLAN LTD

In Memoriam

This book is dedicated to the memory of all those members of No 8 (PFF) Group RAF who failed to return.

First published 1989

ISBN 0 7110 1826 X

Published by Ian Allan Ltd, Shepperton, Surrey; and printed by Ian Allan Printing Ltd at their works at Coombelands in Runnymede, England

Contents

Acknowledgements

In truth, were I to acknowledge all the contributors to this 'ill-favoured thing, sir, but mine own', it would be as long as the book itself. I fear that I can only scribe those occasions which I remember and the people thereof, and here I am reminded of my dear and lamented friend Roddy Banks who wrote his memoirs called *I Kept No Diary*.

I should like to acknowledge Departments in general rather than personalities in particular that I have been associated with, not only in my movie activities but also in the more rarified atmosphere of high technology. I have dealt with several Assistant Chiefs of the Air Staff over the past 30 years and I am indebted to them and their Staffs for the courtesy and extreme kindness I have always enjoyed.

I should like to thank the RAF magazine *Air Clues* and the Director of Training (Flying) RAF, for permission to quote excerpts from an article in Chapter 12, written by myself and published in the April 1988 issue of the magazine.

This also applies to the Ministry of Defence's Air Historical Branch and its various heads of department who, from time to time, have been a crutch that I have been pleased to lean on.

I trust that my family will not be too embarrassed by *Hamish*, although I am certain they were aware that something was in the wind.

I am indebted to the late Chris Wren, the aviation cartoonist, who triggered me off on this project some 10 years ago but on his untimely death I lost heart; but the timely Christmas present of an Amstrad computer from a friendly Solicitor, W. R. Toozs-Hobson, started it all up again.

But by far the best of all spurs, a young girl volunteered to transpose my dialect from tape to type and painfully (ever so slowly) something of these 60 years emerged; this treasure we call Yvonne, and how she was able to translate a complete new range of Service verbiage into some kind of order I shall never know. The credit is hers alone and she can never be repaid.

I am also pleased to acknowledge help I have received from two 'ferrets': first Alan Cooper, researcher and author, and in equal status Ray Callow who has stored a rich harvest of Bomber Command memorabilia which I have been permitted to plunder.

Last but not least I am indebted to Dr Alfred Price, one time Electronics Officer within the RAF's V-Bomber Force, for drawing my attention to the Luftwaffe Staff paper highlighting AVM D. C. T. Bennett's activities with his Pathfinders.

6

1 The Prologue

'As this was to be my 45th bombing operation, after which aircrew members on Pathfinder squadrons were rested, it was therefore with a little trepidation that I approached this evening's trip.

'For reasons best known to themselves, the powers that be had decided that because of the lack of height attained by a Stirling over the target, all armoured plating, except for that shielding the pilot and the flare chute, should be removed. This included not only the rather large piece behind the wireless operator, which protected him and the radio equipment, but also the small piece that formed the seat of the mid-upper turret, which was replaced by a canvas sling.

'It was a cold but dry February afternoon with some cloud as we trooped into the Ops room for the briefing. The Station Commander welcomed us as usual and gave us the news that tonight's target was Cologne. There was the black tape with its doglegs to the target and back, the Met Officer with his usual "some cloud cover en route but clearing over the target", then the instructions from the various leaders. We gathered our flying rations (which contained a can of orange juice, bar of chocolate, small packet of biscuits and a few sweets) then the NCOs amongst us made our way to the YMCA hut where the people in charge always filled our flasks (it tasted better than the coffee that they dished up in the Sergeants' Mess). From there we went to the crew room in the hangar to get kitted up in the electrically-wired inner suit and the leather outer suit, Mae West and parachute harness, picked up our parachutes and boarded the crew bus to take us to Stirling "C" Charlie standing in line on the perimeter track, at the southwestern end of the main runway.

'They were certainly a magnificent sight, a dozen large aircraft in a curving line around the edge of the airfield, a small knot of men clustered about each giant Stirling, quiet subdued talk coming from them as they completed their various tasks. We climbed into "Charlie" and stowed our 'chutes and rations in their respective places. Next we checked our own equipment — in my case cocking my guns a couple of times to make sure they worked smoothly — the rear gunner fired a short burst into the ground at the rear of the aircraft. With everything looking OK we left the aircraft for a last stretch and, if necessary, relieved our bladders under the tailplane. As was my usual practice, I gave my pack of biscuits to the flight mechanic and we then got back on board.

'One by one the engines roared into life: the aircraft now belonged to the skipper and engineer. The rest of us tended to our own duties, for my part the testing of the turret and the gun-release mechanism with the guns on safe.

'The skipper called each position over the intercom in turn, and we were ready to take our place on the end of the runway. It was our turn next: a green light from the Aldis lamp and we were away. Bags of chat between the skipper and Jock the engineer — rich mixture, flaps, full power etc — then undercarriage up, course setting from the navigator and we were off. Time 19.15hrs.

'This was only our second trip with H$_2$S equipment on board, the first one being two nights earlier on a raid on Hamburg. The equipment went u/s over the Zuider Zee and the mission was aborted; this time however, all appeared OK. As we climbed over the English countryside I kept thinking that this was my last trip, I hoped everything was going to be OK; my mind went back to the other crews I had flown with since joining the squadron in September '41, some of whom had completed their tour of Ops, more who had not made it. Half of me was sorry to be leaving this very closeknit crew of ours, the other half glad I was nearly there.

'We were over the North Sea by then, eyes were accustomed to the darkness and from Alec the rear gunner the request "Permission to test the guns skipper". On the affirmative we both gave a short burst; we were on the alert from then on.

'More thoughts as we flew out over the sea. I wondered how Joan (my ex-WAAF M/T driver wife) was this evening, she was five months pregnant and living with my parents in North Buckinghamshire; maybe I'd get some leave after this Op to see her.

'Enemy coast ahead, there were a few searchlights sweeping the sky and the occasional flak burst. As we were among the first aircraft in the bomber stream there was not a lot of opposition at first, but it got heavier as we crossed the coast. A new heading was received from the navigator: the skipper turned to the new course and started a gentle weave. There was a certain amount of cloud cover, for which we were thankful; we had dodged the searchlights so far, but others were not so lucky and were having quite a hectic time. It was not long before the navigator gave the final course correction to take us into the target. As we approached, some of the early birds were already there; the flak and searchlights had increased and the cloud cover had decreased. The skipper increased his weaving and the bomb aimer left his front turret ready to drop our bombload; in the mid-upper turret I now had to cover the front of the aircraft as well, doing a 360° search for enemy nightfighters. The bomb aimer now gave his instructions to the pilot and we were flying straight and level with the target coming up in the bombsights. Bomb doors open with a "left left, steady, right, steady — bombs gone". The aircraft gave a lurch upwards, from the bomb aimer came "hold it steady for the photo". Suddenly there was an almighty explosion as a flak shell burst on our starboard side, at the same time there was the sound of cannon shells ripping through the fuselage and the smell of burnt cordite filled the plane. I felt a sharp pain in my right buttock, as if a knife had been stuck in me. My first thought was this is it, so much for the canvas seat.

'The turret went dead, the hydraulic pipes giving me power had been shot through. I tried to speak over the intercom but this was dead also. The aircraft went into a dive and my first reaction was to get out. As no instructions could be

8

given over the intercom and my turret being u/s, I got down from my seat to find out what was happening. The inside of the aircraft glowed like a Christmas tree; there were green spots everywhere — I presumed them to be some sort of phosphorus.

'As the aircraft had now come to a more even keel I went towards the rear turret to see if Alec was OK; he appeared to be moving his turret by hand, so I assumed he wasn't injured. Looking forward I could see several large holes in the starboard side, then I noticed a torch being flashed amidships. Making my way towards this light I found the engineer at work, repairing the aileron controls with pieces of wire which he had conjured up from somewhere. Going on into the wireless cabin I found that Eddie the wireless op had been badly injured in the hand, a cannon shell had ripped open the sleeve of his flying jacket, severed the two middle fingers of his right hand and gone on into the W/T set, wrecking it.

'There was a first-aid pad on his wound by then. I gave him a shot of morphia in the arm and put a tourniquet on it; by then another member of the crew had come back and relieved me. I then went back to my turret and kept watch — trying to work my guns manually, which proved next to impossible. Luckily we were not attacked again.

'Meanwhile, the skipper was fighting with the aircraft. Having had the aileron controls badly mangled by the cannon shells he could only fly the aircraft by varying the power of the engines. Jock, our engineer — clambering in the wing root — did some very good work with his pieces of wire which enabled the skipper to gain partial control of "C" Charlie and set course for home.

'With all special equipment u/s, Tommy our navigator guided us with the astro compass, and did such good work that we broke cloud over Waterbeach — just five miles from base and on our home circuit. Never was I so pleased to see the homing searchlight that invariably shone over Oakington. By word of mouth we received orders to take up crash positions, and a red distress cartridge was fired.

'Alec Clift and I sat with our backs to the bulkhead facing aft, and just before touchdown put our hands behind our heads. My hands felt all wet and sticky, having banged my head a few times during the return flight. I wondered what on earth had happened. The skipper made a very good landing and the emergency crews raced up to us as we taxied to a halt. Alec shone his torch on my hands and head. The sticky liquid, although red in colour, turned out to be tomato juice; it had dripped from the dinghy pack, stowed above my head, which had been punctured by the shrapnel.

'As soon as we had rolled to a stop and climbed down, the first thing I did was to kiss the ground — the 45th Op was over. The injured wireless op was taken away by ambulance, the rest of us were taken for debriefing. When I reported the sharp pain in my rear the MO had my trousers down. I was given an injection and shipped off to Ely Hospital for X-rays. It was found that a small piece of shrapnel was embedded in my right buttock, but it was left there and I was told it would work itself out. To this day it has never done so.

'In the cold light of day the aircraft looked a sorry mess, the H$_2$S cupola and scanning gear had been shot away, and according to what the ground crew told the skipper, there were 174 cannon shell hits on the fuselage and wings. One of the rear wheels was punctured and there were one or two large holes from a flak burst. I still have in my possession a 20mm cannon shell that buried itself in the skipper's seat parachute . . . Hamish was a very lucky man that night, as indeed we all were.

'It wasn't my last trip however. On 8 March the original crew flew in Stirling "V" Victor one last trip together, taking 24 SBCs of incendiaries to Lorient, luckily with no untoward incidents. This was my last trip and the skipper was whisked away to Pathfinder HQ to be chief poacher for AVM Don Bennett.'

The crew

Skipper	Wg Cdr T. G. Mahaddie DSO, DFC, AFC	(Hamish)
Navigator	Flt Lt F. D. J. Thompson DFC & Bar	(Tommy)
Bomb aimer	Plt Off I. R. S. Luton DFC	(Jock)
Flight engineer	Flt Sgt C. Stewart DFM	(Jock)
*Wireless operator**	Flg Off I. J. Edwards DFM	(Eddie)
Mid-upper gunner	Flt Sgt R. C. Pointer DFM	(Bob)
Rear gunner	Flt Sgt A. Clift DFM	(Alec)

* Plt Off A. H. Bywater DFC (Archie), the regular W/Op with this crew, was on leave for one week having just got married

Bob Pointer DFM

2 *In the Beginning . . .*

I was born, Thomas Gilbert Mahaddie, on 19 March 1911 in Leith, Scotland. My earliest memory was being handed around a railway carriage in the Waverley station, Edinburgh, and being kissed by a crowd of drunken Gordon Highlander Reservists on their way to their depot in Aberdeen, to join the Colours. The date — 4 August 1914. As soon as my mother saw the train on its way, we took the renowned Edinburgh cable car to a photographer at Piershill to have my very first picture taken, which was a shouted instruction as my father disappeared into the darkness of a Princes Street tunnel and the acrid smoke of what I was told to be a 'Puffing Billy'. I have never been able to identify the photographer Alec Roberts' establishment, but I think that it had a balcony. I was told that each train which passed just happened to be the one that was taking Tam Mahaddie away to kill the Kaiser and win the war.

My mother was a delicate creature and a cripple who had to wear a large, specially made boot as she had a shortened leg. She was, nevertheless, an expert dressmaker and as I was to learn later, was the only reason that we lived with some degree of plenty during the Kaiser's War.

During the war my mother worked in a factory making endless ground sheets which I was told could be turned into trench capes. This I wondered at. The factory which was in Leith had what would now be called a crèche where the children could go and play and be looked after whilst the mothers got on with the ground sheets . . . and the war.

By contrast, my father was very much the soldier and something of a mystery. Whereas many of my Army friends can trace their ancestry back and produce forebears who were generals and colonels, some of them were surprised to learn of my Army background but shocked to learn that Tam somehow managed to join the Gordons as a drummer-boy and, 22 years later, reached the rank of Private soldier. This has always been a great mystery to me because I remember seeing photographs of my father in hospital uniform wearing sergeant's stripes (which I understand was the practice then) and later, after the war, he was a corporal. The reason for demotion was never made clear to me.

Despite these fluctuations in his status I remember him fondly on his infrequent leaves as someone with a great sense of fun. He could tell endless tales, normally with himself as the butt. In his youth he seemed to be involved with many sports and I have seen evidence of his playing goalkeeper for a select Scottish hockey team — on roller-skates. In fact in our tenement 'penthouse' I once unearthed several roller-skates which I cannibalised until finally there was only one, at which point I gave up the unequal struggle on a solo skate.

One of these many memories I find myself repeating, even today, is to retrace our Sunday morning walks from my home in Pilrig, Leith, to a hotel near the Tron Kirk (where my aunt worked as a housekeeper) stopping first at a statue, halfway up the Mound, of a kilted figure representing the Black Watch who died in the Boer War. The same litany took place every Sunday. Dad Tam: 'You promise me you'll never tell anybody 'til 'am deed that I stood for the man who made that statue.' I duly promised, crossed my heart and spat — which was the custom of small boys at the time — and I never did break that promise to Dad Tam whilst he lived, and to this day I believe in my heart that the figure overlooking Princes Street Gardens is in the image of my father, complete with a handsome Kitchener moustache.

My mother told her version. Soon after they married my father was out of work (he was a house painter). He answered an advertisement in *The Scotsman* asking for ex-Black Watch volunteers to pose for a sculptor. In his desperation Tam gave the name of a Black Watch friend, got the job and donned the Black Watch kilt for a few coppers an hour — the shame of it. Years later, long after Tam was 'deed', I did some research at the Black Watch archives in Perth and was assured that no such thing could ever have happened. After all 'no Gordon would know *how* to wear the Black Watch tartan'. I fared no better with the Gordons in Aberdeen: 'but no Gordon would be found deed/dead in the Tartan of the Black Watch.'

I was told they know how to honour their dead in the Highland regiments, but the next time I go to Edinburgh I will gaze up at Dad Tam, and see both of my sons in that solid likeness (despite the Kitchener moustache). I will spring a tear, come to attention and salute that old Scottish soldier who took an alien handout to feed his family and still bring honour to the 91st of Foot.

My most vivid memory of that period was the bombing of the Leith Docks. We lived on the boundary of Edinburgh and Leith in a District called Pilrig and our home was on the top floor of a tenement. A neighbour sent for us to take shelter in a basement further along the street, and I was dragged along Arthur Street. I could see this vast sausage-like shape in the sky, dull silver in colour, and actually heard the explosion of the bombs which hit a bonded whisky warehouse on the edge of the Docks.

Exciting stories emerged the next day of many killed and, particularly, the whisky running in the gutters from the warehouse; many claimed to have collected the whisky in jam jars and all kinds of handy vessels. Oddly there seems to be very little official recognition of this incident, save a soldier and a girl who were casualties in different areas of Leith. A baby died later from unknown causes.

I was only three-and-a-half when I saw the Zeppelin, although I cannot claim that it kindled any positive interest in flying. But I do remember being impressed by the various fathers who came home on leave and the colourful uniforms they wore, more especially those who wore the 'maternity jacket' of the Royal Flying Corps. The very first RAF uniform I saw was worn by Flt Lt Wedgwood Benn

DSO, DFC — father of Anthony Wedgwood Benn MP — who was the Member of Parliament for Leith when he visited my school.

When the war ended my father remained in the Army, and my mother became a dressmaker to her friends and the neighbours. I also shared the fall-out of her skills: she designed and made all my clothes. I was very proud of those she made for outdoor wear, perhaps because they were different; they were generally made from offcuts of the various dress lengths being made up into ladies' costumes. Apparently the demand of the fashion of the time was for Navy blue, and I never even noticed that the slightest change in shade was incorporated into the front and back panels of a jacket or trousers. I was not even aware that, until I had my first bought suit, that flies had been invented! The exclusive 'Annie Thompson' design had only a small flap — that was adequate in normal circumstances — but near disaster in an emergency, when I could not even resort to the era of the 'Flapper' in her cami-knickers, and go down one leg. The 'Annie Thompson' design had pre-empted the Bermuda shorts and they were so tight that there was no escape save struggle with the tiny flap. Quite apart from the unique trousers, the jacket was similar to those worn by cavalry officers as dress kit, buttoned at the throat and falling away at each side.

I was never conscious that my attire was odd until I had my first normal boy's gear. The sheer joy of having pockets and flies was something that lasted for weeks. My shirts and nightwear were still 'Annie Thompson' exclusives (which was her maiden name) and she would frequently scold herself when she made a mistake in her work and oddly I find that I do the same thing, even today, a sort of 'pull your finger out Mahaddie'.

Although I can recall so clearly seeing my father off to the war, and even more clearly the Zeppelin, the mid-twenties are not so clear. But in what seemed like a very short period my mother died after a long illness. She was confined to bed and had infrequent visits from a nurse; since my father was still in the Army I looked after myself and skipped school to visit my mother who, by this time, was in a hospital for the terminally ill. It never occurred to me that my mother would die, and it was a profound shock when she did. After a year or so my father left the Army and remarried a Highland lass who seemed to adore me, but did not seem to take to my sister who lived with an aunt.

I left school before my 14th birthday (which could happen in Scotland) and started work the same day in the employ of a grocer and wine merchant. The shop was called Russell's and was opposite the Theatre Royal in Edinburgh. My main task was to bottle wine — Red Biddy it was called, at 1/10d a quart bottle — and Guinness at 7d a bottle. I very much enjoyed this change of life, especially the 15/- a week, of which I was allowed to keep half-a-crown. In those days the licensing laws were very strict, expecially for off-licence sales, except that all kinds of liquer could be ordered and delivered. This produced a rich seam of tips, much of it from the artists at the Theatre Royal during rehearsals. This I overplayed by spending too much time in the rear of the stalls watching rehearsals, and an assistant would take over the Royal deliveries. But when he took just as long the 'boy' was back on call.

By this time I had joined the Scouts and had reached the dizzy heights of Patrol Leader. For a brief spell I became a Troop Leader, which I enjoyed because the

Troop Leader carried the flag, but unlike 'Sister Anna' (who also carried a banner in the song which I was to learn much later) I had a handsome leather pouch which went over one shoulder. My Troop — 10th Leith (Balfour Melville) — frequently marched with the rest of the Edinburgh District Scouts and I found the flag holster a great comfort — as it would have been to 'Sister Anna' — since, in the song, she only had a 'banner-carrying navel' as I recall.

3 When Beech Leaves are Falling

In the late twenties I was attracted to an article which appeared in the *Scout Magazine* written by the Chief Scout, Lord Baden-Powell, about Halton and the Trenchard Experiment. This I discussed at once with my Scoutmaster, who had served as an officer in the Gordons during the war and was now a schoolmaster. He was most enthusiastic and sent away at once for specimen examination papers. When these arrived I realised that my dream of Halton was not to be. But not so my Scoutmaster. I had each Wednesday afternoon off from Russell's and he enrolled me, secretly, into his school for lessons with his normal classes. He and his wife held a weekly open house and these cramming sessions prepared me for the coming Halton entrance examination.

I looked forward to the exam with dread. When it came I tried frantically to remember all that had been forced into me by my mentor, and to the utter amazement of all around — but mainly myself — I passed into the 17th Entry at Halton in January 1928 with, I believe, 305 out of a total of just under 400 starters. But somehow I just managed to miss Leading Aircraftsman by two per cent when I passed out.

My joy of getting into Halton was short-lived. In the first term I was up before the Head, a delightful fellow called B. A. Smith who kindly explained in a most embarrassed way that in spite of appearing to have satisfactory results in other departments, my school results were as poor as he could recall in all his experience. Despite all this he gave me one term to show some improvement. I never really shed the 'below average' tag at the Halton style of academy. After all, most of my contemporaries were ex-grammar school, and at the other end of the scale dealt with the mysteries of each stage of calculus. The workshop classes were a mixture of all grades of academy, and it was here that I found common ground absorbing my trade instruction; and happily in this field I was able not to be as conspicuous as I was at school. Perhaps it was a great help to me at this time that the RAF introduced a new trade into the Service — Metal Rigger — and to the horror of the old 'Chippie Rigger' who fashioned the ancient wooden aircraft, and claimed 'we used to have men of steel and kites of wood . . . sadly now the process has been reversed'.

Another help at this critical time was that Halton won a county title at cross country when I was a junior, and I also won a boxing medal. But it is only fair to record that the lad who won the 'best loser's' medal broke his wrist on hitting me on the head (watch this space) as a flyweight (special gilt one 1/9d), which led to a most embarrassing situation. I foolishly sent this medal home. Immediately my father started matching me with all kinds of licensed murderous thugs, and one in particular who had become the amateur flyweight champion of Scotland. Happily I had been at school with this fellow and was able to contact him on my next leave, and to persuade him that it would be a pity to spoil his good name by killing me. He saw the wisdom of this ploy and invited me to his next fight, when he lost his title. As the saying goes 'you can't win them all'.

In all other respects it seemed that I was winning. I heard no more from the Head (could someone have come worse than me?) and also I found myself in a new dorm filled with chaps who were in the top classes at school. This faster stream chatted about the mysteries of calculus, and were happy to help me as I was anxious to be helped — but not with calculus.

At about this time I was able to discard the dread of the 'chop' from Halton and a balm to my ego was a gain in my outdoor activities, particularly in cross-country and track. I felt very comfortable at the workshops, I also adored the evening sessions at school when we were lectured by such great names of the day as Churchill, Trenchard, Beaverbrook, General Smuts, a host of politicians, and near our own field, such fine names in aviation as Handley Page and others; splendid names in their day.

I began to feel more a part of this vast foundation of the great Halton Experiment. However small it was (and whether it is just or not), I have felt over the years that the Halton experience has enabled me (despite my background) to bridge the gap between those far off days, and reaching the rank of sergeant pilot, and the mid-war years when, in a few months, there was swift passage through the roles of flight commander, squadron commander, staff officer and station commander.

I am certain that the transition could only have been made possible through the dedication of those Mr Chips at Halton, who gave their entire working life to the charges of all their students. Men like A. C. K. Kermode, Whittaker, Latimer Needham, Pillars, B. A. Smith and last but not least my dear friend the maths master.

He in particular helped me considerably. Quadratic equations were a great mystery to me, and seeing me struggle with a problem he would call me out and painstakingly take me step by step to a solution. Then he would ask the class if anyone had an answer, and before they had a chance to reply he would add 'Mahaddie and I have arrived at this conclusion'. I adored that man.

Another splendid fellow was A. C. K. Kermode who taught 'Theory of Flight' which seemed to embrace in a single formula, at least to me, the entire majesty of flight.

Also Whittaker, the English master, must have suffered with my transposition of a simple sentence in basic english, but nevertheless seemed to enthuse over anything I did in the manner of an essay.

Whilst I was not physically built as an athlete, I found by hard training I could make the track and cross-country teams. This was a boost to my ego and helped to offset the ever-present dread of getting the chop from Halton. Perhaps some indication of how this reacted on me may be gleaned from memory. One of the medical wing commanders at the hospital — H. E. Whittingham, later Sir Harold E. Whittingham KCB, KBE, LLD, MB, ChB, FRCP (Lon), DPH, FRCS (Ed), FRFPS (G) etc, etc, had a wager with the Commandant, Sir Norman McEwan, that by medical examination he could forcast the first, second and third places in any track event over 220 yards. Now I was keenly aware of where I ranked in the mile, half-mile and three miles. I enjoyed a secret determination to upset the medical theory. Came the intense medical examination, much of which is commonplace today, but by no means in vogue in 1928/29. For example, all the competitors had to blow into what resembled a gas meter and the capacity of the lung was recorded. I failed to see the point of this exercise, and that, with other medical experiements, only fired my resolve to upset the doctors' wager, which I believe was for a box of cigars. On the day of the Station sports I tried harder than I had ever tried in any of my events, and the results were exactly as predicted by old Doc Whittingham, 'not in the first three, could make fourth if he really tries hard enough' (which could be the story of my life).

Thus the years at Halton fell away like the beech leaves from the trees around the camp, some golden, some dark brown, but only one black that covered the parade grounds and even got into our billets on a windy day in the autumn. At long last came the passing out. I was confident by this time that I was safe, despite retaining my poor showing at school, but I was in a new trade — Metal Rigger — and was, by result, as good as most.

My interest in sport helped and apart from three days jankers (for being late back from weekend pass — could not afford a taxi from Wendover station), this vexed me as many of my Entry had zero days but many, like my dear friend the late Roddy Morgan, did more than 300 days. He was possibly one of the most brilliant boys ever at Halton, whom I have always claimed, if Whittle had not invented his jet engine, he certainly would have come very close in his time. He was killed at Shoreham in an experimental microlite machine.

One of my colleagues in the billet during the very early days at Halton was known as Buster. Buster bought a very old and very large American motor car — I believe the price was £10 and, being probably one of the poorest of apprentices at the time, I had a 10/- share in this syndicate. To glamorise the whole thing (the car obviously could not be kept at the camp), it was kept in some out-of-the way garage, possibly in Aston Clinton, which was the nearest village to the camp at Halton. Buster felt that he could make the vehicle — which was a very dismal thing to look at — a real sort of Bonny and Clyde affair. He could glamour it all up by putting in a phoney dashboard and to that end he thought that perhaps he could borrow (borrow is a word we use a lot in the Air Force) some instruments from an old aeroplane down on the aerodrome — I believe it was a Boulton Paul Sidestrand. There it was in all its glory abandoned outside in all weathers. It seemed a good idea at the time, and it was agreed that all the shareholders would get an instrument of any description. It did not matter whether it was the oil pressure gauge or anything else. I was detailed to get the altimeter.

I should add here that even as a junior at Halton I was in the senior cross-country team — which only people in their very last year were normally eligible to join and at this stage I was in my first year of three. I was allowed to go out on any occasion, in running gear, to train as I was a *bona fide* member of the team; and so on one of these occasions when I was out training — I always wore a sort of towel around my neck which looked very professional at the time and quite unnecessary — I managed to conceal the altimeter, which had become very very hot property by this time because it was known that several instruments were missing and we could have a visit from the gendarme. So out I went. Halton is ringed with beautiful beech forests and one of my training runs just happened to take me through one of these forests where I felt I was utterly safe except for the birds and the bees. I dug a hole under the root of one of the trees and deposited the altimeter. The only reason I went this rather dicey route was that we heard a buzz that all the billets were going to be searched. We were not sure what they were looking for but it was almost certainly for these 10 or 12 instruments that were now gaping holes in the dashboard of the abandoned aeroplane down on the airfield. So up until then, being very cautious and a canny Scot, I hung the instrument wrapped in a piece of rag outside the window of my bed space on a nail, just in case somebody came round whilst we were either at school or the workshops. However, the altimeter was buried and no doubt if it still has not been found, someone roving round the forests with their metal detectors today will come across it and will not be able to understand what an ancient altimeter is doing there after 60 years.

Buster somehow or other was found to have one of the instruments, and so he was put on a charge and ultimately he was sentenced to be flogged as this was still the practice in the Services. This is not something from *Mutiny on the Bounty* or *Cowardice in the Face of the Enemy*. Incidentally, in World War 1 you were shot — and many people were shot — by a firing squad of their own regiment, thus Buster was sentenced to be flogged. He was adamant — although all the shareholders in the motor car felt it was time, as one did at school, to say 'look I am involved', but Buster was quite insistent that it was pointless 10 or 12 of us being flogged. So the whole Wing and a mustering from the other wing on our camp, about 600 boys in all, assembled in the square with Buster in the middle, still determined that it was pointless us all being whacked. I think (I cannot remember the number) that it must have been at least 20 lashes he received and I felt every one of them. If I dip deep into my memory these 60 years hence I can feel them still. Buster bent over a table, on trestles (airman's, six-foot, for the use of), and received his punishment from a great monster as we thought at the time, a flight sergeant RAF policeman with a cane. In the meantime, someone had found that there was some sort of balm that we could rub on his bum before the event, but an echo that I will tell you and I will never ever forget, I can honestly say that having witnessed that ordeal and experienced the aftermath, and having seen the vicious weals on Buster's backside, I have never ever stolen a thing of any value since.

When people ask me about the deeds of some of our very great airmen, and I go right throughout the war on both sides, there are shining examples brighter than anything in the constellation that come to mind; I think of Cheshire's 100 sorties and, no less important, Fraser Barron — a little Kiwi not yet 21 with two DSOs, two DFCs and a DFM — Pathfinder squadron commander, killed with his deputy Master Bomber on one of the interdiction targets before the Invasion, and a host of others. I can think of half-a-hundred, but I have never met anyone — in fact I have never walked in the shadow of anyone — braver than Buster. Buster — one time aircraft apprentice, 17th Entry, Halton, 1928 — but all time and forever will be a rare English gentleman, in the tradition of Titus Oates.

4 Cranwell

Thus, Aircraftsman First Class Mahaddie left the chalk hills of the Chilterns with some regrets, and a deal of thanksgiving for the blessings bestowed, to enter the RAF proper. And proper it was at Cranwell — the RAF College. A fortunate posting indeed, straight into the College workshops with an endless work rate, repairing the ancient Avro 504, Siskin and the Audax — work I really enjoyed. I was also lucky in working for a sergeant who happened to have only three figures in his official service number, a relic of the old Royal Flying Corps. Whilst the College was in recess we had a great deal of spare time. Once the backlog of prangs had been cleared one was able to enjoy the taste of Service life of the early thirties, in which sport figured in balance with the work in hand.

I was never to get beyond the most minor rugger stage at Halton, because the Wing standard was very high. So I set out to have a go at the Station side, but it just happened that there was also a scratch side called the C. N. Lowe 15. Lowe had been a well-known wing threequarter for England — Wg Cdr C. N. Lowe, Chief Flying Instructor, RAF College, Cranwell — and his side drew players from several RAF stations in the district; he was also a very good coach. The real object of his 15 was to provide a chopping block for the College 15, who trained incessantly for their annual fixtures with Woolwich and Sandhurst, whom up to then they had never beaten. Lowe's side never beat the cadets, but at least provided reasonable opposition and enjoyed a form of coaching from Wg Cdr Lowe.

This led to another form of coaching. I just cannot remember how my interest in tennis arose, save that I used to practice for hours against an airman's table top fixed to the netting of an old tennis court. Because I must have been noticed, I was invited by the families to play in mixed doubles. Cranwell enjoyed excellent tennis courts, beautifully secluded with 12-foot high hedges, in excellent condition. Arising from this, I was offered coaching by the College coach; I think his name was Pearse, and he was one of Dan Maskel's assistants at Queen's Club. I understood that the fees were a charge on some obscure NAAFI rebate fund. Pearse coached me for two years. When I went overseas I had graduated from the 'Pat and Giggle' stage and could join those who had served several years in Mespot. Uncoached I was at least able to survive a couple of rounds in the local tournaments; a stroke of luck at this stage was that I was paired with a newcomer to the Command — a Flt Lt Reep who was in a different league to mine — and we entered for competitions and this raised my game quite a bit. In fact we did very well in doubles. This, in turn, improved my singles game considerably and I won the Baghdad Open one year playing against Indians in the main, who were horrified that I insisted we played in the heat of a Baghdad afternoon when it was normally well over 110° in the shade, and there was no shade — mad dogs and Scotsmen! This was a minor tournament and played at the YMCA in Baghdad.

After the trials of Halton, Cranwell was a haven. With my pay now being nearly 30/- a week, I invested in a motorcycle — a square tank Rudge of questionable vintage — for £4 (at a pound a week), but soon cured myself of the motorcycle bug that seemed to affect us all at the time.

After some 20 months I was able to take a trade test and become a Leading Aircraftsman getting nearly £2 a week. One of the notorious figures at Cranwell at this time was Aircraftsman Shaw (the legendary Col T. E. Lawrence — Lawrence of Arabia) whose mind-bending task daily was to sit outside 'C' hangar and record the cadets' flying times. He was, of course, revered by all and sundry in the hutted West Camp, Cranwell. He was a form of Guru to the airmen who frequently took their problems to him, rather like the simple Arab in the desert who treated him as some form of God. Many tales are told of his judgements that hovered between those of Solomon and Sanders of the River. On one occasion the old crone who managed the NAAFI decided that she would have to charge an extra penny for a cup of tea. Now in the early thirties this was too much for the troops to take, so they took their problem to Shaw who then went to the NAAFI and bought all the cups for a penny. When the NAAFI ran out of cups, the old dear was at her wits end and sent for the orderly corporal, who in turn sent for the orderly sergeant. He also realised that this was a situation far beyond his *métier* and summoned the duty staff officer who arrived resplendent in full ceremonials, pantaloons, highly polished knee-length riding boots, and regulation yellow walking stick, and visited Shaw in his billet and confronted him in a corner, where he held court. After a short and unequal debate, Shaw conceded the surrender of the cups, provided the NAAFI no longer charged a penny deposit on a penny cup of tea, and West Camp, Cranwell, returned to its normal tranquility.

The other story I recall to mind about this time is that Cranwell in those days must have been the coldest spot south of the Arctic Circle and the ration of coal to fire the single stove in a billet of 22 erks took little account of the temporary hutment. Some genius had laid down that the ration of coal would be 1lb of coal every other day as sufficient to ward off armies of brass monkeys that descended on Cranwell in winter. In even the mildest winter, the situation was desperate enough for those in the workshops to make a form of briquette from any form of rubbish bound by rags — and sometimes wired flex — that would give the slightest measure of heat.

Now the ration per airman, meagre as it may have been, was four times for an officer — ie 4lb every other day. The coal compounds were side by side, and whilst the officers' compound was generally well filled, I can recall sweeping dust from the airmens' compound floor to get a wee bit extra for the billet. The Shaw solution to the inequality of the coal ration was simple: just change the signs on the compounds. A perfect balance system was introduced and there was no complaint from the officers' batmen — well they would not would they?

And so some two-and-a-half years slipped away at Cranwell. I practiced my trade, I simplified my life, I was on my way to becoming the 'Compleat Airman', I also felt that I should get an overseas tour out of the way, and was quite pleased when I found my name on the PWR+; I then awaited eagerly to learn where. In those days I was going, and was only intrigued to learn that it was Mespot — or Iraq as it became.

Goodbye Cranwell, thank you for all your favours and 'Sydiha' Baghdad. . .

5 Mespot

Having been duly warned about an overseas tour, in time a boat list appeared and all the old sweats started horrific stories about the various places we were destined to go. If it was in the Near and Middle East the stories generally centred round what would happen to you if you were ever caught by the Bedouin — or the Bedou, as the old sweats termed the colourful Arab in the desert. There was a sense of adventure about it all, despite the warnings 'don't forget to carry your goolie chit'. This was a warning to the adventurous Arab in the desert, if you did force-land and you suddenly found you were his prisoner, and in several dialects of Arabic. It claimed that a large amount of money would be the immediate reward if you were delivered unharmed to the nearest British post. This was a very comforting thing, although I must admit that I heard of no cases occurring in the period that I was in Mespot. But the tales that were told were not only gruesome but frightening — in fact sickening is probably a better word — of what happened to you if the desert Arab got hold of you and handed you over to his womenfolk.

However, that did not stop the sense of adventure to a 20-year-old going off in 1933 in a very strange vessel called the *Somersetshire*, of which a very famous Air Force song will be sung for evermore. It was a British India troopship and somehow managed to cram 600-700 troops into the sharp end, and the rest of the ship — quite two-thirds — was reserved for one hundred officers and a few, very few, Princess Mary's Royal Air Force Nursing Service. But once more, in the words of the song, 'it was a nice tiddley ship and the skipper looks on her with pride'.

It took 21 days to get to Basra, through the Suez Canal, down the Red Sea (that was not) sharp left at Aden and up the Persian Gulf. There in front of us was Basra. It was a great joy to get ashore after being cramped with our fellows, not all of them Air Force. I recall that there was a battalion of the Highland Light Infantry (HLI). They had very strange habits and hygiene was not something that they practised very seriously. One of our fellows claimed that, within half a day out from Basra, one of the RAF chaps was stopped and a HLI lad said, 'Hey Jock, can you tell me where is the wash-hoos?' That might be pure fiction but nevertheless it was a very amusing story at the time.

On sentry duty one night, in the magazine of all places, I propped myself with my rifle on guard in a corner and somehow or other managed to let my feet out at about 30° to 35° to the vertical, and I fell asleep. The orderly sergeant missed his footing coming down the rather steep gangway into the magazine and cursed 'Oh bother' or some similar word you hear often in the Sergeants' Mess. He was followed by a very young and very clueless officer. The sergeant came straight up to me and said: 'Sentry you were asleep.' By that time my eyes were wide open and I replied: 'Oh no, sir, I was just leaning in the corner.' 'No you weren't, you were fast asleep,' and he turned to the young officer and enquired: 'Did you see him asleep, Sir?' 'As a matter of fact sergeant I didn't' he said.

After giving me a bit of a rollocking they went away telling me what happened to sentries who fell asleep guarding the magazine.

There were many amusing things that happened on the way out, to distract us from the utter boredom of slogging through the Med and down the Red Sea. I doubt if we sailed at anything more than eight or nine knots, maybe 10, if we had the wind behind us. One of the things that some chaps found amusing when they went to the 'heads' (the head is what the Navy calls the loo), you sat in a long row and a great flush of water ran right through a row of 20 or 30. It was very common that the duty wag at the time would make a little paper boat, and probably get some fat or grease from some convenient part of the ship. He would then set light to this and let it sail down the waterway whilst there was a great row of people sitting attending to their needs of nature.

Baghdad at last, and a short trip to Hinaidi — the large RAF base and home to No 70 Squadron. It was a great event on the squadron when the boat arrived; in fact it was the greatest event of the year, save Christmas. Next day I was a second rigger on a Vickers Victoria — a large troop carrier known as the 'flying pig' because of its girth. The squadron had a general-purpose role and just how general can be gauged by my first flight, which was only a couple of days later — to deliver a coffin-like box to RAF Shaibah near Basra. The journey only took a few hours. On arrival the coffin was decanted and refilled with ice and shark meat in exchange for the pork we had brought from the squadron pig farm.

The squadron also flew the Iraq Levies. A sort of RAF Regiment of the day, they were mainly Kurds who came from the far north of Iraq — excellent soldiers but poor airmen who generally laid their breakfast on the cabin floor whilst we were taxying to take-off. That, mixed with the mule's contribution, produced an atmosphere in the cabin that stood me in good stead for the rest of my flying career.

We also had a strong liaison with the RAF Armoured Cars. These were manned by RAF personnel, but were Rolls-Royce-engined devices that resembled a large, extended bully-beef tin. Their main task seemed to be to inspect the landing grounds that extended across the route from Baghdad to Damascus. The landing grounds were linked with a furrowed track which a motor company called Nairn Transport used as a guide to Rutbah Wells — a kind of *Beau Geste*-type of fort, or staging post — between Baghdad and Damascus.

As this was my first experience of squadron life, I quickly fell into its easy way. I was rather surprised to find I was already selected to play rugger for the squadron the following Sunday, and also went straight into the squadron tennis team. Someone was taking a frightful chance I felt; these games were always held on a

Sunday and the English community in Baghdad came out to the camp as several matches were played in the afternoon.

I enjoyed the complete change of life at Hinaidi. There was plenty of flying, sport, and my work on the aircraft was nearer to the pulse of the Air Force than I had been before. The following is a typical example of the character of the RAF as I saw it for the first time about a couple of months after I got to Baghdad. We were called out in the middle of the night to man the Bund (a sort of wide wall that encircled the entire camp). There was a danger of the rising River Tigris flooding the camp, and the hospital was the first building to be endangered. When I arrived on the scene there appeared to be hundreds of people there, but a civilian — the works and bricks engineer — seemed to be the boss, and even the station commander was happily taking orders from him about filling sandbags and placing them on the Bund to strengthen it against the rising tide. A very new officer (judged by the colour of his drill shorts, which had a yellow rookie look about them as if they had come straight out of Millett's window) appeared in his drill which was never meant for him; it was meant for a much larger person. He rather looked like one of the comics on television who will always wear his khaki shorts halfway to his ankles. This fellow went up to a chap (you could not tell who were NCOs or who were officers) who was just resting because it was very hard work and we were working under pressure, and said sharply: 'What is the trouble with you, have you run out of sandbags?' The chap was a flight sergeant, a very aged flight sergeant, and he always had words for very young stupid officers. He said, 'No Sir, we have run out of sand.' Now considering there was at least 1,000 miles of sand between Baghdad and Damascus, everybody who heard this remark had hysterics, everybody except for the stupid young officer who went off to think about this.

The station commander at Hinaidi was a very famous RAF character called Jackie Hunter, who was an amazing example to all. He was a giant of a man and did the work of three, and when someone flagged with exhaustion he would appear like a genie by his side and with a quiet word help him over the temporary crisis. Towards the end of my Baghdad tour I had regular tussles with the group captain in friendly games of tennis, but I was never able to take a set off him, which never surprised me since he was more or less the permanent Inter-Services Tennis Champion in the UK. (Oddly enough, Jackie Hunter was my station commander early in the war and saved me from the wrath of my Air Officer Commanding — 'Maori' Coningham — when I brought my bombs back when everyone else had 'found the target', but this was before the days of the night camera.)

At this stage in my Mespot tour I had a bit of luck. The Cranwell tennis coaching I had received was paying off and my rugger was improving. Whilst I had nothing in the way of academy to display, I had won an open competition at the YMCA Baghdad Tennis Tournament, and was scrum-half for a 15 that was scratched up to play odd sides like the Palestine Police, or a crew from a Red Sea sloop on a visit. I thought that I would have a go at getting a pilot's course, which I did — and was soon sharply put in my place. Paraded in my immaculate 'dhobied' drill I presented myself to my commanding officer who glared at me, and dismissed me with these words: 'I am astonished that you have the gall,

Mahaddie, to apply for a pilot's course . . . if anyone is foolish enough to ever recommend you, you would only kill yourself, and probably others. Good day!'

Happily, my AOC had other ideas. Frequently he would stop on his walk around the teams on a Sunday, and at least on one occasion he advised me to break from the scrum more often (in those days airmen scrum-halfs played to orders). It so happened that on one of these Sundays my CO strolled by at the same time, and the AOC asked him why he had not seen Mahaddie for a pilot's course. The CO lied, of course, and said he had no idea, whereupon the AOC demanded 'put him up at once', and up I went. And it could have been a disaster.

The AOC's personal assistant was an airman like myself and he warned me not to stand on the mat in front of his desk. When I was ushered into the presence, I did stand on the mat. Due to my forward speed the mat and my feet ended up under the AOC's desk at the same time I saluted, and my Wolseley sun helmet sped to the opposite corner of the room. The great man put me at my ease at once: 'What does your father do?' 'A school janitor . . .' 'Did he serve in the war?' 'Yes, he was a Gordon.' 'A Gordon?' exploded the AOC. 'Which battalion?' 'The 1st . . .' 'I was a subaltern in the 1st Gordons!' I was home and dried.

It would be quite unjust to end the story there, for years later, a very pretty WAAF officer I knew came and asked if my wife and I would come to her wedding reception to be held at Claridges. We were delighted, and at a convenient interlude she took me to a favourite uncle, an Air Vice-Marshal. On being introduced, and when I repeated my name, he mused, 'Mahaddie . . . MAHADDIE. I seem to know that name . . .' 'You recommended me in Mespot for a pilot's course' I enlightened him. 'Of course' said the AVM, 'I well remember I said to myself at the time, "there is a lad who will go a long way".'

So it came about that there was a vacancy for a rigger in No 70 Squadron, Hinaidi, and off to the Canal Zone, Egypt, I sped to learn to fly. A pleasant change from the heat of Mespot, but with a deal of other diversions that I found easy enough to take. Practically on arrival I was caught up with what was a slightly better standard of rugger and tennis. No 4 Flying Training School (FTS), Abu Sueir, was a pleasant station, well-established and well-run by one of the oldest group captains in the RAF, and the adjutant was none other than 'Happy' Day — or 'Wings' Day — perhaps one of the best known officers of the pre and postwar RAF. 'Happy' was indeed a character much larger than life, and even today when I meet a fellow student from my course in the RAF Club, he related with tears streaming down his cheeks an incident when 'Happy' was taking the course on rifle drill. Now 'Happy' was a fugitive from the Royal Marines, and he knew his rifle drill. Each pupil had to detail a movement in front of the squad pretending to be a drill sergeant and my detail was to get my squad from the stand easy position, slope arms and march them some 50 yards, then bring them back to the original position, order arms and stand at ease. Quite simple you might think. So thought I. The first part was okay when we got the squad marching the 50 yards, but I was the only one that did not see that someone had dug a trench in the line of march, and in one step leapt over the trench in perfect style. I dared not even glance at 'Happy', but to add insult to injury I gave the order 'About turn!' and they repeated the gazelle-like jump even better than the first time. When I think of that occasion and what 'Happy' had to say to me (but not in private), I blush.

But the Gods were once more on my side. I took very kindly to flying instruction, but again I was lucky. My instructor was a Sgt Williams and he was remarkable for his quiet voice and stable temper. For years afterwards my fellow pupils would remind me that he got a gong — an Air Force Medal — for teaching me to fly. Years later during the war when I went to Central Flying School to get an instructors rating, he once more instructed me and this time got another gong — Air Force Cross — for conduct far and beyond the call of duty, trying a second time to teach me to fly (or so my mentors claim).

Whilst at Abu Sueir I managed to get a great deal of tennis but my rugger was curtailed slightly. I played for a scratch side called the Canal Zone but was not allowed to take part in away matches because of the time I would have to spend away from the course due to travelling. In any event, I was loathe to miss any flying. Once more I found that the Gods were smiling on me. The Chief Flying Instructor (CFI) was a well known — in fact, famous — character in the days of the skirmishes with the tribes in Mespot after the League of Nations had proclaimed Mespot (Iraq) and the country a Mandate under British protection. He was also a very keen observer of rugger, to my everlasting relief.

To this day I have no idea how I nearly managed to kill my flight commander during a taxying accident, but I did. Suddenly I found that he and I were on a collision course, both in Atlas aircraft. It all happened so quickly. In a flash I realised that my propeller was tearing great chunks out of his cockpit and he was quite literally trapped. I switched off immediately but the propeller was determined to make yet another turn, and another, and eventually stopped — embedded in the side of his aircraft. Naturally, he was speechless with rage and he seemed to go a funny colour, rather like the top range of a steel tempering chart — cherry red. He was bigger than I and he grabbed me by my Sidcot collar and hauled me in the direction of the CFI's office. I did not even have time to shake off my parachute before we burst into the 'Holiest of Holies'. The moment the CFI caught sight of the flight commander, he said crisply 'What do you want? Come back later'. The flight commander, without having the chance to say one word, retreated in haste. Seeing me the CFI said 'Ah Mahaddie, I wanted to have a word with you, sit down'. He then embarked on a long tirade about the tactics we should adopt for a forthcoming game with an Army side. He took his duties as the non-playing captain of the Canal Zone scratch side very seriously, I am happy to recall. I still adore that man, one-time CFI Abu Sueir George Gardiner.

I was also favoured by this delightful fellow when the instructors had a sort of 'Wing Ding' towards the end of the course. They did a mass formation practise for some show in Cairo, and he would get in the back of an Audax, throw off his parachute and Sutton harness, then kneel looking backwards and control the formation like the leader of the Hallé. Happily, it was generally very stable air when we did this. There would have been no reprieve had I deposited my CFI over the side and I suppose that could have happened. I was to learn many years later, however, most of the formation complained that I steered a very erratic course, and I thought it was the CFI touching the control column in his cockpit, and with his feet (suggesting that I move to the right or the left). However, I was always quite relieved when he resumed a proper attitude in the back of the cockpit and was safely attached to his parachute and using the Sutton harness.

And so my tour in Mespot came to an end. I gained my 'wings' on 13 June 1935 and was promoted to sergeant. It had been most enjoyable with a tremendous amount of flying: I had been in every part of the Command — Persia as it was in those days, down the Gulf and all the way round the Gulf to Bahrain, Salalah. I took part in the search for the Imperial Airways Argosy airliner *City of Glasgow* that landed on the beach and was literaly lost for a couple of days before one of the Shaibah crews found it away down beyond Sulwah Wells. I did two tours all the way round to the Gulf and right round to Aden which was very pleasant. We staged with the Sultan of Oman and Muscat, and Salalah, and I can recall one evening a bit of a commotion, when one of the Wapiti crews of No 55 Squadron caused an uproar by trying to get on to the roof. He did not feel very well and he felt that some air was called for. A large Nubian slave — the Sultan had removed his tongue so he could not speak — was manhandling this fellow because he wanted to get on the roof. It was not until an Indian secretary arrived and said 'Well I'm sorry, you can't really go up, the Harem is up there.'

So these things came to an end. I recall that on one occasion I was offered the eye of a sheep that had been cooked on a vast platter. We all sat around cross-legged picking at bits of the sheep and I was offered the eye by the Sheikh, which I understand was a kind of honour. Whilst I took it, I was about to flip it away somewhere when my CO said, 'You must eat it, YOU'VE GOT TO EAT IT!' under his breath. How I put that eye into my mouth and how I swallowed it I will never know, but swallow it I did. The things we do for England!

When my tour ended we were taken across the route to Damascus in the Nairn transport. This was a vehicle with all mod cons at the rear of the bus, which I had followed many times and checked on its progress flying over the route; oddly enough, on my last night in Mespot I was to sleep in the Imperial Airways rest fort at Rutbah Wells. I had refuelled there many times and had wondered with awe at the vast ugly route-flying Imperial aircraft — Handley Page HP42s — and even more so at the passengers who took an even greater interest in our tiny single-engined Wapiti aircraft, and furthermore asked endless questions about our aircraft and of our life in Baghdad.

So at last I was to savour the delights of staging at Rutbah Wells fort and, after travelling most of the daylight hours from Baghdad, it was bliss to get into the fort with all its comforts. Far and away superior to those we had at our base RAF Hinaidi, and certainly better than those enjoyed by officers in the Mess.

Whilst the nine-month period I spent at Abu Sueir in the Canal Zone, Egypt, was intense and highly concentrated, it did have some dramatic moments, such as my taxying accident. After all we were all leading aircraftsmen on the course and the officer element were acting pilot officers on probation who generally referred to themselves as the lowest form of animal life within the RAF. But they were all quite delightful fellows about the same age as most of the airmen pupils, and we seemed to fit in very well with each other; although most of us had spent several years in the RAF the acting pilot officers had only spent, say, a couple of months. But also on the course, and I believe one of the earliest, was a pilot scheme for Medical Officers to take flying training. On our course we had the most enchanting fellow — a flight lieutenant doctor and his name was Tom MacDonald — who eventually became one of the most senior Medical Officers in the RAF. He was treated a little harshly because he was aged and equivalent in rank to the vast majority of the officer instructors. In other words he was a flight lieutenant of medium seniority in the rank.

Now it was an established custom that we very often used to go out to a strip in the desert away from the camp where we could indulge in circuits and landings to our hearts content without being related to the hour by hour flying that went on at the Base camp. Naturally, amongst other things that we took out into the desert with us was the long-established tea swindle, which we all subscribed to. It was considered a most heinous offence if pupil or anyone else taxied within the proximity of the tea swindle and the great volume of sand engulfed those who were engaged in making the tea — indeed, getting any sand anywhere near the brew as it was being prepared was considered a serious offence.

On one occasion Doc MacDonald did. He must have forgotten there was a wind change. In any case a great mass of sand was blown in the direction of the little Base Camp and smothered the tea swindle but, worse still, it also smothered the various Instructors who were resting whilst the pupils were carrying out a detail in the air. One of the Instructors was an Irish gentleman by the name of Fagan who had all the Gaelic charm of the Irish and, more especially, a great mass of raven-black hair exquisitely waved from his brow to the nape of the neck. He was very proud of this crowning glory of his and he was incensed with Mac's indiscretion in his taxying too near to the tea swindle and, more especialy, too near his hair-do. When Mac got out of the aircraft Fagan stormed up to him and said: 'You are a bloody fool, Mac, look what you've done with your inconsiderate taxying, blowing this shit all over the camp.'

Now it was a rule and the custom at the time that any of the staff could impose a fine on the spot and in this circumstance Fagan imposed a fine of 10 'ackers' — that is 10 piastres, which I cannot remember what the value was at the time, but let us say it was something in the order of 5/-. So the doctor was most apologetic and went. Whatever the state of the tea that was being brewed, he still had his cup. But before he got into his aircraft to complete his detail he presented 20 piastres to Fagan. Fagan looked at the 20 piastres — and the 20 piastre piece was a great thing like a cartwheel, very large and bigger by far than an old-fashioned crown, some 2-2½in wide. Fagan looked at this and the doctor said: 'I am sorry about the shit I blew over everybody — there is my fine.' Fagan looked at it and said 'Doc, the fine was only 10 piastres,' 'Yes,' replied the doctor in his delightful Scottish accent (and rather I think with a lovely Highland lilt to it), '10 is for the shit I blew over you and 10 is for the shit I am just about to blow over you. Good-day sir.'

In Alexander Frater's book *Beyond the Blue Horizon* I found another echo of my Mespot days when he follows the footsteps of the early Imperial route as he called it and, strangely enough, he has a chapter called 'Following the Furrow'. These were the deep furrows etched in the sand to help the Nairn transport, but I rather think more so to help the pilots of the period to find their way across the route from Rutbah Wells to Damascus, or indeed from Baghdad to Rutbah Wells. But the other echo which really gripped me was his reference to some of the Imperial flights down the Gulf that were not as straightforward and as simple as they are today. I speak now of when I was awakened from my afternoon siesta by someone from the guardroom telling me to get down to flights as quickly as possible and have my overnight gear with me. When several of us got down there the CO informed us that we had to fly down the Gulf to look for an Imperial Airways airliner, one of those Armstrong Whitworth Argosys which was named *City of Glasgow*, and had been overdue for sometime.

So in a very short time we were in the air. We bypassed Shaibah of the famous and immortal song *Shaibah Blues* — which will be belted out by our sons and their sons I hope for evermore — and on to Bahrain where we landed and had a bit of a briefing by the CO of No 84 Squadron based at Shaibah, and so on down the Gulf to look for the *City of Glasgow*. At the briefing it was not actually uttered, but there was a rumour that there was a woman and child on the Argosy, so this had made it even more important that we keep a good look out and try to find *City of Glasgow*. We had a very impromptu meal which was brought out from somewhere near Bahrain because our landing area was in a small offshore sand strip where the Nos 55 and 84 Squadron aircraft (also a Valentia from No 70 Squadron, which was our support aircraft) were all based overnight and I went to sleep in this hot and humid place. The humidity factor at Bahrain was very high indeed, in the 90s, but I went to sleep quite comfortably on a groundsheet having dug a little hole for my not very considerable hips, weighing very little above 9 stone, and I settled down for the night. But I had a nightmare. It was a nightmare about this child. Oddly enough, I was not with the rest of the aircraft that were in the search; in fact my station was offshore — not on the coast, or inshore — but quite some distance out in the Gulf. So it was indeed a classic nightmare where I dreamt that I was the only person searching for the child, and the only person who saw that this vast Argosy was down near the coastline, and I landed in a most difficult position near the aircraft and found nobody else about. Possibly they had all gone off looking for help but I found the child and I cradled the child round my neck with some sort of rag and headed off back to Basra. Why I headed for Basra I do not know. On the way the child seemed to do nothing else but take a great deal of delight in wetting me thoroughly.

I woke up in the middle of the night to find that I was completely and utterly saturated. But it was the precipitation running off the wings through a gap in the frieze ailerons that we had on the Wapiti aircraft at that time, that had soaked me. This channelled a complete stream of water — and quite cold it was — on to my stomach and woke me up. But no child. So I got up and changed into my khaki drill and was just about to throw the water off the groundsheet that by this time had collected in the hole that I had prepared for my sleeping, to find that there was a black scorpion wallowing in the slight indentation I had made in the sand. It seemed to be enjoying the water that somehow or other had seeped through, and

I often wonder what would have happened to me if that black scorpion had indeed swung its deadly tail backwards and on to me.

We pressed on down the Gulf and after an hour or so my radio lad in the back gave me a chit — 'The Argosy has been found, return to Bahrain' — and so, led by the squadron commander, John A. MacDonald commanding No 55 at that time, we were led back to Bahrain. We refuelled and went on to Shaibah and spent the night. By this time several of the aircraft crews that had found the Argosy made arrangements to ferry its crew and passengers to safety. Having arranged a guard on the aircraft we all went back to Shaibah, where we were entertained by the one lady passenger in the Officers' Mess. For the first time in my life I tasted champagne and I did not care for it very much because I was a complete and absolute non-drinker at the time. I would like to warn anybody that this was something which did not last for very long: I have since acquired an insatiable thirst and desire for champagne.

When the celebrations were at a height the lady who had been rescued said she would present a piece of silver when she got back to England to the squadron and what would they like. One wag, and I believe it was a junior officer of No 84 Squadron, said 'I wonder, please, we would prefer something from you.' 'What have you in mind?' she entreated. He became very confused and it was suggested that the squadron would like something which she was wearing at the time. So she dashed off to her room and came back with a piece of underwear that I had certainly never seen before. This was long before all things that girls wear could be studied and were exhibited on the way up the escalator at Piccadilly Underground. So she produced a very exquisite and delicate garment called French cami-knickers. So the plot was that the squadron would make a mould in mahogany to fit the cami-knickers and this became a very prized trophy of No 84 Squadron.

I only heard of what we will call 'the-carving-of-mahogany-to-fit-the-cami-knickers' years and years later from my dear friend Bruin Boyce. Bruin many years later became the CO of No 84 Squadron in Greece — that is before we were all thrown out by the Germans and, let me say at this stage, aided and abetted by a rather unmentionable faction of Greek insurgence. So having got back to Egypt (and he was being harried from one end of the Western Desert to the other by Rommel) Boyce found himself in a caravan which was his headquarters and also where he lived, when he received an order to hare back as fast as possible to El Alamein.

So he jumped astride a tractor and was being driven at maximum speed when he was told by somebody landing one of his aircraft alongside 'You are not so far in advance of Rommel's recce tanks'. At that stage the airman suddenly realised that he had left the carving and 'Jane's' pants in the caravan. All the paperwork had been removed and burnt, but the caravan had been the working place of the squadron — the squadron headquarters in other words — and so against the CO's most urgent requests and orders the airman turned the tractor round and raced back, grabbing 'Jane' and her pants off the caravan wall, thrusting them into the arms of the CO and then retraced his steps in the direction of El Alamein.

6 *The Dark Clouds Gather*

When I returned to the UK in 1937, just as the Expansion was getting underway and when the RAF was some 33,000 strong, one could see more people at a mid-week match at Arsenal. Such was the style of the Service at the time that it was known as 'The Best Flying Club in the World', but measured against today's standards, utterly amateurish and grossly incompetent.

If I should wander into the uncharted minefield of personal opinion, it is only with the benefit of hindsight. It was a profound shock to return to a very different Air Force than the one I had left before my overseas tour. I feel that a typical true story of this period may well illustrate the sense of the time.

In Mespot you were allowed to purchase a bolt of blue serge and have the squadron tailor make up your uniform. Likewise, your shoes were made by the squadron 'Moochie', costing less than a pound. Shirts and ties were also non-regulation. So when I was confronted by the station warrant officer (SWO) in my very best turnout I was somewhat aggrieved at his tirade about my flouting regulations when a strange apparition approached, an airman acting as the station postman. It was still in the days when airmen's tunics were buttoned up to the neck. His was undone to the waist, he had no cap, his slacks were dirty and crumpled, he was unshaven and badly needed a haircut, he wore plimsolls, loosely tied with bits of string. He was a complete mess; and please, let me claim, in complete contrast to my own turnout. The SWO stopped his flood of words about my rig (the airman also had one eye bandaged with a filthy pad). The warrant officer was speechless, but not for long and he thundered at him as he had on me a few minutes before. Starting at the airman's feet he moved up and raved at each disaster until he came to his head. He paused as if to draw breathe, and bawled: 'What's the matter with your eye?' The airman just replied, 'It's full of bullshit,' and he did not alter his sloppy slouch on the way either. I had returned to a very different Air Force indeed. Oddly enough I met the same warrant officer some years later when he was SWO on a station near Warboys and we had many a chuckle about that. In fact we became quite good oppoes in a way.

It should be remembered that a serving sergeant pilot (as we called ourselves in those days) had little clue about the policy that emerged from Arthur Marshall (Air Ministry) when the plans for one White Paper were never implemented before another White Paper overtook it. And so it went on in what was styled —

even in the ranks — as the Baldwin Air Force, and it was in this environment that I found myself a mere fragment within a daily expanding Air Force.

Thus the RAF commenced its preparation to meet Hitler's Luftwaffe and within a handful of years added roughly one million, including WAAF, to Baldwin's original figure. With hindsight it was a remarkable logistic achievement.

My own case at this point was by no means typical of the average or a product of the time — some 12 years service, and my five years as an NCO pilot coming to an end. I had, however, a great deal of flying experience, but unfortunately measured only in hours in the air. This in the main was from following the pipeline in Mespot to Damascus, or better still a rough track from Baghdad to Damascus, linked by a series of emergency landing grounds, staged on their way to Egypt. Thus, in spite of the large amount of flying experience I had accumulated overseas, I found that it was of little use to me back in the UK. I did find, however, that my seniority as an NCO seemed to attract functions that I found difficult to avoid.

I had been trained in Mespot in the art of aerial survey by the Royal Engineers, which I felt was of no practical use to my squadron, thus I became the squadron photographic officer (small p and small o). I was also the squadron instructor and the Link training instructor. Sadly, I failed daily to get any of the pilots to use the Link, so I used the periods myself and, in time, overcame my shortcomings in bad-weather flying. I am convinced to this day that those stolen trips in the Link could well have prolonged my flying life in later years.

There were, of course, some hidden benefits to being the head boy amongst the junior pilots. I seemed to be something of a senior subaltern, and as such donned the mantle which brings to mind the old chestnut about this essential character in regimental life who enters the Mess, sees a great array of flowers and demands 'who put those bloody flowers there?' A very junior subaltern leaps to attention and says 'the colonel's wife SIR!' A slight pause and the crafty reply was 'how charming, how utterly delightful'.

After Munich in a very short year we were at war, and by all accounts it was a very different manner of acceptance of war than we are told of the 1914 war. After Munich there was a positive lurch to prepare as best we could with the near-hopeless equipment available. On that lovely September morn the Prime Minister entoned, calling us to battle 'and consequently we are now at war with Germany'. The thin, dreary voice trailed away. There were no cheers, just a stunned silence. And yet, speaking for myself, something stirred within, and I would expect each and every one of us felt this something.

As a boy at Halton I had devoured every book available on the exploits of the RFC in World War 1 and my mind went at once to the great deeds of Ball, Bishop, McCudden, Mannock — why not Mahaddie, I thought? And that euphoria lasted quite 4 minutes until the first siren wailed and a bile settled in my gut that lasted until my Commander-in-Chief sent me a signal: 'Personal for Station Commander from C-in-C — Hostilities cease at midnight tonight. Signed Harris.'

I would like to add here that after the PM's announcement and the start of the siren wailing there was a dignified stroll to the shelters, but as the tempo of the siren note seemed to get more urgent the pace quickened and no one wanted to start a sprint but I, being a scrum-half, anticipated this and was in the shelter first. After all, the head boy must show the way.

And so to war, and at first a very strange war. On either side it appeared that no one wanted to start the bombing war which in our way had been our long time plan — in fact the Trenchard theory that fighters are for defence, bombers for offence. It is only fair to put on record, so that the student of war today can trace Trenchard's early thinking, by recalling that the Harris war aircraft were laid down in the mid-thirties. In spite of the struggle Bomber Command endured and the casualties suffered, particularly in the first two years when the bombers did so badly, and the only positive result we could measure was the shocking number of losses in aircrew, we were squandering our seed-corn.

Left:
'Wee Bertie' pictured at the age of three-and-a-half on the day war broke out — 4 August 1914 — by an Edinburgh photographer.

Below:
When we were very young: I am in the back row, fifth from the left. My little sister, Mary, is in the front row on the extreme right.

Above:
'Shire, Shire, Somersetshire, the skipper looks on her with pride . . .' Converted to a troopship in 1927, the MV *Somersetshire* weighed in at 9,787 tons and was built for the Bibby Line in 1921. *Real Photographs 2625*

Below:
Hinaidi was the principal RAF base in Iraq during the early 1930s, and home to Nos 45 and 70 Squadrons. In the foreground is one of No 70 Squadron's Vickers Victorias.
A. E. West collection/Ian Allan Library

Above:
My namesake — the original Hamish; a blue roan Arab, 14/2 with legs like a 'tiller girl'.

Above:
The way we were in 1939 — me with my No 77 Squadron crew.

Below:
When the war started the very first sortie I did was to take pamphlets to Germany, flying in at the top end near Kiel and going throughout the Ruhr. *Flight*

VELKÁ BRITANIE ČESKÉMU NÁRODU

ČECHOVÉ!

Demokratické národy celého světa sledují s obdivem a sympatiemi váš skvělý boj proti útisku. Ohavné činy nacistických násilníků a zvláště obludy, která se jmenuje Karel Herrmann Frank, vzbudily rozhořčení celého civilisovaného světa.

Buďte trpěliví! Nedejte se vyprovokovati k předčasnému krveprolití.

Dokázali jste nám, jako již tolikráte v minulosti, že váš duch je nepřemožitelný.

Naše společné súčtování s naším společným nepřítelem, kterým jsou brutální Hitlerovi pomocníci, již přichází. Právo je na straně svobodných národů a váš národ bude brzy opět mezi svobodnými národy. Důvěřujte nám; jsme s vámi právě tak jako jsme s vámi byli před dvaceti pěti lety.

PRAVDA ZVÍTĚZÍ.

267.

Above:
Of Britain to the Czech Nation
Czechs! The democratic nations of the whole world follow with admiration and sympathy your marvellous fight against oppression. The dreadful action of the brutal Nazis and especially of the monster whose name is Karel Herrmann Frank, rose the admiration of the whole civilised world.

Be patient! Do not be provoked by premature bloodshed.
You have proved to us, like so many times in the past, that your spirit is indomitable. Our mutual reckoning with our common enemy, which are Hitler's brutal supporters, is coming. Justice is on the side of the free nations and your nation will soon be amongst the free nations again. Trust in us, we are with you just the same as we were with you twenty-five years ago.
Truth will conquer

For Hamish
who found the way to Victory
Arthur T. Harris
C in C Bomber Comd MRAF
1942/5

Above:
The High Master — ACM Sir Arthur Harris, C-in-C Bomber Command 1942-45.
RAF Official

7 The First Tour

I quote from Laddie Lucas who, in his recent book entitled *Out of the Blue*, talks about fate, chance, luck, destiny and a lot of other factors which affect ones lives so curiously. I take two examples which I find seem to embrace the fateful aspects of my life in the Service. They are, you might say, the minimum and maximum in this area of fate and chance.

The first is a quote from Al Deere, one of the most famous Battle of Britain pilots: 'Fate is a strange master and I have always been a fatalist.' He should be a fatalist — he has baled out nine times in his air-fighting life. I also find an enduring quote from a friend of mine, a Pathfinder, who makes this comment: 'The way all my crew were picked was a sheer gamble. I think, therefore, I was exceedingly lucky.' This was from Maj Johann Christie DSO, DFC, of No 35 Squadron (PFF), later General in the Royal Norwegian Air Force.

Now within these two parameters I seem to find all the chance, the luck, the destiny that have been my fellow passengers or fellow crew particularly throughout this the first tour. Oddly enough I may never have had an operational tour had it not been for one of these fellow travellers. And I will leave it to you, dear reader, to make a choice.

The very first sortie that I did when the war started was with No 77 Squadron in a Whitley to take pamphlets to Germany, flying in at the top end near Kiel and going throughout the Ruhr spreading these horrors of war on the Germans telling them 'you are wicked naughty Germans and if you don't mend your ways Hamish will come back tomorrow night and drop some more paper on you'. Not that it would have done the slightest bit of good. Oddly enough — and those of you who may recall what it was like in the Ruhr (or as crews called it 'The Happy Valley') — on this occasion there was one searchlight waving about near the top of the Ruhr, and for one agonising moment it waved over the Whitley, and there was another one at the bottom by the Cologne end.

My second pilot was Spike Edmonds, a well-known character in the RAF, but also an excellent navigator who seemed to have God on his side. By the time we eventually turned to starboard and headed off towards the UK I was most anxious to get home; I was to be the best man at a wedding that day, and I had to get back before high noon. When the dawn really appeared we were flying very sedately over (and we were not aware of it at the time) Belgium. Suddenly the Whitley was entirely surrounded by strange aircraft (I learned later after much research that they were Fairey Foxes). In the rear of one of these biplanes there was a gunner with a Scarfe ring who selected a pan of rounds which he put on the gun. The next thing I knew I was looking straight up the barrel of this gun because the Fairey Fox was no more than 12ft away from the cabin and the pilot was very annoyed. He kept shaking his fist at me, and with the other hand he pointed downwards; and I kept putting my thumb up. Spike, of course, kept saying 'He wants us to go down for a drink.' Now I did not have the slightest intention of going down for a drink; all the drinking I was going to do was at the reception — if I ever got to the wedding. So I kept putting my thumb up implying 'Yes, it's alright I'll land'. Spike also said 'We are of course quite near the coast'. The gunner of the Fox gave me the final two fingers and I knew the third finger was coming up which meant the 'K' gun would be right in my starboard earhole. I put my finger up and gave the impression I was going to land, whereupon all the Foxes — by this time four or five of them — were given a signal by the leader, and they all turned on their backs and headed where they wanted me to follow. But I then put the Whitley into the most desperate dive, everything in the cabin was floating, and before the Foxes could turn round and do anything about it I was over the Channel. I landed at Manston where I was put under arrest immediately. My guns were inspected and a statement was taken from all the crew and I was released, as I said many times later, 'without prejudice', but darkly adding 'subject to re-arrest'. However, I did not make the wedding but I did get some of the grog and a piece of the cake, and kissed the bride by proxy (her maid of honour was stand-in).

As an interesting echo, the flight commander of the Fairey Foxes was a Lt Donnet, whom I met later at RAF Sylt, and I was very amused to hear his version. The Belgian's claim was that a Whitley had fired on one of his Foxes and wounded the observer, although they were able to land safely. They were obviously very annoyed and when another Whitley flew straight over Brussels (Averre, I believe it was) they all went up and forced this aircraft down. One of my friends — Flg Off Murphy — was interned, and in point of fact spent five years in 'the bag'. So when the third Whitley appeared overhead (incidentally, Murphy said that could only have been Mahaddie) Donnet recalled thinking 'that was no gentleman, and that was no Englishman. He gave his word that he was going to land but he didn't'. And, after all, would you have done so in the same situation? Providence, destiny — although I would like to treat destiny with a very small 'd' in my case — inevitably played their parts but nevertheless I got away with it, and my crew got away with it. Considering that we were completely and utterly untrained at this stage of the war, this was no mean achievement.

On my birthday, 19 March, we went to the German island of Sylt. It was in direct reprisal for their raid on British ships in Scapa Flow a few nights before when bombs had been dropped on land and killed one civilian. We were to bomb the seaplane base at Hornum on the southernmost tip of the island. Now, I served on the island many years later and became friendly with a host of people, and I personally researched a great deal on our raid when not a single bomb fell on the seaplane base. And I would dare those of you who would look up the newspaper clippings of that occasion and challenge that view, because you would find a much different reading in those newspaper clips than what I learnt many years later, trudging round the island. Personally I thought that I was being particularly clever bombing a seaplane that was taking off. It was only when I was serving on Sylt in the fifties that I learned that this was in fact a tug (or you might call it a barge, a sea-going barge) on the end of 100 metres of line, that was being towed. The lights of an aircraft were stretched on timbers, but no seaplane — and I did not hit one. I do know that some of my colleagues tried but you will not read about that in the newspaper clippings of the period.

And we trudge through the winter and into the spring of the first bombing year. We visited Oslo Fjord with only six 250lb bombs and that would not do much damage even if we had found a target (which we did not). We also went a few nights later to Stavanger, and I do believe that my bomb-aimer at least claimed he saw, through broken cloud, what he took to be hangars on the airfield at Stavanger and these were bombed. Whether it was ever verified that we did I doubt.

Then we started, in May, to go to Germany — München Gladbach in the Ruhr area on 11/12 May. Happily it was not the Ruhr that I knew on my second tour, a desperate place to be at then. On this occasion we did get shot at. A vast area of towns all spilling into each other, we must have hit something. Geilenkirchen, we were looking for oil. This, interestingly enough, was the one thing the boffins told us: get oil and we will stop the war. That was a very shrewd thing to say in 1940 but it did not happen for nearly five years. Later on when we had returned to the daylight offensive with the 8th Air Force, escorted by hundreds of fighters, could we go searching for oil. When I went to Germany within a few days of the end of the war, it was rather remarkable to go to a Luftwaffe airfield with many aircraft, all intact and fully serviceable, but with their tanks dry — not a drop of oil was to be found on those bases. In 1940 we had the will but neither the know-how nor the equipment. So we waited five long years before we could go in daylight, find the oil, and deny the Luftwaffe and the tank crews of the substance that they so desperately needed.

I see from my logbook that Geilenkirchen, Abbeville, Hirson, Hannover and Hamm amongst others appear as targets but I was never convinced that we either found, damaged, or even delayed the German masses' progress through the Low Countries. Hamm seemed to be a favourite target; although our numbers were small in these raids we never seemed to achieve any worthwhile concentration.

Despite this period there was always a mass of cloud and it was quite normal for us to go down to see if one could identify some feature. Fortunately for us at the time there was not the amount of light flak associated with later years, or that which was spawned by some of the Cheshire low level attacks. Neither was there the more deadly flak which confronted the interdiction or pre-Invasion attacks on railway centres, which accounted for some of our best PFF crews.

I recall at this period that I had a new second pilot by the name of Saltzgaber, who was a first generation Canadian but German born. The target was Mannheim. When we got into the area we found that thick cloud covered what we thought was the target, so we went down. But there was no way we were going to get under. Fortunately we had an alternative target so I asked for a course. When we reached the new target and found gaps in the cloud and bombed, my second pilot just remarked that he was glad we did not bomb Mannheim, and I asked why. He replied that he had a grannie down there.

In one of my lectures to the Staff Colleges, *The Bombing Years — A View from the Cockpit*, I can say as pertinently as I can that my first bombing tour was a complete and utter waste of time. I was lucky enough not to be court martialled, quite apart from getting away with it the first night. We were briefed that if we could not sight and identify the target we had to bring our bombs back. I brought my bombs back on many occasions, because I am quite certain we never got anywhere near anything that looked like a target. Please remember in these early days — and I am talking before we really started the bomber offensive — we were just trying to halt the mass of Germans who were rolling through Holland and Belgium. There were no real strategic targets; they were in fact tactical targets, and they were virtually impossible to find. I will take just one example. In mid-June 1940, when the Nazis were sweeping through Belgium, we were sent out on one occasion to find a very large wooded area near Rotterdam. The first I ever heard of 'pathfinding' was after briefing in June 1940, when most Whitley crews in No 4 Group, Bomber Command averaged 25 sorties that month after the breakthrough in the Low Countries. Flg Off 'Jimmy' Marks of No 77 Squadron (later Wg Cdr J. H. Marks DSO, DFC, killed whilst CO of No 35 Squadron) got a few of us together and suggested that we made a time-and-distance run from the seemingly everlasting fires of Rotterdam to the target — a large troop concentration some 35 miles away. It was a relatively easy business to navigate from Spurn Head to the Dutch coast since the glow of Rotterdam could be seen 100 miles away. Marks suggested that after a careful time-and-distance run from the centre of Rotterdam, we would all drop a flare and at the same time fire a red Very light. The interesting thing about this — in my experience the first ever co-ordinated attempt to find a target — was that despite the assurance of all the enthusiasts to the scheme (one Plt Off Leonard Cheshire included) that the run was made with great care, not one of a dozen or more taking part in this quite unofficial experiment claimed to have ever seen one of the other's flares or Very lights. This occasion was really under ideal conditions, from an easily-defined startpoint and with no opposition. An afterthought, but one which may be taken as a portent of the future, was that Marks was not deterred by this initial failure. He then selected crews for another attempt the following night and reduced the numbers to the four best navigators.

Please remember that the navigator at that period was also the second pilot. I considered mine was as good as any on the station — he was included. On this occasion the timed run was made with a stopwatch, all compasses had been re-swung and the ASI recalibrated. At the end of the run from Rotterdam, and within three or five seconds, four flares and four Very lights were visible in a radius of approximately three miles and one flare had pinpointed the target — a large, distinctly-shaped wood concealing troops and armour. At once more flares were identifying the target area and a fair concentration of bombs directed on the aiming point. This was confirmed by the immediate reaction from the ground. The time, it should be recalled, was June 1940, and take note of the name — Jimmy Marks.

Just glancing through my logbook of 1939-40, I find it astonishing how little we seemed to do before the advent of the German breakthrough in the Low Countries. I see what are described as security patrols, where we flew, and in daylight. We had to fly all the way to the Danish coast or within sight of the Danish coast; happily this was very low and the Germans did not appear to have our style of radar at the time. The value of these occasions was very doubtful. We flew also to France (Epernay) which was one of our bomber airfields and we operated to places like Prague. Now Prague is a very long way from Epernay. The airfield's codename was 'Vino' and was near Epernay. The only thing I can remember of that occasion was that we got lost and had to ask for a radio steer from the ground station. We were anxious to get back there because the next evening Gracie Fields was performing for the troops in a local theatre. Of the visit to Prague (which we never found), I recall that we showered thousands of leaflets all over Czechoslovakia but I doubt if one fell on Prague. This was telling them — trying to bolster their morale — that we were coming to their aid when it was virtually impossible for us to aid them at that time. Certainly, it was impossible with the gear we had, and certainly with our lack of skill for getting to a positive point on the Earth that could do some good.

I well recall walking the 11 miles from the airfield to Epernay. We could not get in to see Gracie Fields and, together with hundreds of troops, we stood outside and they relayed her performance. I listened to this glorious voice singing 'Sally' and all the rest of her favourite songs, and then walking the other 11 miles back — in flying boots. It took my poor wee feet weeks to recover. That was my first and only visit to Prague.

Duisberg and Frankfurt were visited towards the end of June and then, after 33 sorties, I was posted 'tour expired' to Kinloss in the bonnie land of Moray to instruct at No 19 OTU. So here ended my first tour and I could not claim that I ever actually had a clear view of any German target, save that which we did locate with the aid of Jimmy Marks' experiment northeast of Rotterdam in mid-June 1940.

I might have broken my luck had I been able to get over the Alps on a raid to Turin on 11 June. This sortie was planned to attack Turin on the evening that Mussolini was going to declare war on England. No 4 Group's Whitleys flew to Jersey in the morning, refuelled and awaited instructions to fly to Italy; I believe that there were about 20 of us. In the early evening we took off and, speaking for myself, I was very glad that there was a drop of about 100ft to the sea when the heavily laden Whitley cleared the airfield boundary. We took off into the last of the evening sun in poor visibility and I do not recall seeing any of the aircraft that took-off in front of me rise in the evening murk. I was too busy putting the nose down and squeezing a bit more speed out of the lumbering Whitley as we cleared the boundary.

The events that followed have been chronicled by several of those that took part. My fate was similar: we were to listen out for a coded signal from Group at Lyon if we were to proceed to the target. I certainly received that signal and pressed onwards to the Alps. On approaching the high ground before the Alps themselves we all encountered thick cloud, despite the season, and icing. Now Spike, apart from being an excellent navigator, was also something of an amateur Met man and would quote yards of Pick (an authority on Met forecasting) at anyone who would listen, and at first he could not believe that we were in an icing situation. The first indication of this predicament was the ice slipping off the airscrews and splattering against the side of the cockpit. The control surfaces became sluggish and in spite of full power we were not making any height. So I went on to reciprocal for 10 minutes to seek a more friendly environment, which I did, and then set course again. We got a little higher on this occasion but again ran into severe icing and again we turned back in order to find less cloud and less icing. On the third attempt we were getting quite near the Alps and we were collecting a great deal of ice. My wireless operator reported that several of our Italy-bound contemporaries had abandoned the sortie and were returning to Jersey. Of that No 4 Group party which set out to bomb Italy the night they declared war on England, I know that four — and only four Whitleys — did get over the Alps. Somehow they bombed the target in perfect weather and unopposed, and returned to Jersey. I find it almost amusing to listen to several of my contemporaries tell me about that ill-fated occasion and how they found a means of getting over the Alps. But they are never the four that *I know* did actually make it on 11 June 1940. I know I did not . . . but I *do know who did*.

Overnight I was posted to the other end of the country and the war seemed to recede, but the need for bomber replacement became more urgent.

On one of the occasions that we flew to Italy, we turned for Switzerland once south of Paris and there was the glory of Geneva — a bright smudge on the darkened horizon that was the city all lit up, with the lights actually being reflected on the lake — but several hundreds of miles away.

*It was common for the skipper, once safe from flak and fighters and well south of Paris, to engage 'George' and fall asleep. Immediately the skipper was full fathoms five, captaincy was assumed by the navigator — Tommy Thompson, one time Metropolitan Policeman (Special Branch) whose father just happened to be Churchill's bodyguard. A certain amount of discipline was engendered during the period the skipper was non compos mentis and inter-crew conversation broke out followed immediately by a remonstration from the acting captain: 'keep quiet keep quiet for * * * * * sake, you'll wake the skipper up'.*

8 Kinloss

From being with a squadron on a war footing at Driffield — which was a pleasant oasis in the East Riding of Yorkshire — to arriving in the Highland town of Forres, which seemed to welcome the inmates of Kinloss, was like fumbling through a series of dark curtains into some broad sunlight. There seemed to be no sense or reason for war at Forres; in the bonny land of Moray there did not appear to be anything such as rationing. You could buy salmon (which I suspect could have come from the King's Reach skirting Balmoral) for 2/6d a pound; and there was no dearth of whisky, for which I had yet to acquire a taste.

There followed a period for the next 18 months where my family, having joined me from Yorkshire, came up to Scotland. We lived in a series of pleasant digs until eventually we settled on the outskirts of Forres, very near the local satellite airfield of the same name. Now the selection of pupils was another gamble and they were allocated to us straight from the various flying training schools. They had been trained in their own callings — pilots, navigators, gunners and wireless operators — and came together at No 19 OTU Kinloss where they were to be trained on Whitleys. We all got a rough average of the scale and the standard of these people, but somehow or other — and I never understood why this happened — I seemed to get the occasional chaps that were given a last chance. These 'no-hopers' were probably given to me because I may well have been overheard to say I did not believe that there was such a person who had gone through ab-initio training as a pilot who could not get on step by step until he became an operational pilot. I might vary this if one was arguing that it was easier for a chap in some circumstances to become a bomber pilot than it would be to become a fighter pilot, and I would concede that argument.

However, among the several people I had there was one rather unique fellow. He was a highly educated gentleman, a very well known Varsity athlete, but he came to me with a bad report that he was completely and utterly clueless about some of the finer points of simple take-off and landing procedures. We had a simple code about the immediate drill before take-off — TMPF we called it. T was throttle, M was mixture, P was pitch and F was flaps and undercarriage. On several occasions I would find myself at 1,000ft or above, and the undercarriage was still down; the flaps, if we had put any out, were still down; the engines were belting away in fine pitch; and the mixture control remained where it was — in rich. This was something we had to put a stop to straight away and after relaying time and again the simple formula TMPF: *TRIM — MIXTURE — PITCH — FLAPS*, which he repeated, he always forgot to take action.

Eventually when we found ourselves nearly at 1,500ft, I said to myself, and into the microphone, quite plainly so he could overhear: 'This puts the undercarriage up.' I then put my hand on the throttles and said: 'This reduces the power.' I then went on in the proper sequence to the pitch control: 'And this reduces the pitch,' and so on. Now I though he would have hysterics; he could not get down on the ground quick enough to carry this action out. We had barely got off the ground again when he grabbed the undercarriage lever and shouted into his microphone 'this puts the undercarriage up,' followed by the most hysterical laughter. He went through all the drills saying exactly what I had said previously, and did everything right. We had not the slightest trouble with the landing codes: 'This puts the undercarriage down; this puts the flaps out; this goes into fine pitch . . .' I never had the slightest worry about him from then on. He could land averagely well and take-off. Nevertheless, I had an odd feeling about this fellow and it came to me many times during my short period as an Instructor. I suppose it is what the Scots, particularly in the Highlands, call being 'fey'. Now that is a word you seldom come across in England, but away up in the Highlands and Islands being 'fey' means that you have a certain sixth sense — you are the seventh son of a seventh son, or whatever the drama is on that score. I did not think this fellow would survive very long, he was what I call one of my 'oncers'. I always felt frightfully embarrassed and equally sad about this. Why was it right to train a fellow and you knew, or you felt that, you could not go to the flight commander or the wing commander and say 'I think this fellow should go down the pits,' or 'I think we should remuster him to the Army or the Navy'. He had been trained and he had passed all the standard regular practices. I could not. Fey was something they would tell me I had just invented, but it is something that never left me during the entire period I was an Instructor and sadly I was to learn very shortly after he left Kinloss that he did not survive very long on the squadron that he joined. Also it was particularly strong in the latter years of the war, particularly in the last 18 months, when many, many first and second tour people were coming back to do a further tour. I have wept many a tear for some first class fellows that pestered me, pestered me beyond belief, writing to me every week. I knew in one case that every Saturday morning I would get a letter from a lad who was having a very trying time at an operational training unit, and he begged me week after week. I eventually relented and brought him back; he nearly went through and completed a second Pathfinder tour. He even got himself a VC in the most alarming circumstances, but that did not stem my tears that I shed for this man. But I did not stop him coming back, and do not, I beg of you, ask me to try and explain that.

Kinloss was a pleasant environment and the locals were extremely kind to the alien invasion, but one felt so very much out of the hurly burly of wartime England. This was made particularly clear when pupils I had trained returned for their rest period, and one did get the message that my operational background was no longer valid or right to pass on to the crews coming forward for conversion to twin-engined aircraft. I suppose that a better expression would be to frankly admit I was getting stale.

I had a spell off instruction and became the assistant to the chief ground instructor and, in that capacity, I also was instructed to carry out preliminary inspections of crashes that happened at Kinloss during that period, and a most unpleasant task this was. I was normally the first RAF person to view the scene, and I find it quite unbearable to attempt to describe the desolation and carnage that confronted one on a hilltop in the isolation and splendour of the Scottish Highlands. If there had been a fire the tragedy was doubly sickening; frequently there was not a fire and it all seemed so unreal rather like some still life tableau. The entire scene was compounded by the thunderous silence that covered the scene, save the wind which seemed to whisper in condolence. Once a huge golden eagle circled above a wreck and I intercepted a couple hiking to call at a Crofter's cottage for assistance because I was loathe to leave the area to the eagle.

Towards the end of my sojourn at Kinloss, and after I became the assistant to the chief ground instructor under a squadron leader, I was also seconded to the engineering wing. The purpose of this wing was to test aircraft that came out after a form of garage servicing; this was before the garage system introduced by Bennett in the earlier days of Pathfinding at RAF Wyton. So as an aircraft came out of the engineering wing I gave it a test. Here I am not trying to give the impression that I am a Test Pilot as such, not in the way of Roly Beamont, or a host of other of my friends in this particular field; this was just a question of an air test rather than a flight test.

So I took this Whitley up for 10, 15 maybe 20 minutes and just made quite sure that all the engines were running perfectly, made a spot check on each engine and tested its flying capabilities — hands off — and a few simple things in everyday testing. I took with me a very young airman from the engineering wing and I understood that it was his first flight. He was sitting beside me in the jump seat or that generally occupied by a second pilot because in those days there were no flight engineers on twin-engined aircraft.

So we carried out a test very satisfactorily and then made overtures to land. Now we were using a rather old radio set at the time called a TR9 that was not one of the better things that our radio and radar boffins produced for us in the early days of RT air-to-ground and vice-versa. This was a very old set and did not always work; as I did not make contact with the control tower I came round and I saw that it was all clear for me to land, so I put my wheels down and made my approach. No sooner had I selected wheels down than I noticed that the port wheel had not come right down because I did not get a green light on that side of the undercarriage indicator. Starboard was alright but there was no green on the port. So I selected 'up' once more and went round again. I went away from the aircraft circuit and tried this once more and still no green. I decided to get a bit of height and do a gentle dive with power off and I made a rather ham-fisted upward climb in the hope that I could jolt the wheel down. Still no green. Again I was making no contact with the flying control and as I did not have a WT operator I could not use my wireless set to inform the station that I was in this predicament. However, we had in the aircraft a rather antiquated device (certainly World War 1) of a message bag with a coloured streamer and I put a message in the bag and I dropped it near the control tower. I saw the airmen of the watch come out and gather it up, and all the time I was trying to make contact with the control tower. In my message I told them that I was going to fly close to the control tower to see if they could tell me what was wrong with my port wheel, but again no reply from control. However, they gave me a green Very light which I assumed was 'clear to land'. So I made an approach, a long low approach and happily there was a bit of a crosswind from the portside. I decided to use this crosswind to help me place the aircraft at the end of my run off the normal line of landing and nearer to the engineering hangar. The whole thing went very well.

Oddly enough, I found that I could keep the port wing up for a considerable time and, as I lost flying speed and I came nearer and nearer to the Engineering Wing area, the port wing happily stayed in the air until my speed was very low indeed and then gradually — and I did not think of this — one (and only one) of the prop blades gently ploughed into the rather soft earth. My port wing was still in the air, and ever so gently we made a beautiful semi-turn to port. Gradually the port wing tip fell on the ground and we came to the gentlest of stops some 70/80 yards from the engineering wing perimeter.

All the while I had been telling my young passenger what I was going to do. He was well strapped in: 'The moment the aircraft stops,' and I showed him the escape hatch in the cockpit, 'open this hatch and get out and get as far away from the aircraft as you can'. 'Yes, sir,' he said. We could talk to each other with our internal RT.

So we came to the halt, everything worked perfectly and I was astonished how easy this all was. I rather fancy it was the one blade digging gently in and scribing a beautiful arc to port, all the time into wind; it was the gentlest of one-wheel landings that could ever have been attained. So as we came to a stop the hatch was opened and this young fellow put one foot on the throttle quadrant, another on my shoulder and the next one on the top of my helmet and he was out. But not before he kissed the top of my helmet and shouted at me: 'Oh, my mum's going to hear about this.' And he was off. There was no fire and I had switched off long before the port wing touched the ground. I saw him hare across the airfield diagonally opposed to the direction of the hangar, and indeed the aircraft, and at the same time he was haring away towards Findhorn. I saw that the wing commander engineering, who also was a pilot (but in those days they did an engineering course as we had no Engineering Officers, at least I do not remember any) opened his window in the office and climbed out. He came racing towards me just as I got out. I had already shed my parachute in the aircraft to get out a little more schnell before he accosted me. I got the most bitter rollicking for leaving the aircraft outside his engineering hangar area. I recall one of his demands was: 'What on earth possessed you to leave the aircraft here?' I replied: 'Well it never occurred to me to put it anywhere else; this is the engineering hangar area and you could find out very quickly, once you jack up this port wing, what happened to the undercarriage.' There did not seem to be a satisfactory answer to that and indeed to prolonging this very bitter rollicking that he was bent on awarding me.

Oddly enough, later on in the Mess I heard him repeat part of the rollicking, but not my reply, to the station commander. The station commander, who just happened to be a bit of an oppo of mine called 'Bull' Jarmen — a great monster of a fellow and a Kiwi to boot — who was heard to say: 'Well, it was very convenient him leaving it there; you did not have to travel very far to collect it or find out what happened to the undercarriage.' So no more was said about that.

Also, the other reason that I did not leave it in the centre of the airfield was that the flares, the gooseneck flares (a device with paraffin and a sort of rough wick), were laid out for night flying. If I had left it on the night flying path I would have had a serious rocket which I would not have forgotten as easily as I had forgotten the first one — from the wing commander flying. So I found myself in one of those 'Catch 22' situations and I chose the lesser one, and the one I thought I could defend.

I was commended by my station commander, but relations with the wing commander engineering were never quite the same I am sorry to say. The poor fellow could not accept and believe that a person with active flying experience, slight as it may have been, could land an aircraft in a relatively confined space. This possibly had something to do with my early days in Mespot, where the Wapiti had huge doughnut wheels and literally you could choose a very restricted area and get the aircraft down. But the wing commander sadly decided he should return to GD duties. In those days a wing commander engineering officer was still a GD pilot but after the long course (I think it was at Henlow, on engineering) they devoted all their energies to full time engineering. It happened that he decided to go back and found himself commanding a squadron on operations at about the same time that *Salmon* and *Gluxstein* as we called the two German battle wagons, decided to leave Brest, head up through the Channel and escape the wrath of the Navy and whatever airborne effort we could produce in the teeth of extraordinarily adverse weather conditions at the time. I believe he was one of the many aircraft that General Galland's flying wing and the German Navy shot down on route through the narrows of the Channel.

Thus the idyllic lifestyle came to an end; back to Ops and the upheaval of the family and the relative pleasures of a training establishment. But the stark reality of the Highland scene described reminds me of another idyllic circumstance that went the rounds about this time. Imagine a similar hilltop in the lovely countryside of Aviemore and a small stone-built lodge providing shelter for a corporal and two airmen at one of the quadrants of a bombing range that Kinloss used for practice. How one afternoon in the blaze of the Highland summer one of the airmen roused the corporal and entreated: 'What do you make of yon?' 'Yon' just happened to be three WAAFs toiling up the brae each with a kit bag. The corporal and the airmen first put on some trousers and literally threw themselves down the brae to meet the girls. In the breathless explanations that followed, apparently the WAAFs had been sent to relieve the airmen of manning the bombing quadrant, but no action had been taken about withdrawing the RAF. Oddly enough, there had been no similar arrangements about the second or right angle quadrant. Now this yarn had long since passed into history of ancient Highland folklore, and the WAAFs and airmen could have lived happily ever after. They had settled down to happy domestic bliss and a couple took strict turns to collect pay and rations from Aviemore railway station at regular intervals. It was, of course, by far and away a situation too good to last and in time, gazing down the glen, a solitary figure was spied struggling up the brae — without a kit-bag — the WAAFs identified their squadron officer (known as Belladonna) apparently about to make her first call on her troops in the wild. I was never able at first hand to witness this airmen's paradise but it is a story that passed the rounds at Kinloss. I was questioned about this in recent years when I visited the Camp during one of my lecture rounds to the ATC in the Highlands, but I only add this yarn to illustrate that it takes all kinds to make any air force station, and I am sure our childrens' children will be told and the tale will no doubt be embroidered to suit the occasion.

9 Pathfinder Force — The Background

Seen purely through the eyes of a bomber captain, the year 1942 saw the awakening of the 'sleeping giant', but although no dramatic results ensued in the first half of the year save the '1,000-Plan' (surely the most well-conceived confidence trick of the entire war) hope for the future was clearly manifest. The most pertinent thing was the advent of Arthur Harris as the new C-in-C. His arrival at 'The Petrified Forest' (Bomber Command HQ) coincided with the publication of the Butt Report — one of the most deadly denunciations of the only serious offensive we were able to mount against the enemy. Whilst the Butt Report 'scourge' had a devastating effect on the staff at Bomber Command, the Directorate of Bomber Operations at the Air Ministry were under no false illusion as to how able the Command was in striking its targets. Moreover, since the admirable 'con trick' of the 1,000-Plan, they had been extremely active in a certain field. This had been talked about by a few experienced bomber squadron commanders, notably Wg Cdrs 'Willie' Tait, Charles Whitworth, Syd Bufton and, of course, 'Jimmy' Marks who, as bomber pilots, Flight and Squadron Commanders, knew where the great weight of effort ended up but, more importantly, knew why. This select cell and others knew the most experienced 'bomber barons' who had endured nearly three years of bombing, but were now with a 'three ringed' voice. The most active of these well-disciplined 'rebels' occupied an office in the Air Ministry and were all agreed that the basic cause of our dismal failure to date was navigation. Disregarding the gallantry and the will to 'press-on', if — in the face of all the efforts of the enemy, his flak defences, searchlights, decoy targets and, most lethal, ever-increasing 'fighter boxes' of the Kammhuber Line — we simply could not find and destroy targets, the task was virtually impossible in the face of such odds. Thus, this 'think-tank' at the Air Ministry started talking about a target finding element which evolved into a target marking force and, ultimately, the Pathfinder Force (PFF).

Long before the actual birth of PFF in August 1942, the concept of the target finding/marking force was being well received by the hard-pressed bomber crews but, oddly enough, not by the staff at Bomber Command. It took many months to get the Staff to evaluate the possibilities of such a scheme. We are told the new C-in-C vetoed the suggestion from the outset and, in the absence of evidence from the archives, this is surely inconsistent with his demand for the agreed build-up of the Command, his determination to shed the twin-engined bombers in favour of four-engined Stirlings, Halifaxes and Lancasters, and his bitter and seemingly endless feud with the Navy (and, to a lesser degree, the Army) about the 'milking' of his Command. It should be remembered that Harris inherited a virtually bankrupt concern, achieving little and suffering appalling casualties. The incredible thing at this 'halfway' stage was that crew morale was as high as it was. This was due to many reasons but, in my view, mainly to the excellent field rank officers — the flight and squadron commanders — and in no small degree to the basic training of aircrews, and the support of the Empire Air Training Schools in Canada and Rhodesia.

The sadly-lacking mainspring of the entire offensive was the slow build-up of planned routeing and the lack of any scientific devices to assist the navigators and bomb-aimers. It is extremely odd to reflect today that whilst the 'boffins' managed to save the country in 1940 with radar in the Battle of Britain, no parallel device was being developed to help Bomber Command. But please to remember that the Battle of Britain boffinery first saw the light of day in the mid-1930s. There was a scientific hiatus and it took the Butt Report and the prodding of the C-in-C to trigger off an effort in this direction. GEE was an excellent start, but soon negated by jamming. It did, however, assist in the concentration of bombers on route to the target and was invaluable in getting aircraft back in contitions of bad weather. GEE's most important occasion was perhaps the 1,000-Plan, when nearly 1,000 aircraft passed through the target area in about 90 minutes, making Köln a watershed in the history of the British Bomber Offensive. Some 600 acres of central Köln had been devastated, and although the other two targets within the 1,000-Plan were not a success due to poor weather, Harris had made his point. At the same time the Air Ministry element renewed their efforts to get the Command to consider some co-ordinated system of condensing our bomber streams through the target and, more importantly, the concentration of damage to the aiming point. The Air Ministry firmly believed that fundamentally it was a question of pure navigation, and furthermore they were convinced that they knew one man who could lead such a formation to meet the planned Bomber Force envisaged by the Chiefs of Staff — but he was not even in the RAF. He was a professional Imperial Airways pilot with an international reputation — a host of 'firsts' in world aviation events and, even more importantly, he was an outstanding navigator. By name — Captain Don Bennett, the Operational Director and founder of the Atlantic Ferry who persuaded first Lord Beaverbrook (and he in turn Churchill) and finally a reluctant Air Council that delivery of aircraft by air from the USA was feasible; and on 10 November 1940 Don Bennett delivered seven Lockheed Hudsons; six landed at Aldergrove in Northern Ireland, and another nearby. Harris is believed to have said on receiving the Directive to form a Target Marking Force, that this was one more occasion where a commander in the field had been dictated to by junior officers at the Ministry. It is difficult to understand why the Bomber Staff was so reluctant to even consider the Ministerial direction. We are told that the main reason given was the weakening of squadrons by withdrawing the best crews. Nevertheless after much procrastination, all of which is still clouded in the veil of 'security', the Pathfinder Force was formed on 15 August 1942 and its first Commandant was Gp Capt D. C. T. Bennett DSO (later AVM, CB, CBE, DSO) who was officially appointed on 5 July — the master airman extraordinary and navigator par excellence.

Once the formation of PFF was *fait accompli*, and apparently against the personal wishes of the Bomber C-in-C (and the majority of his Group commanders) the Bomber Groups were instructed to send selected volunteer crews to a squadron raised by each Group and, thereafter, each squadron would be supported by its parent Group. Thus, at the outset, No 1 Group raised No 156 Squadron (Wellingtons), No 3 Group — No 7 Squadron (Stirlings), No 4 Group — No 35 Squadron (Halifaxes), and No 5 Group — No 83 Squadron (Lancasters). By the end of the war, PFF comprised eight Lancaster squadrons and 12 Mosquito units, plus the Met Flight Mosquitos and the PFF Navigation Training Unit. The early problems of the PFF gave its critics much to enjoy since the Force was Pathfinder in name only. The four initial squadrons, each with a different type of aircraft, had essentially different operational capabilities. The one redeeming feature was that Groups initially did select good crews, many of them second-tour types. All the original crews were expected to volunteer for 45 sorties: by and large this meant in effect that each PFF crew would start a full Bomber Command tour of about 30 sorties. Very few, in fact, claimed the 'let-out', and 60 sorties was nearer the average. This incredible sense of duty should be considered against the average sortie life of aircrew in the Command which was never higher than 9.2 and, at one time, as low as eight sorties per crew. Whilst 100 bomber sorties was quite normal in PFF Mosquitos, particularly in the OBOE squadrons, many 'heavy bomber barons' did achieve over 100 sorties, and all in Western Europe.

Some very bad-luck cases come to mind of apparently indestructible characters who were chopped on the last few sorties — 97th or 98th. Two that seemed particularly sad cases were Sqn Ldr 'Danny' Everett DSO, DFC, of No 35 Squadron who was killed on his 99th sortie. Everett, who had been ordered to take a rest at 98 trips, was testing aircraft at the Group Maintenance Unit when he heard that there was a spare aircraft going a-begging at his old squadron. Without mentioning it to anyone, he took a scratch crew and was posted missing, believed killed in action on 7 March 1945. But if Everett's chop was a severe blow, the advent of Alec Cranswick's death on 5 July 1944 ended a living legend. Alec Cranswick was the perfect Englishman — quiet and retiring, but as a bomber captain in an exclusive class of his own. At that time he had flown nearly 60 sorties in the Middle East before joining PFF and his total trips are somewhat obscure, but it was certainly not less than 147 (AVM Bennett, in his book *Pathfinder*, credits him with 143). Few bomber crews — if in fact any — exceeded this total, and certainly not in heavy bombers.

One of the most fascinating aspects of the Pathfinders was its attraction for characters, and the very nature of the Force seemed to beckon to the most unusual types. PFF crews had to volunteer which meant, in effect, that they were volunteering twice — first as aircrew and then, if selected again, to do an extended tour as Pathfinders. Although originally we demanded experienced crews, many actually started their operations with PFF. These I personally selected at training schools, generally those with 'Distinguished' passes. After the initial flush of good intentions by Groups, within six months there began a steady deterioration in the standard of crew replacements. In many cases they were not even volunteers. After a further period of three months or so, Don Bennett appointed me Group training inspector — and I became virtually a horse thief! My function was to tour the squadrons daily, using the previous evening's raid as my theme, to explain the difficulties and, in general, to make contact with the Main Force. And, I suppose, to make a plea on the spot for greater support in the shape of better crews, because I believed the best was only just good enough. Another source of crews was the instructional staff at flying and navigation training schools. In my endless lectures to the training Groups, I charged a fee — two tour-expired instructors. A great number of the OBOE pilots were in fact Blind Approach Training (BAT) instructors and the hurdle was 1,000 hours on a BAT Flight, the relationship to PFF OBOE work here being too obvious to detail.

Possibly the main strength of the PFF lay in the hotch-potch of nationalities. Approximately half the force were from the Commonwealth — Aussies, Canadians, New Zealanders, South Africans, Rhodesians and even from as far afield as Hong Kong, Fiji and the West Indies. This all made for healthy competition. I have in recent years got into a deal of trouble in certain Commonwealth countries by claiming that any all-Canadian or Australian squadron was not as good as a mixed squadron. In fact I have gone further and said a 'mixed' crew was, in my view, infinitely better than any 'national' crew. One of the reasons, possibly, for the high proportion of Commonwealth crews was my established policy of spreading my selection net as widely as I could in view of the poor co-operation of the Groups; to this end I literally plagued the various HQs in London — the Aussies at Kodak House etc. I was able to have the pick of excellent crews practically at the dock side as they arrived in the UK. An excellent seam of Dutchmen was worked; these were all Dutch naval pilots and navigators, not particularly experienced but the lack of hours was more than compensated for by their almost embarrassing zest for flying. Amongst the first of these was one Erik Hazelhoff, at one time the aide to Queen Wilhelmina and who held a Dutch Knighthood on arrival in PFF. He was the bait that brought many Dutch aircrew to our Mosquito squadrons.

Amongst other nationals was an outstanding Norwegian, Maj Christie — later to become a General in Norway's air force. Several Americans served, but were thinly disguised in RCAF uniforms. These were first-rate press-on types. One, a Texan, would never wear the issue flying boots but preferred the cowboy-type with high heels! It took the whole of his crew to hold him on a table whilst I got a hacksaw and cut at least two inches off his fancy boots; somehow he managed to get them restored. My objection to his high heels was that he would do himself a mischief if he had to bale out!

An interesting aspect concerning my widely-flung net for Pathfinders was that Groups after a short while sent crews who had not volunteered to join the PFF and, in many cases, had made a nuisance of themselves. By mid-1943 it was made very clear to the Main Force Groups that their 'selection' was unacceptable as I sent more crews back than we kept. About this time I noticed that those crews who consistently got aiming point pictures on the bomb plots issued by HQ Bomber Command after each raid were never selected for PFF. In my lecture tours round the squadrons I sought these crews out and, almost without exception, found they had in fact volunteered for PFF but had their applications rejected by their CO. It was a very simple matter to reverse this procedure, generally after some unpleasantness with the appropriate squadron and station commander.

When we had a regular flow of sound, keen material and the PFF Navigation Training Unit was in full swing, we saw the steady development of tactics geared to the constant production of new and better 'stores' — target indicators, hooded flares and many other innovations, all of which was more than matched by the improvement in navigational techniques. Whilst all this was going on, the enemy night defences were of course more than keeping pace with our ever-changing methods. It is true to say that the German nightfighter dictated the tactics we were forced to adopt. It was a critical struggle — a battle of wits between ourselves and the Lufwaffe with the edge always in favour of the Germans. Occasionally we had a relatively trouble-free raid: Dresden, for example. We were never given any long period free from a fight from the coast to a target and back . . . Happily, there were few disasters like the Nuremburg raid of 30/31 March 1944. Of 795 aircraft which set out we lost 94 which failed to return, some 74 badly damaged which reached England — 22 of which being write-offs after crash-landing. The total loss of these aircraft and crews was the bitterest blow Bomber Command had to suffer in the entire war, and it is difficult to understand why it happened. Normally, the PFF planned the route, which took account of many factors such as the avoidance of heavily-defended areas and the upper winds. The usual dog-legs associated with a bomber raid were inserted into the route to give a false impression of the ultimate destination, and the Mosquito Light Night Striking Force carried out spoof attacks on either side of the main track with 'Window' attacks and actually dropping TIs on probable targets along the route. In the case of Nuremburg however, the PFF planned route was rejected by the Group commanders (save one, the AOC No 4 Group), and one single-leg inserted of some 260 miles. Willi Herget, a Luftwaffe nightfighter ace with 74 confirmed kills, told me that halfway along this track it was easy to guess at the target, because a line of burning British bombers pointed the way to Nuremburg. This disaster was written-off as an 'accident', 'one of those things'. But Nuremburg was no accident. It was caused. Oddly enough, to the best of my belief, the PFF routeing was never challenged thereafter.

Possibly the greatest compliment that could be paid to the PFF — and that accidentally — was near the end of the war when the Command was strong enough for each Group to mount an attack on a single target, but generally supported by the full paraphernalia of hard-won pathfinding techniques. True, there were a few exceptions to this rule-of-thumb, plus OBOE and GEE-H, the main agents for precision marking.

It has been claimed that these free-for-all/do-it-yourself Group attacks justified the early Command view that it was wrong to form a *corps d'elite*. But such a misguided view fails to take into account first the 'fusing' of the many experienced crews that served in the Force, and the pooling of operational expertise that followed the hard-won tactical procedures, and last but no means least the steady improvement of the boffinery devices that were tried and tested on the job by no less than Bennett in person. And finally the determination of his crews to influence an ever greater weight of bombs to be left in the right place in Germany.

A secret report issued by the Luftwaffe in March 1944 on *British Pathfinder Operations** (see **Appendix I**) declared that 'the success of a large-scale night raid by the RAF is in increasing measure dependent on the conscientious flying of the Pathfinder crews'. And at the same time to quote 'Bomber' Harris, 'the customer is seldom wrong'.

I also must add that as far as the war moved to its close, crews became increasingly better; the output of the Empire Air Training Scheme gave us crews with more experience; second and even third tours crews were returning to Operations; and in the final phase, in daylight, the casualty rate dropped dramatically. All of this was happening alongside the steady decline of the Luftwaffe which did not enjoy our operational tour scheme and rest periods.

The chief architect of this incredible advance in bombing efficiency was unquestionably Don Bennett. His single-minded pursuit of operational perfection had to be witnessed to be appreciated. He was the only Commander in the field that was able to change the entire concept of strategic bombing; moreover he was the only Group commander with any worthwhile operational background, my personal researches accredit him with more than a full bomber tour of operations, and that includes his escape from Sweden. Yet Bennett was the only wartime Group commander not to be knighted. *We in the Pathfinders, who survived, wear this slight like a mark of Cain.*

It is ironic to reflect that had he served the Luftwaffe in a similar role to that which he graced in the Royal Air Force, there can be little doubt that he would have been invested with the highest order of the Knight's Cross of the Iron Cross — with Diamonds, Swords and Oakleaves. And those doubters should read *Great Britain — British Pathfinder Operations as at March 1944*. Whilst I would commend you to study the German Staff Paper in its entirety, I would also draw your attention to its personal citation of AVM Bennett, and note the dateline — March 1944:

'This 35-year-old Australian — known as one of the most resourceful officers in the RAF — had distinguished himself as long ago as 1938 by a record long-range flight to South Africa . . . an example of his personal operational capabilities . . . may be cited in the attack which he made of the German Fleet base at Trondheim.'

Wg Cdrs Peter Cribb and 'Shadey' Lane were at one time during the war Flight Commanders on No 35 Squadron. They lived in what I believe was called a half-Nissen hut for senior officers.

Now they lived in this hut together in perfect harmony. There was a sort of phoney partition hanging from the ceiling which divided one bunk space from another and, unhappily, the light that they shared was in the middle of the Nissen. When they came home from the Mess

---

*No 61008 Secret Ic/Foreign Air Forces West; A/Evaluation West: *Great Britain — British Pathfinder Operations as at March 1944*; Luftwaffenführungsstab Ic/Fremde Luftwaffen West.

after a bit of a Wing Ding (and these Nissens were like refrigerators) they would hurry into bed and neither was keen to get out of bed to switch off the light. So when it became obvious that neither of these senior gentlemen was able to persuade the other to get out in the freezing cold and put the light off, Peter Cribb — who was a man of great resource, as indeed so was 'Shadey' Lane — decided that the best thing to do was to resort to his .38 revolver, with which he then took pot-shots at the light; in the condition that he was in and hampered by the freezing cold, he had a series of near misses. Then 'Shadey' Lane thought that this was a good idea — 'I am a better shot, I am Canadian, I am better at everything than he is', so he took his .38 but served no better.

Now both these gentlemen were served very much better by a most extraordinary batman, and we had many like him. He was a very superior gentleman's gentleman in the fashion of Jeeves, and when both chambers had been exhausted he came in resplendent in the most magnificent silk dressing gown — better by far than either of the officers could afford, and with the most magnificent cravat — and he approached both gentlemen after the last shot had missed the bulb. 'Sir, have I your permission to reload?' he enquired.

10 Able-Oboe-Charlie

'Able-Oboe-Charlie' was the aircrew phonetics used by the early Pathfinders to identify their Commandant, although at the time he was officially a Commander of the Pathfinder Force, with the acting rank of group captain under the control of No 3 Group for day-to-day administration.

Thus the tempo of development within the Pathfinder Force kept pace with the events of the times. Early 1942 saw the doubts that lurked within the minds of many inside and outside Bomber Command that all was not well with our bombing of Germany. Fortunately, there was a small cell of opinion within the Air Ministry that passionately believed they knew the reason for the failure and, more importantly, felt that they also knew the answer.

At the highest level, Churchill's Scientific Adviser, Prof Lindemann (later Lord Cherwell) was also looking at this state of affairs and originated a study of some 600 aiming-point night photographs to be analysed of our best results to date. This emerged as the Butt Report and was immediately rejected out of hand by the incumbent Commander-in-Chief, Bomber Command, but not so by the Army and Navy to whom the report had been leaked and who were bent on carving Bomber Command up between them for their desperate needs in the Western Approaches and in the war in the desert. Fortunately, as so frequently happens in our military history the right man — and many would claim the only man — that was available at the time, assumed Command of Bomber Command in February 1942, and I have no doubt that future historians will claim that Sir Arthur Harris inherited a bankrupt concern, a sum total of 374 aircraft with only about 40 four-engined bombers in that total. And it should be recalled that in a very short time (less than three months) Harris mounted his 1,000-Plan to demonstrate what strategic bombing was all about, but more especially the main reason was to get the Navy and the Army off his back with their insistent and regular demands for bombers to bolster the parlous suituation in their theatres of war.

There is little doubt that Harris's 1,000-Plan saved the Command for the planned strategic bombing of Germany that had been his Directive from the Chiefs-of-Staff Committee who set aside some 3,500 heavy aircraft for this task. (It is worthy of note at this stage that Harris never received his full complement of aircraft and in the final days of the Bomber Offensive his maximum strength of first line aircraft was only 1,625 of which 200 were Mosquitos.) In one of my Staff College lectures, *The Bombing Years*, I stress and support the Harris claim that the Allied strategic bombing was the main contribution to the downfall of Hitler's Reich and our victory in Europe. I also say, with tongue in cheek, that the Harris 1,000-Plan should be dubbed the most outrageous confidence trick of the entire war. Let the Staff College student consider how Harris was able to conjure from his original strength of 374 frontline aircraft, and in a few months have some 1,047 aircraft set course for Köln in order to devastate 600 acres of the city (plus the admirals and generals in Whitehall). I invite the student of the air war to compute Harris's achievements with 1,625 aircraft and consider how much sooner we could have achieved victory in Europe had he the support of the promised 3,500 aircraft, and the entire Chiefs-of-Staff Committee.

Sir Arthur Harris does not, and never has, claimed that the Allied victory in Europe was the sole achievement of his Command. He had unstinted praise for the part played by the US Eighth Air Force as an equal partner in the Allied Bomber Offensive. He did, however, reserve some individual praise for the vast professional contribution that Don Bennett brought to the Command. And it should be remembered that despite a tremendous volume of criticism that heralded the Bennett appointment as the Commandant of Pathfinder Force, it was but a murmur compared with that when he was appointed AOC of No 8 (PFF) Group at the tender age of 31. I have in my possession a letter from one of the RAF's most revered names, a great wartime C-in-C and possibly one of the RAF's foremost Chiefs-of-Air-Staff and, in peacetime, a dear friend of mine these many years, who said of the Bennett appointment: 'I cannot understand what Harris was thinking of making that airline fellow a Group Commander . . .'

Donald C. T. Bennett, the youngest of four boys, was born at Toowoomba, Australia, on 14 September 1910. Destined to take over his father's cattle station, he quickly defected and headed for Point Cook — the RAAF 'Cranwell' — but not before several obstacles, which might have deterred many a lesser lad, had been overcome. He was deeply influenced by the great aeronautical pioneers of the day, notably Kingsford-Smith and Ulm, whose epic flights in the southern hemisphere shone like the target indicators he was to introduce years later over Germany.

His period at Point Cook seems to have been distinguished only by his getting a first in flying, and a second in the academic studies — by his standards, a poor start. For reasons best known to the RAAF at the time, they started cutting back on pilots and offered his course a transfer to the RAF. He accepted and joined No 26 Squadron at North Weald to start a Short Service Commission.

At this time he developed a feeling for courses and put in for every course in sight. Oddly enough, this must have sickened him because he banned *anyone* going on a course whilst he was AOC Pathfinder Force. In fact, he claims that his flyingboat course was his last in the RAF and certainly the most fortuitous for himself and subsequently the RAF.

His posting to Pembroke Dock, then commanded by Wg Cdr A. T. Harris, was a meeting of great minds and it is interesting to recall what Harris said about him in the early thirties, and later in the war years: 'he was, and still is, the most efficient airman I have ever met'. But also added that he easily became impatient with any intellect inferior to his own.

During his flyingboat period he added to his natural aptitude as a pilot several academic qualifications — a First Class Navigation Licence, 'B' Pilot's Licence, Ground Engineer's Licences, 'A'-'C' and 'X' categories, a Wireless Air Operator's Licence and an Instructor's rating — in preparation for the period when he entered civil aviation.

On leaving the Service in August 1935 he spent several months looking around and also being looked at by the family of the lovely Ly, his Swiss wife, a scrutiny which was reciprocated when Ly had in turn, to be looked at by the swarm of Bennetts in Brisbane, Australia.

In January 1936 he joined Imperial Airways and quickly became known as the 'Boy Wonder' and it was during this period, he later admitted, that he committed the only error of judgement in his entire flying career. Coming into Brindisi Harbour, he noticed that on the roof of a high rise block of flats under the wing float, lay a lovely Latin sunbathing. She gave him a rather languid finger wave and just as she disappeared under the wing float, he then realised she was only wearing a black sporran. The result unnerved the 'Boy Wonder' and he 'dropped in' from several feet.

In 1938 he was given command of *Mercury*, the top (seaplane) half of the Mayo composite, the lower carrier element being the *Maia* flying boat. In July that year, he flew *Mercury* on the first ever commercial Atlantic flight with a half-ton payload, starting at Foynes and landing at Montreal some 20 hours later, navigating by astro. The return flight was made via Horta in the Azores due to not having a *Maia*-assisted take-off, which would have allowed a heavier fuel load.

There followed DCT's attempt to fly the *Mercury* nonstop from Dundee to Cape Town, which failed by a relatively short distance, but nevertheless added considerably to the world's seaplane records and is still the record today. This particular flight can take its place with those of his boyhood heroes, Kingsford-Smith and Ulm.

It would appear that the real importance of the *Mercury* records was lost in the 'peace-in-our-time' sentiment which swept the country at the time, and despite the world record and some 42 hours 26 minutes air time, Bennett returned to duty in a week and to nonstop flights to Egypt carrying mail, logging about 14 hours each way. Again, these nonstop flights between England and Egypt were commercial firsts.

In August 1939, Don Bennett inaugurated two-way regular Atlantic services, aided by Alan Cobham's Flight Refuelling Company — yet another first, with Capt Jack Kelly Rogers starting at the New York end of the route.

The outbreak of war saw Bennett still in the navy blue of Imperial Airways and he heard the Prime Minister's broadcast, declaring war on Germany, with much the same feeling as most of us who remember it. Later that evening, over the Atlantic, he heard the SOS of the SS *Athenia* with its 1,000 complement of women and children *en route* for the New World.

Wedged neatly between his route flying at this period was a rescue operation to collect Gen Sikorski's staff who were making their way to the South of France, hotly pursued by the Germans. The only hitch in the operation was when the Royal Navy fired on the flyingboat as it took off from Bordeaux with the Polish General and his staff aboard.

The Atlantic Ferry now figures largely in the Bennett saga in which he was joined by several of his old Imperial Airways colleagues. The Ministry of Aircraft Production under Lord Beaverbrook was keen to fly the badly-needed aircraft across the Atlantic, instead of crating, shipping and uncrating — and a good proportion being sunk by U-boats.

The Air Ministry was emphatic that it 'was suicide to attempt air delivery — more especially in winter time'. Despite this, Bennett led seven Hudson aircraft, with captain, co-pilot and wireless operator and made the first formation delivery flight across the Atlantic in November 1940; similar formation flights followed at regular intervals, DCT personally leading about one in every four flights.

It was around this time there were grave doubts about what might be called the cost-effectiveness of the results achieved by Bomber Command. The C-in-C of the day utterly refused to believe the Air Ministry's suggestions that we were wasting our effort and losing many crews to little purpose. During one of his staging trips, Bennett was invited to the Air Ministry ('by some friends') when the sad tale of Bomber Command's failure was laid bare. The quite unprecedented step reflected the deep concern felt by a cell of opinion within the bomber department at the measure of the Command's worth at that time.

The fact that an unknown 'civilian' should have been consulted about what was indeed a purely Service matter, should be weighed against Bennett's unequalled background and experience. No serving officer — at that time, or since — could match his enviable array of qualifications and experience. Despite the 'Boy Wonder' tag, he countered the quite genuine complaints that with the elementary aids available — basically just a compass and air speed indicator — it was virtually impossible to find a German target in the face of spoofs/dummies and the mounting numbers of fighters, as well as flak and searchlights.

From that quite informal meeting at the Air Ministry, and others subsequently, the idea of setting up a Target Finding/Marking Force was imperative to the saving of Bomber Command as a vital contribution to winning the war.

From these secret meetings evolved the idea of a Force that would actually lead the assault and would be responsible for finding and marking the target for the Main Force. When the new C-in-C, Sir Arthur 'Bert' Harris, assumed command in February 1942 he was compelled to accept the concept, against his adamant belief that a *corps d'élite* was damaging to the Command. But he claimed that '. . . this is just one more example of a Commander in the field being overruled by a junior staff officer at the Air Ministry'. I had a feeling when I read those words over 40 years ago, and written in the heat of the aftermath of a long and tiresome period of war, that Sir Arthur might have wished he had put it differently. The whole vexed question associated with the gestation period of the 'Target Marking' element has not been, to date, documented. Ultimately, Harris conceded that if this was the Air Ministry's will, the addition to the Command would be called the Pathfinder Force and demanded Bennett would be the first Commandant.

Prior to the Ministry's ultimatum, Bennett had been removed from the Atlantic Ferry and was replaced, oddly enough, by the Air Chief-Marshal who had resisted the actual formation of the Atlantic Ferry as 'suicidal'. An interesting comparison between the two periods of operations was that in the Bennett era, only one aircraft failed to make the crossing. Students of wartime history will find a study of the post-Bennett era revealing.

On re-entering the RAF, DCT was made an acting wing commander and, after a short period, was given command of No 77 Squadron flying Whitleys which, with his background, must have been a daunting experience. Happily, after a short period, this was rectified and he commanded No 10 Squadron with Halifaxes.

Shortly after joining No 10 Squadron he was shot down during an attack on the Tirpitz at Aasfjord near Trondheim in Norway. Despite having one wing afire and disintegrating, he managed to get his crew away but only after his flight engineer, FS Colgan, found a parachute and attached it, and had gone to the aid of the wounded tail gunner. Bennett was the last to bale out. He evaded capture on his adventurous journey from Norway to Sweden and this is best savoured by his own description in *Pathfinder* which, unhappily, does not report details of his encounter with Count Bernadotte of the Swedish Foreign Office: this must have been a very unequal contest. He was back in the UK exactly one month after being shot down.

On his return to duty, and the award of a DSO, he was ordered to Bomber Command where Harris confirmed that he was to command the Pathfinder Force. Although the C-in-C had initially resisted the formation of the PFF, he gave the Commandant virtual *carte blanche* in the selection of airfields and staff; the Command however, insisted that the Force operated the night it was formed, despite an adverse weather forecast. This did nothing to alleviate the poor opinion of the whole PFF concept held by senior officers inside and outside the Command. Bennett was considered an upstart, and a civilian upstart to boot, in spite of Point Cook and his Short Service Commission, not to mention his formidable flying experience and technical background. And, I hazard a guess, more logged flying time than the sum total of all the senior officers in the Command at the time.

Nevertheless, he set about the seemingly hopeless task of making a bankrupt Command a going concern. At the time of his appointment to PFF, the Command was just getting used to GEE, thought originally to be a bombing aid but really at best an aid to navigation. Nevertheless, it was very welcome until its worth was diminished by enemy jamming.

It must have been a testing time for the boffins at the Telecommunications Research Establishment (TRE) at Malvern to find an operational RAF pilot in their midst, competing with them and reducing by months the time-scale normally associated with getting things done. Here was the case of the user in desperate need and the boffins equally keen to deliver the goods.

Quite apart from the endless experiments to be carried out in developing H_2S and OBOE, there were countless visits to the Air Ministry, HQ Bomber Command, the aircraft makers and TRE where he had to fight — and fight hard — for the priority he felt his PFF must have to survive. It was during this latter period that the anti-Bennett lobby really closed ranks on the 'civilian upstart'. It is only fair, however, to place on record that he never felt that a tiny measure of diplomacy was worth trying.

A typical example — and there are many of these — was when he patiently sat through a high level Air Ministry conference listening to the Mosquito being castigated for its poor night flying qualities (because of the glare from the exhausts), and Boscombe Down recommended that it should never be flown at night. The chairman, as an afterthought, suggested Bennett contribute his views: 'I wish someone had told me about all these faults', he replied, 'because I have been flying the Mossie on OBOE night trials with excellent results'. End of conference — but not the end of 'civilian upstart'! What Bennet did not tell the conference was that he had designed special shrouds for the exhaust ports, and his Group engineer had them made up in the local village smithy. They only lasted a short period, but the Command engineer followed up at once with proper drawings and specified the correct heat resisting metal.

Not only was the question of PFF navigation imperative to the success of the Pathfinders but there was the vital question of armament 'stores' — hooded flares and target indicators in all sorts of colours. A special form of coloured route marker had to be developed and approved and it was in this field, as with TRE, that Bennett had the least of his problems. It was a love affair between thinking minds as opposed to that 'bloody jumped-up airline chap' which seemed to be the anthem of his air-rank contemporaries.

Whilst the need for 'stores' and all forms of ancillary equipment was being chased, the matter of operating a hotch-potch of five squadrons, each with a different type of aircraft, brought its own problems to the PFF. But the Command insisted that the Pathfinders must pathfind with what they had and make the best of it. Small wonder that there was high glee within the Command when the first sortie to Flensberg was such a debacle, due in the main to weather. I remember — I was there. Nevertheless, methods were being developed to allow the mounting weight of Bomber Command to inflict an ever-deeper mark accurately on the allotted targets.

Whilst DCT would not accept an Australian squadron, he did accept a Canadian squadron — No 405 — because he said the Canadians were actually getting their replacement crews direct from No 6 Group, which was the Canadian group wholly supported financially by the Canadian government. Perhaps the close proximity to No 4 Group — and Roddy Carr, the Group Commander — might have influenced 'Black Jack' McEwan, the Canadian Air Vice-Marshal, since they were the only two Groups which supported Bennett entirely during those troublesome times, from the PFF's formation to the end of the war.

I felt that it should now be placed on record that the monumental and disgraceful row which was a feature during the Battle of Britain between the two Air Vice-Marshals — Keith Park and Leigh Mallory — was in no way comparable to the discord that appeared to exist between Bennett and AVM Sir Ralph Cochrane, AOC No 5 Group. Here were two superior intellects — 'Cocky' with a vast Air Force-trained mind (and as Bennett quoted in *Pathfinder* '. . . an energetic and conscientious man . . . no Air Force officer with more zeal . . . a magnificent brain . . .') and I, as one who basked in the favour of them both, fully endorsed these views. Bennett had added to his original Australian Air Force training, albeit with a Short Service RAF Commission, but had accumulated almost every qualification known to aviation and beyond this, had a wealth of practical experience. In flying experience alone he came to the Command with nearly 10,000 hours. I claim to have seen this conflict at closer range than anyone. As the PFF 'horse thief', I would be told to visit the Group commander when I next called on No 5 Group to explain some aspects of our techniques, or indeed a lapse in recent sorties. I was always made most welcome and enjoyed 'Cocky's' confidence. He would gently put his point of view and add 'go tell your master'. It was on one of these occasions that Guy Gibson was ushered into 'Cocky's' presence and, just prior to his appearance, the AOC had given me a slip of paper with the names of about 20 pilots whom he asked me not to recruit — as a favour to him — which was his style. When Gibson and I left the office, Guy turned on me and bluntly told me the fate that would overtake me were I to steal one of his crews. Now 'Cocky' did not tell me what his list was intended for, I had assumed that Gibson was referring to his own unit, No 106 Squadron. He did, however, add '. . . and keep your sticky fingers off Searby'. Now up to that moment I had never heard of John Searby, one of Gibson's flight commanders, and he did not appear on 'Cocky's' list. That same day he (Searby) was posted to command No 83 Squadron, and won renown at Peenemünde as the Master Bomber. Guy quickly evened the score by removing, through stealth, one Dave Shannon from the PFF Training Unit at Warboys, to become one of the outstanding Dam Busters.

There is a sad ending to this tale. 'Cocky' had grounded Guy Gibson after his epic Dams sortie, but he pestered his Group Commander to return to active flying. Eventually 'Cocky' agreed with the proviso that he undertook a short course at Warboys on the Mossie before he attempted what was known as the Cheshire low-level marking technique. This technique was highly dangerous and required the skills that Cheshire had certainly acquired over a long period, but was equally within Gibson's exceptional abilities. However, Gibson had no experience on the Mossie and would have benefited a great deal from a few hours with the PFF Mossie Unit at Warboys — perhaps a couple of low-level bombing attacks on our bombing range. Sadly he rejected this dual instruction and was lost on a low-level marking attack that, had Cochrane been aware that Gibson was not checked out at Warboys, his AOC would have forbidden him to fly that night.

Thus the RAF and the nation were deprived of one of its most gallant battle leaders, amongst the bravest of the brave — I knew them all, I walked in their shadows. As I make my way through my lecture tours overseas I am frequently asked who was the best, and I have to evade a proper answer because each group had its Gibsons, but at different times. However, I can debate with anyone and at any stage that Gibson was right at the time for the Dams. He was right at that time because he was, shall we say, 'in season', an exceptional pilot. He had the arrogance and the charisma of a Bob Stanford-Tuck or Doug Bader, but I will also add that he had that indefinable something that was an essential ingredient in an outstanding bomber pilot. He also had the same stock-in-trade qualities that were clearly visible in Len Cheshire, Willie Tait, Jimmy Marks, Pat Daniels and the youthful Fraser Barron to name but a handful.

Oddly enough many years later — and shortly before his death — 'Cocky' and I often had breakfast together in the RAF Club and he never berated Bennett or in any way referred to the difference of opinion that certainly existed in the

Pathfinder era. Sadly much of the animosity generated about Cochrane and Bennett originated from within No 5 Group and a great deal I was able to counter before it reached tap-room levels. I never felt I was running with the fox, because I had great feeling and admiration for both these Olympian figures. In fact, Cochrane invited me to move to No 5 Group with him when he left No 3 Group, but I declined as I was in mid-tour. When the war ended he sought me out to offer me a choice of jobs; I chose his Transport Wing in Germany, on loan to Sholto Douglas, then the C-in-C Germany, to operate the air transport requirements for Germany in the early days after the end of the war, with aircraft based in the UK. Bennett was less discreet and, by virtue of his unsurpassed practical experience, was less patient with 'Cocky's' theory and lack of operational experience. I have been the catalyst in the fusing of these two remarkable characters at postwar reunions and have been warmed by their adult behaviour, long after the flak had faded.

I have always understood, and believed, that you just cannot 'dance at two weddings', but I admired and respected Cochrane as the most efficient serving officer I had encountered in my short 33 years in uniform. Bennett, on the other hand, had my absolute loyalty and to witness him in action led one to understand in later years what Lord Reith — founder Director of the BBC — meant when he said 'I was never fully stretched'. DCT's tongue-lash never really hurt because a moment's reflection made one realise that he was right. He generally was.

The Battle for Control of 3cm H_2S

Whilst the Pathfinders had the original control of H_2S, developments were going on with a fair measure of practical input from Bennett and his friends at TRE, and eventually a superior set was devised and known as the 3cm H_2S. Immediately — and this can be well understood — Coastal Command had more than a passing interest because it was having a desperate struggle with the U-boats in the Atlantic and, naturally, it was very keenly supported by the Admiralty and the Navy to boot, to get hold of this latest model.

Oddly enough, Bomber Command seemed to feel that if Bennett was so impressed and believed that the Pathfinders should have this latest version, then it was up to Bennett and the Pathfinders to fight and debate with Coastal Command. So Bennett was instructed to go to AM Sir John Slessor, Commander-in-Chief, Coastal Command, and literally fight it out for their share of the new 3cm H_2S. Viewed entirely from a technical standpoint, this was rather an unfair struggle. Whilst AM Sir John was generally acknowledged as a very rare intellect and, particularly, an excellent scribe in the best Staff College style, he was no match whatsoever for Don Bennett with his mass of technical knowledge and practical hard-won experience.

It may be of interest to many, particularly Bennett's detractors, to know that he disapproved originally of the Main Force having H_2S, even the earlier versions. He made a very sound case that only the Pathfinders should receive the benefit of H_2S developments and that it was wrong for the Main Force to have the device. He did have (and I know this as I was on his staff at the time) some sympathy with Coastal Command in view of its plight in the Atlantic, particularly in the Western Approaches and more especially in what was called the 'black pit'.

This was an area in the Atlantic where the RAF could not give air cover to the convoys either from Ireland, Iceland or the Eastern seaboard of Canada and America.

What struck me at the time about the 'battle' between Bennett and Slessor was that Bennett acted as an agent for his C-in-C as well as in his own personal interest. Nevertheless, he did feel that Coastal had a strong claim to the latest 3cm version which could well have been made available to assist with the war at sea if large resources had not been diverted to equip the Main Force of Bomber Command. This diversion was unnecessary, thought Bennett, and I fear this and many similar instances were to befall him whilst commanding No 8 Group — for example, the introduction of the Master Bomber role, and the Group commander's broadcast prior to the distastrous Nuremburg raid in March 1944.

It would be a very revealing item of Bomber Command's history were a tape to be made available today of that unfortunate telephone link-up, and for a cold assessment to be made of all the circumstances as known at the time. But perhaps the most surprising 'own goal' scored by the Command was the length of time that it took to appreciate the value of Radio Countermeasures (RCM).

11 Some 'Odd Bods'

Sqn Ldr Tommy Blair DSO, DFC*

Perhaps I should start with one of the most colourful characters that we ever had in the Pathfinder Force — unhappily now dead — Tommy Blair of No 83 Squadron. He was a very much larger than life character who it is understood, although it may not be strictly true, was sacked three times by his company for which he worked as a salesman. Although he was sacked he was taken back a fourth time and he did indeed die in harness. I can recall one memorable evening when we met in the Pathfinder Club just as soon as it had opened in the evening; I was attached to the Air Ministry at the time and it was very soon after the war as we still wore uniform. 'Hamish, oh I am so pleased to see you', he said. 'I have got a very important job tonight, one of my clients is over from France with his wife and daughter and I am entertaining them. Now I find that in entertaining three people I cannot quite devote as much time to the two ladies as I would like to, perhaps you could assist me.' He continued, 'they are coming in here shortly and there will be papa, mama and a daughter; we will go to the Savoy Grill where we will have a little meal'. Now Tommy's idea of a little meal was quite different to that of my own, a serving Wing Commander living in London whilst my family were up in East Yorkshire. My idea was more Lyon's Corner House than the Savoy Grill but, nevertheless, we went to the Savoy. After a delightful supper we just tottered across the forecourt of the Savoy Grill into the Savoy Theatre — very intimate — and we saw a nice show.

We then all got into taxis and we went off to the *Coconut Grove* at the top half of Regent Street where we spent until the small hours of the morning, Tommy dancing with everyone in sight and paying court to the French ladies.

We were wined and dined at great expense and the next time I met Tommy he thanked me profusely for assisting him on that evening. He told me that he got an awful rocket from the Director of Accounts when he handed in the bill which worked out at several hundred pounds — and here we are talking of the year 1946!

He completed a Pathfinder tour and came to Warboys when I was the High Master there. Whenever I wanted a guest to be really entertained at one of our functions I would send for Tommy and ask him to look after them. We had no Balls as such in those days, we would have a dance, and when I was entertaining any of my theatrical friends from the West End it was always Tommy that I selected to do some special entertaining — well within the reach of the station commander's entertaining fund. However, this was very limited indeed in comparison with the vast sums that we can associate with Tommy's expense account!

Incidentally, Tommy had a dog of 57 varieties called Sammy who was predominantly Spaniel by looks and devoted to him. Sammy had his own log book and the number of sorties he did over Germany varied according to the time of night and the amount of beer consumed in that period. Sammy slept under the navigator's table and never seemed to have any reaction to the gyration of the aircraft or the attention of the natives with their flak and fighters outside.

Wg Cdr Fraser Barron DSO*, DFC, DFM, RNZAF

I have difficulty from time to time in persuading some of my colleagues to believe that a boy not yet 21 could amass so much experience in such a short time; he had completed two tours and looked like completing a third. Nevertheless, this happened to many, but I would question if anyone in the Command had amassed the experience of Fraser Barron in such a relatively short time. I was particularly distressed when I personally sanctioned his return to operational flying after a short period as an instructor at an OTU.

When highly decorated and very experienced operational pilots were posted to training units within Bomber Command, they invariably suffered some difficulty within these establishments. The main reason for this was that the units themselves resented a very young officer, heavily laden with acting rank, which meant that an existing officer of the same rank had to be disposed of to make way for an operational type doing a rest period.

After considerable pleas in writing and phone calls, I brought Fraser Barron back to command No 7 Squadron; during the interdiction period prior to the Invasion he was outstanding not only as a squadron commander, but also as an inspiration to all. Sadly, as the Master Bomber on a raid against Le Mans railway yards on 19/20 May 1944, he collided with his Deputy and it was indeed ironic that they both actually marked the aiming point with their burning aircraft.

Wg Cdr Roland Winfield MD, ChB, DFC, AFC

'Mad Doc' Winfield was one of the doctors at the Institute of Aviation Medicine at Farnborough and he was also one of the earliest of qualified doctors to take a full pilot's course. Now Dr Winfield — and I have ratified this — made 127 sorties; he could not have enjoyed his period at the Institute very much because he never seemed to be there. But he would come on a station with some project he wanted to fully research and he believed the only way to fully research these things was to 'try them out on the dog'. Although he was a fully qualified pilot, he never to my knowledge (certainly not whilst he was with No 7 Squadron) was ever captain of an aircraft; he had been second pilot, or flown as mid-upper, or rear gunner, or had taken some other crew function, but at the same time he would be researching and demonstrating some aspect of a project that he was currently engaged with at the Institute.

For instance, I recall one evening he came to me and took out a matchbox and he gave it a couple of shakes; I thought there were matches inside, but he opened the box and inside were some very evil-looking pills, about the size of, or a little larger, than a Beecham's pill. They were generally of a mottled colour and looked most unappetising. 'Try one Hamish' he invited. I would take one and taste it and then he would say: 'What do you make of it?'

'If it wasn't a pill I could almost be certain of a taste and an odour of liver and bacon, and probably some onions. Are there onions mixed?' I asked. 'Why yes,' he exclaimed, 'it's liver, bacon and onions'.

Somewhat perplexed I asked him what was the purpose of these things. 'Well,' he said 'we're very concerned about gunners — particularly rear gunners. On the way back they get past the enemy coast and usually they light up a cigarette'.

'None of my crew would, I'd know instantly,' I told him. 'I'm a non-smoker and if anybody smoked in my aircraft I would know at once. I know of anything that is happening down at the rear, I can tell you I have a very keen sense of smell.'

'Well,' he said, 'we think we lose a lot of aircraft, because we have been monitoring quite a few — they just disappear from the radar screen 50 miles off the coast, sometimes more, sometimes halfway across the sea if they are making a dash for Flamborough Head. This is a great worry to us and we believe we can help to prevent these losses by giving them something to distract them from smoking like liver, bacon, eggs, or steak and onions. We've got all sorts of mixes'.

Then he would take another matchbox out and say 'try these'. There was a very positive taste and odour about what he was trying to illustrate.

He was also the fellow who sat on the ground in what was called a 'Robinson Jacket' and was snatched from an absolutely stationary position on the ground by an Anson with a hook; this was a device to snatch injured personnel off the battlefield and into the air. What happened to them when they got to the other end I have never dared to ask, but perhaps these few illustrations (pages 82-83) will convince you that Doc Winfield actually sat in this contraption and was hooked from a completely static position by an aircraft into the air and probably (and I never found out) delivered to some hospital none the worse for the experiment. Wg Cdr ('Mad Doc') Winfield DFC, AFC — and no braver man ever took to the air, after completing 127 sorties — was found dead by his wife halfway up the stairs with a tray of morning tea, which might be a sort of warning to those of you — and there may be a few — who do get up to make your wives cups of tea.

Erik Hazelhoff-Roelfzema

I told you in another part of this saga of mine that I took over a flight in No 7 Squadron from a Flight Commander, Sqn Ldr Leigh-Smith, that I believe had ditched. I found all his clobber in the flight locker swimming in salt water, and his aircrew sweater and all his other gear dyed yellow by the colouring that aircrew used to put in the water to help identify their position to searching aircraft.

Now this fellow had a very attractive girlfriend called Midge and I got to know Midge through my predecessor, about the time I was due to leave No 7 Squadron and go to Bennett's headquarters. I met her in Cambridge and she introduced me to her new boyfriend who was a Dutchman called Erik Hazelhoff-Roelfzema. I was most impressed with this keen and very handsome young man, but I knew nothing whatsoever about him save that he was anxious to get into the Pathfinders.

As my new job in Bennett's Headquarters was ultimately to recruit Pathfinders, I felt that this was possibly a chap I should look at — quite apart from the fact that I knew little of him except that he had somehow or other got out of Holland and become the ADC to Queen Wilhelmina at the Dutch headquarters in London.

However, I was not prepared just to accept him with no experience at all and I asked him to give me some sort of evidence about the amount of flying he had done. So after one or two other visits to *The Bun Shop* or Joe Mullins' *Volunteer* in Cambridge on nights off, he eventually presented me with a log book detailing some 280/290 hours of flying, which was about the average of the normal straight-through pilot that came from the training machine and could then enter an Operational Training Unit. So there was nothing different about that save that years later I found out that it was not his log book at all. It was in fact a log book that he had bought from somebody and changed the name. Now had I known abut this at the time, of course he would not have stood a chance of getting into the PFF. After the war he also confessed to me that his eyesight was very bad and he would not have passed any normal eye test that we used in the RAF, but he did have contact lenses.

Quite apart from the bizarre situation of a bought log book and contact lenses, you have got to also measure the style of a fellow that goes to those lengths to do something he wants to do, and wants to do badly. But this, of course, was the stock-in-trade of any of these people — Dutch or anybody else — who managed to get out of German-occupied Europe and fight with the Allies.

Erik Hazelhoff-Roelfzema was accepted eventually, but I still felt he wanted more experience. It was not until about a year later, when I became the High Master of Warboys, that I took him into Warboys and made him a sort of Staff pilot flying Oxford aircraft on special navigational training exercises; this was something that I could physically check and I do not know why it is, and I am not being clever now, I just accepted the evidence he gave me of this phoney flying. Later, when I felt that he could do with even more experience than he had got at Warboys, I sent him up to RAF Grantham which at that time was training navigators. He could fly all day long and all night long if he wanted, but I wanted him to get 100 hours at night and I felt that despite his enthusiasm I would like to be shot of him for a period. So it would take him, in my view, at least three or four months to get 100 hours night flying. Although he was on Oxfords, or even Ansons, he was nevertheless getting experience at night and this was important if he wanted to become a Mosquito Pathfinder. So off he went to Grantham.

I think it was within a month or so of his departure that I received a phone call from a friend of mine at Grantham: 'Look, for God's sake let's get rid of this Dutch friend of yours, he's a menace.' 'What has he done?' I asked. 'He hasn't done anything except fly at night,' was the answer. 'He has asked to do at least two details at night and if anyone falls sick he will ask to do a third and even a fourth. If he had the chance he would fly all night long and also do any day flying. He's got his 100 hours, can I send him back to you?'

I agreed and I put him under training for Mosquito, and to the best of my knowledge (and this is only a guess) he did over 70 sorties, got himself at least one DFC, if not two, and became a very worthwhile member of the Pathfinder Force.

Wg Cdr Jimmy Marks DSO, DFC

I always had a strong feeling that, once 'Bomber' Harris was forced to accept a Target Finding/Marking faction within his Command, one of the very first people to be considered as founder member would be Jimmy Marks.

By the time the Force (now called the Pathfinder Force by Harris himself) was being manned, Jimmy Marks had become the Commander of No 35 Squadron and so arrived on the day that the Pathfinders were formed with his hand-picked aircrews from No 4 Group. Sadly, Marks did not last very long and he was the first of the Commanding Officers of the four founder squadrons to be lost in battle; this was not only a great loss to the squadron, but certainly to the Pathfinders. I possess a letter from one of his crew who was the last to leave the stricken Halifax whilst his Commanding Officer struggled to keep the aircraft airborne, losing height rapidly and beseeching all the crew to get out before it struck the ground. It is difficult to understand why Mark's action was not brought to the attention of the authorities then, because his action as the captain of the aircraft dwells within many heroic and desperate actions that under normal circumstances would have been considered for high award. His flight engineer WO W. G. Higgs wrote:

'On the night of 19/20 September 1942 we were attacked by a Bf110 from below; he hit us in the port mainplane and set fire to numbers five and six fuel tanks; the ailerons were jammed and the fuselage was also on fire. It was impossible for the skipper to get out; although I put his parachute on for him he remained at the controls and ordered the crew to bale out. I wrote to my parents in POW camp telling them that the crew were alive because Jimmy Marks had stayed with the aircraft in order that we could escape.'

I served with Marks before the war and he showed great promise even as a junior officer. Earlier in this tome I recalled his experiment with target finding, and remember the dateline — June 1940, attacking a target near Rotterdam.

Gp Capt Johnny Fauquier DSO, DFC

Johnny was a Canadian bush pilot before the war and was fortunate to survive the trough of despair in the spring and early summer of 1942 when survival chances were at their lowest (see graph on page 85).

I recruited Johnny at the *Golden Fleece* in Thirsk, one of the No 4 Group watering places, and he came down and commanded No 405 (PFF) Squadron at Gransden Lodge. Fauquier was a hard CO, very much after the manner of the Royal Navy chaplain whose Gospel appeared to be 'don't do as I do, do as I tell you'. He survived an outstanding Pathfinder tour as a group captain, was snatched by the AOC No 6 Group to become his SASO and got a 'thick 'un' but chucked it all in to drop two ranks to command No 617 Squadron, wherein he finished the war. He gave me the most trouble by returning more potential Pathfinders than any other CO; but not only aircrew — he walked about Gransden with a wad of railway warrants in his pocket, and anyone who offended got one on the spot. The AOC No 6 Group complained to me about this, so I suggested that he keep the culprit for a week and then send him back. It never failed.

He found himself stymied by an old oppo of mine when setting out on one of the Bielefeld Viaduct sorties with Tallboys. His R/T went u/s as they were taxying out and he called for control to stop 'Jock' Calder (his Deputy) and tell him to get out of his aircraft and hand it over to Johnny's crew. 'Jock' overheard this plea, switched off his R/T, took-off and led the sortie, but was never forgiven.

Johnny was surely the 'Billy Bishop Canadian' of World War 2: only the war ending when it did denied him the highest award.

Wg Cdr E. E. Rodley DSO, DFC*, AFC, AE

Wg Cdr Rodley, a distinguished Pathfinder, commanded No 97 Squadron which, together with No 83 Squadron, was hijacked by No 5 Group towards the latter part of the war to provide pathfinding expertise for No 5 Group's bombing sorties.

Possibly the most terrifying of Rodley's activities whilst attached to No 5 Group was a remarkable escape from destruction when he took off from Coningsby on a special mining raid, with a full load of Admiralty aerial mines, and suffered engine failure almost immediately after take-off. There was no possibility of jettisoning the mines and fortunately, right ahead on the preliminary climb, Rodley sighted a sandbank awash ahead. He landed wheels-up on the sandbank and he and all the crew escaped certain death. Aparently, some years later the whole story broke and Rod and the crew — those that survived the war — were awarded the Freedom of the Town of Boston. Rodley, having survived a complete Pathfinder tour and beyond, became a senior captain in BOAC and is today happily retired and an active member of the Pathfinder Association.

Gp Capt Leonard Cheshire VC, OM, DSO, DFC

Leonard Cheshire and I were pilot officers together in No 4 Group at the beginning of the war; he came from the dreaming spires of Oxford and I had just been commissioned as a pilot officer after serving a stint of five years as a sergeant pilot. Thus together we became one of the lowest forms of animal life in the Royal Air Force, the most junior — a very thin single ring — but, nevertheless, Leonard Cheshire had a stamp of his very own.

First of all I recall that there were not too many varsity entrants in the Air Force, probably only one on each station at the time, and Leonard Cheshire was our first university entrant and viewed with considerable suspicion and a certain amount of distaste. He was not one of us; he did not quite fit into the measured compartmentalised minds of the Service at that time. However, from the moment he entered the Mess he was quite an outstanding character — and I hope he will not mind me mentioning it — against a rich harvest of exceptional characters at that time.

Something that struck me personally at this period was that he had a most strange and cultivated sense of humour. Being such an 'odd bod' he was the butt of many who took the opportunity to make it known that he was different from us, and whether we thought we would in time change him was something that was a hope — happily a fond hope.

One of the things that always intrigued me, and still does, concerned his Oxford tailor who seemed to think that the practice of having the brevet just above the left breast pocket on the tunic should be reviewed. His brevet (his flying wings in other words) was situated some two or three inches above the pocket and when this error was pointed out to him by the more die-hard RAF characters he pointed out that the space was to make room for the VC, the DSO and the DFC. He obviously had never heard of the Order of Merit or I am quite sure he would have mentioned it at that time. Truly one of our outstanding men of the war (and any war).

Another side of the coin: when Don Bennett lavished high praise on my finding and training of Pathfinders in the final phase of the war, I have never quite understood why 'Chesh' as we called him at the time, was the only person I selected for training with the Force that my Master vetoed; my Master also vetoed the selection of Leonard to command No 35 Squadron in the early days of the Pathfinder Force and I was never able to establish why.

12 Second Tour

In the preface to this saga you will have tasted the full flavour of the Ju88 attack from the account by Bob Pointer — my mid-upper gunner — and who better to describe that horrendous shock of the cannon squirt. I, of course, at the sharp end felt but a slight tremor and my concern was with the loss of lateral control and my instrument panel disintegrating in front of me.

Permit me to take up our plight — try to imagine for a moment the straight and level run in to the target, 'bombs gone' followed by the desperate seconds (best described by one of my Canadian pilots as 'when I bite buttons off my parachute cushion') before the automatic photoflash and the aiming point picture taken by the night camera. The instant I realised that we had a picture I made a steep turn to starboard and a downward movement, simultaneously I was aware of a slight tremor in the aircraft in the region of the bomb bay. As I made the turn and dive I realised that I had lost lateral control and the wing 'roll and dive' was increasing alarmingly. My immediate reaction was to reduce power and I grabbed for the throttles. Due to my haste and attitude I missed the four levers and only managed to close the two nearest throttles — in other words, the port engines. This arrested the rate of roll and steepness of the dive and the wing started to return to the horizontal (also aided by the power from the starboard engines and pressure of the elevators). I was then able to assume some lateral stability by careful manipulation of the outer engines. All this, of course, happened in much less time than it takes to explain.

Happily all four engines had been spared the attention of the Ju88 but I was soon to learn from the flight engineer that the aileron control cable had been severed and he went into the wing root to find the two ends and make some sort of connection. I then started to climb through the broken cloud to recover some 10,000ft lost in the dive. When I came out on top I immediately looked to starboard for the Pole Star and was rather shocked to find that it was on the portside and we were obviously heading east, but by careful use of the engines was able to turn through 180°, and the navigator gave me a heading after taking a sight from the astro compass.

Roughly halfway between the target and the coast the rear gunner signalled that we were about to be attacked and my ham-fisted evasive action severed the repair that the flight engineer had made to the aileron controls. I was therefore left to dodge the fighter by very rough usage of the throttles, and shameful longitudinal control of the elevators. Happily we got rid of the fighter and the navigator set course once more by his skilful application of the astro compass readings and crossed the Channel. We were then able to find our way home by the friendly beacons until we reached the searchlight cone at Oakington. Whilst in the circuit we called for an ambulance on the Aldis lamp for the WT/Operator who had lost three fingers on one hand whilst 'tinselling'. I was not aware how badly Eddie had been injured, but understood that he was comfortable; this information came much later.

What the crew were not aware of was when I went into the starboard turn and dive without knowing that my aileron controls had been severed, and the fortunate miss of the four throttles made all the difference to the immediate arrest of the desperate attitude of 'Charlie'. And further, I had no idea I had lost some 10,000ft by this stage. By now I was well under the cloud base and had some idea of horizontal reference and applied maximum boost and revs to regain height.

Having restored stability I quickly got above the cloud, found I had lost the Pole Star and somehow, like a tank commander, turned through 180° by not very gentle use of the outer engines. The odd thing was that once on reciprocal we should have passed near the Köln area, with its attendant flak and searchlights, but not a sign.

Thus all things were bearing an equal strain and we were westward-bound when a frantic signal from the rear gunner warned me that we were about to be attacked again, and my heavy-handed evasive action severed the aileron control repair. Happily there was some friendly cloud; this time I went right through it to regain some horizontal reference, then bob in and out of the cloud until Jock had repaired the damage. I stayed near the cloud base just in case we were jumped again. Soon the Manston cone appeared on the port beam, and my London bobbie (Special Branch) steered me home via friendly beacons. But my bit had yet to come; I had no idea if we had sustained damage to the undercarriage, although we had three greens burning bright. I motored in as if to land on new-laid eggs; all the crew, including Jock the engineer, were at crash stations and we landed 'soft as a mouse's instep', as Spike used to say.

In retrospect, what I found fascinating at the time (and this feeling has only increased with time and further thought) was that all the crew just did what I would have told them had I been able to make contact with them. In point of fact the reverse ruled: I was constantly having chits thrust at me giving me a blow-by-blow account of 'Charlie's' state of health, but I was never made aware of the seriousness of Eddie's wound, and somehow I did not know until I visited him in hospital later that morning.

In August 1942 I was delivered to No 7 Squadron at RAF Oakington by an oppo, Geoff Wornersley, who shortly followed me to PFF. He did not leave the Force until he had completed the 'ton' with DSO, DFC and Bars, and his third tour with No 139 Squadron which later had a modified 120° scanning H_2S that acted as hand-maiden to the Light Night Striking Force.

I replaced a flight commander who I understood had ditched, or so it seemed — his name was Sqn Ldr Leigh-Smith whom I have already spoken of. Oddly, I felt this was a good omen. Early in my first tour I argued with my colleagues that I doubted it would be possible to ditch a Wimpy or a Whitley on water, particularly if there was a heavy swell. By a strange coincidence the first ditching I heard about was in No 77 Squadron in the early months of the war. A sergeant 'Nobby' Hall ditched and the crew got into the dinghy, and somehow Nobby got separated, drifted away from the dinghy and was drowned. A sketch was found on my locker door and I believe the author was Nobby Hall; he had opposed my views on ditching, as well he might, since he was an ex-officer, Merchant Navy, who had joined the RAF as a direct entry sergeant pilot in the Baldwin expansion period, and it was indeed ironic that he should perish and his crew saved.

Quite apart from the sheer mystery of all that I had to behold on arrival at an up-to-date operational station, I was plunged at once into an immediate round of familiarisation of completely new and strange devices that were the work-a-day tools of Bomber Command. What I found startling was the maturity of the crews. At first I was not aware that all the crews in the PFF had been selected by their Groups and, in the main, were either second tour volunteers or were well advanced on their first tour. This was eventually made doubly plain when each member of my crew took it in turn to brief me on his particular duties, and I in turn had to perform in his position.

My first sortie was on 18/19 August with a Peter Heywood, a son of the manse, who gave me a faultless demonstration of captaincy. Sadly it was on Flensberg, the first PFF outing that was ruined by the weather, and did nothing to further this foundling of target finding/marking. I think what impressed me most about Heywood was his absolute control of his crew and, in particular, his assurance that he was the boss, despite his tender years and meagre experience.

My next trip was not so pleasant but nonetheless enlightening. It was with a scratch crew and an experienced navigator who, like myself, had returned to ops after a period in the training world, but also (like myself) utterly clueless about present day operations. On this occasion I felt that all was not well and, although we got round alright, I had a deal of unease about the method employed by the navigator. He had a weird habit of talking to himself or, as I later realised, to God. At times when the flak splattered against the fuselage, he assumed an affected ecclesiastical voice, apparently coming from God: 'Are you in there Algernon?' And the navigator replied in his normal Brummie voice: 'Oh no, he is in the aircraft over there,' and the odd thing was that the flak left us and clobbered an aircraft near us. It was the dead-ringer of God's voice that unnerved me. I put a stop to this impersonation of the Lord and, sadly, Algy used up his measure of luck. I was then given a super navigator with only the sharpest of pencils and the instinct of a homing pigeon who took me through my tour; he perished the first time he flew without me after I was hijacked to Bennett's staff.

I now had a settled crew and witnessed the steady improvement in the PFF methods, but very much trial and error as it was at the time, although in keeping with the Harris momentum. I was enjoying the Stirling, but I was not impressed with its operational altitude. Here we saw the professionalism of Bennett when he made a study of the factors that impinged upon the operational height aspect.

72

When he looked at the tremendous penalty borne by the aircraft in regard to the armour plating carried, the first thing to go was a huge ½in thick slab that could have graced Fort Knox, but which protected the W/Op and the cabin crew, and that must have weighed several hundred pounds. Next he interrogated the gunners and found that the average rounds used by them (that came back) was something in the order of 350 rounds per gun, and they carried and brought back several thousand rounds per gun. He then made careful research into the reserve fuel lifted and found we all returned with about 23% of our fuel. This reserve was cut to around 12% and the result was that the Stirling was able to operate at 18,500ft plus, which was a much better height than the bare 12,500ft we struggled to in the early days of PFF. I remember at the time that all the crews felt a great deal happier being so much nearer the rest of the Lancs and Halifaxes, and no longer were in great danger of our oppoes dropping bombs and incendiaries on us.

Strangely, and almost coinciding with this modification to weight reduction, I found myself in a lack-of-petrol situation. It was on a trip to Frankfurt with a mixed load of several 2,000lb bombs and the varied load of experimental PFF flares and early target indicator devices; Bennett always insisted that we had to carry a full load of the hurtful. Running into the target we were heavily engaged by accurate flak that caught us whilst in a large cone of searchlights. Although we did not appear to have a direct hit in any vital part (and the engines were spared) as soon as we dropped our bombs, and the photo-flash meant we had a picture of where we had left our load, we turned for home. Now please permit me a slight diversion here. The flight engineer and I were one-time apprentices at Trenchard's, Halton, and he had left the Service at the end of his 12 years and returned when the war started. In the meantime, I had attended a special engine-handling course at Rolls-Royce, Derby, and we had different ideas about the engine settings. This led to an occasional resetting of my settings when I may have been distracted. Halfway between the target and the coast the flight engineer announced that we were having a heavy petrol consumption and the dialogue was something like this:

'Skipper to navigator, how long to the coast?'

Navigator: 'Thirty-nine minutes.'

'Skipper to flight engineer, how much petrol?'

'Flight engineer to skipper, thirty-seven minutes.'

At each stage there was always less fuel than there was time to get to the French coast. Then this pantomime carried on from the coast. The next stage was to get to Manston. When we got to Manston with four engines still running there was a heavy undercurrent in the cabin, although no words were uttered, the inference was that possibly we had the wrong engine setting. We entered the Manston circuit and found two Stirlings demanding emergency landings and I recognised the voice of one of my lads, Desmond Ince, and I told him to go ahead and take my turn to land. The other chap I was to learn later was a Sgt Middleton from Mildenhall (later Plt Off, VC). Whilst I was behind Desmond he was on two engines and landed heavily; one of his engines came adrift and preceded him along the flarepath. The Mildenhall aircraft veered away to the left and into a flying club canvas hangar full of light aircraft and churned the lot into kindling. By this time Desmond had nearly stopped on the flarepath and I decided to give him a wide berth. At that instant control called to announce that there was an Air Raid warning and put out all the lights, followed immediately by bombs exploding on the airfield. I knew the airfield well and I stuck to my heading and switched on my landing light just to 'feel' the ground, landed and rolled along until I felt a sharp jerk and a bash or two then a complete halt. In the gloom I felt I was in some kind of an enclosure and told the rear gunner to get out and find out where we were. By this time the 'All Clear' sounded and there was a certain amount of light by which I could plainly see I was in what appeared to be an MT parking lot. When the rear gunner returned he reported that we were in the Manston MT yard. He later told me of the adventure he had walking round the high netting accompanied by an airman on the other side of the wire. When my chap turned to confront the Manston sentry — who was on guard with a rifle and one round, and obviously felt that the chap on the wrong side of the wire could be one of those attacking his airfield — my chap said sharply something to the effect: 'Can you get us out of here?' and explained that he only meant his oppoes, not the Stirling. The sentry is claimed to have replied: 'Now don't * * * * abaht, I've got one up the spaht . . .' but rushed away to get the orderly corporal who, in turn, found the situation beyond his authority, and we were only released by no less than the duty officer. Later when we were enjoying a beer with the station commander were we nearly disposed of when it was announced that the Stirling had clobbered a Coles crane, an ambulance, several minor vehicles and the CO's Humber. The station commander, a well-known Battle of Britain type, suggested that he had wasted more ammo on the Luftwaffe that he could have kept for such an occasion as ours. On the way back to Cambridge we staged at 'Moonies' in the Strand, The nav — Tommy of the Metropolitan Police — rang his wife who appeared, as if by magic, with a large £5 note to feed and water the crew. Not that this, as it happened, was necessary because the landlord's wife saw we had all we wanted. The regulars and the heavy mob from Fleet Street arrived and we just managed to catch the last train to Cambridge.

Something similar must have happened to Middleton's crew because we met together at the station and took the train on the last lap to Cambridge. There I was to have a long conversation with young Middleton, to whom I took a great shine, and was very impressed with him as a person and indeed his crew. I enquired if he had volunteered for Pathfinders. to which he replied that he had thought about it. I told him if he wanted to come he could join my squadron. He agreed, and in a few days — not very long — he was in my flight. By this time it needed reinforcing, we had recently lost several crews.

So Middleton did two sorties I believe, and on each occasion he brought back an aircraft that was no longer capable of flying and was a write-off, it had so much flak and fighter damage. When the same thing happened a second time I had Middleton in and told him that one of his problems was his navigator who was just not able to navigate him round the very heavy flak areas. It was pointless him going right through the centre because he was incurring far too much damage and eventually he would be shot down. Of course, he was highly hacked about this — as only young Aussies of his type can be — and he insisted that he was not having his crew tampered with in any way. I agreed, but reminded him that he had

74

volunteered to come here, so he could volunteer to go back to his squadron. I suggested that he might like to go and have a talk with his crew. I did not want to send him back to his squadron, but with a new navigator I believed he could eventually forge a good Pathfinding crew. Middleton did not want any of that but he said he would go and talk to his crew. Whether he did or did not, he was back in very short order saying that the crew had decided to go back to their old squadron, and I cleared him to return to his squadron that same afternoon.

So back he went to his squadron — No 149 — but he fared no better. The sad thing was, as I said before, his navigator was incapable — and I must say not good enough — to get him round the heavily defended areas, and so in two sorties he still sustained abnormal flak damage. On his last sortie to an Italian target, of all places, he sustained tremendous flak damage which rather belied the sort of opinion that we had of Italian flak. We often said they loaded the gun in the afternoon and took a long lanyard into a dugout some distance away and fired their gun once and never emerged to reload. But Middleton received enormous damage on that last sortie which ultimately proved fatal. As I have heard from his crew, he baled out when he eventually got back to the south coast of England. One of his gunners, FS Cameron, who oddly enough baled out from two aircraft whose captains, ultimately, were posthumously awarded the VC, has his portait in that magnificent War Museum at Canberra. It shows this air crew just as he baled out of the aircraft less his parachute harness which he had abandoned on landing. He is looking up and out to sea in a southerly direction, and looking and listening desperately for sight or sound of Middleton — but that was not to be.

Middleton's body was washed up sometime later on the south coast of England, the country he had fought for so valiantly, and I commend you to read Chaz Bowyer's citation, which embraces the official citation for Middleton's VC, in his book *The Bomber VCs*. The navigator, who I wanted to exchange and who remained with Middleton in his very last moments, his body was never found. And whilst I have gone to Middleton's grave in the village of Mildenhall, I have found that I could in no way criticise his rejection of my plea that he stayed with the Pathfinders. But what I will say — and it must be said because in Australia it has been put about that I sacked Middleton — Middleton, sadly, sacked himself. I needed crews such as Middleton's badly and more especially captains like Middleton, but I was aware there was a weakness and that weakness had to be reinforced. The decision was Middleton's, but I will say — and I have repeated this in Australia, and what better place to say it than here — had Middleton accepted my alternative he would have had a better chance of living; but I would question very sincerely whether he would have had a VC.

The apprentice period followed sorties to Düsseldorf, Bremen, Krefeld, Osnabrück, and visits to the Ruhr — or 'Happy Valley' as the troops called it. Each sortie seemed to bring some added knowledge to the art of Pathfinding although some attacks were better than others. Then we had a period on the Italian targets. Despite being easy trips they did have a valuable effect on crews. The flight right through France down to Geneva, over the Alps down to Genoa or Turin, was something of a rest from the normal German targets. One could almost claim that setting course south of Paris for Geneva nearly 250 miles away was a pleasure compared with the more northerly targets. Strangely enough one could believe that the slightest glimmer of light on the dark horizon could be the lights of Geneva, and the glimmer became a glow and the glow became more positive, and one could distinguish the lights which were real lights and those which were the reflections on the lake. We steered away from neutrality and headed for the magnificence of the Alps in the moonlight; I always wondered if the Stirling would clear the Matterhorn and it always did with plenty to spare. It always was a surprise, the pure majesty of the scene approaching the Alps, more especially in moonlight; it seemed odd to me, whilst devouring this special panorama, that in a short time we would be raining all the horrors of war down on people not seriously willing to fight. But they were, at that particular time with the Germans, giving us a bad time in the Western Desert. It seems odd, in retrospect, that we carried out some excellent Pathfinding, but then we were aided by the lack of any serious opposition.

An amusing reminder of these sorties (I missed one of the larger of these attacks while on leave) springs to mind when, on returning to the squadron, I was told that I would have to take a strange aircraft that night. I learnt that my aircraft had been damaged by flak — and Italian flak to boot — and one of my lads was in hiding as he claimed I had threatened him with dire punishment if he damaged my aircraft. The shame of it: to damage the boss's aircraft — by Italian flak!

But all good things must come to an end; back on the old routine mixing it with the Luftwaffe and all they could muster — and their reaction was tremendous. In the years that I have had to research my 'Bombing Years' lectures I realise now that we never really got to grips with the German defences until the latter stages of the war. I am aware that there was a steady decrease in the casualty figures and this was welcome to the Harris Offensive and also to the Mighty Eighth, but it always appeared to be that the Luftwaffe were just that one step ahead until, of course, the advent of D-Day and the advance of the Allies on the Continent. About this time the appearance of the Mustang with the Packard Merlin engine must have seemed like manna in the desert to the Eighth Air Force. Of course, there was less enemy terrain to fly over, but at this period the sortie value was diminished — 70 and 80 sorties were common for those who elected to complete two tours and soldier on beyond the 60 cut-off.

Thus the entry into the fourth bombing year could be termed a watershed in the fortunes of the Allied bomber offensive. Moreover we see both bomber forces gaining weight and flexing muscle; Harris with his 100 bomber squadrons in sight (but still painfully short of the Chief of Air Staff's promised 3,500 aircraft), and the General commanding the Eighth Air Force in no better state, having to fight and fight hard to arrest the diversion of his build-up in aircraft to other theatres. But it was not all gloom on the side of the Allies: the general trend on the other side was one of gloom and doom. It is very heartening now to witness some of the excellent combat shots taken at the time — Eighth Air Force bombers being escorted to places as far afield as Berlin with a mass of Packard Merlin-engined Mustangs indulging in a leapfrog technique which meant fighter waves could follow the bombers, fight and be relieved by another escort wave. Thus those who had done their escorting and fighting, and had dropped their *papier mâché* tanks, could return to base. This excellent system of continental escorting and fighting-off the Luftwaffe marked the beginning of the end for the Luftwaffe as we had known it up to the advent of the newly-engined Mustang.

A further echo of the Köln Ju88 strike reverberated the following evening when most of the crew were out in Cambridge celebrating survival and, as it happened on these occasions, most crews had their own favourite watering places. The squadron's pub in Cambridge was known as *The Bun Shop* which, many years before, had been a bakery where undergraduates were able to go and buy alcohol as well as buns. On this occasion I personally moved from *The Bun Shop* to a pub I believe was called *The Volunteer* run by a well-known and aged bare-knuckle fighter from London's East End called Joe Mullins. He had an endearing habit at 10 o'clock of calling on each facet of his customers, starting with the lowest rank of airman, to 'piss off'; and worked through the ranks until he got to Kings (and on this occasion it happened to be King Peter of Yugoslavia). His ADC took great exception, but then Joe was able to say 'all Aides des Camps — piss off!'.

Now on this occasion after 'last orders' when Joe had got rid of everyone, save the remnants of my party, we went downstairs into the cellar and were enjoying pints drawn off by Mrs Joe when there was a great thundering on the door. A very authoritative voice shouted: 'Joe, I must come in because I am looking for a wing commander, Hamish Mahaddie, who I believe you have inside.' The police constable who had been hammering on the door was allowed to come in. He came down into the cellar and was awarded a pint and we all seemed to be enjoying ourselves when, once more, there was a banging on the door. This time it was a police sergeant, and when Joe went upstairs the sergeant said: 'I am looking for Wg Cdr Mahaddie, and I am also looking for one of my constables.' Joe foolishly replied: 'We might have a wing commander here but we don't have your constable,' and the sergeant replied, 'that's odd because his cycle is leaning against your door, Joe'.

So the sergeant came down into the cellar and again was awarded a pint; he explained that the wing commander was wanted back at Oakington immediately because someone at HQ wanted to speak to him.

I do not know why but that did not seem to register with me at the time, and it did not until there was a third assault on the door. This time it was an inspector who had come looking for the wing commander, his sergeant and his constable. He refused to come downstairs into the cellar but more or less instructed me to return to Oakington at once, as the Commander-in-Chief wanted to speak to me. By this time it was approaching midnight and when I got back to camp and rang Bomber Command the duty officer was most reluctant to put me through to 'Bomber' Harris. When I was eventually connected with my Commander-in-Chief I was to learn that this was the first night he had been abed in 13 consecutive nights of operations. What my Commander-in-Chief had to say to me is something that I will treasure for the rest of my days — and has only been shared with one other.

The epilogue to this evening's survival devotions was, strange as it may seem, exactly as I should have expected it to turn out. I do not remember when I missed — or at what stage — my flight engineer, but when I returned to camp and was literally wallowing in what the High Master at Command had to say to me, I was roused from my room with a call from the Cambridge police. Stewart had been arrested for disorderly conduct and was demanding that his skipper should come down and bail him out. I had a friend, an inspector in the 'cop-shop', and he advised that after breakfast would be early enough for that procedure. Next morning I was driven to Cambridge, clutching the flight engineer's personal documents which included his Service conduct sheet. In the normal run of events these would never come to my notice, but on this occasion I was going to make a plea of mitigation on his behalf and hoped that the Bench would release their prisoner into my care and he would be summarily dealt with in accordance with Air Force Law. But a brief study of his conduct sheet started warning bells ringing loud and clear — softly, softly, Hamish.

My plea was wholly contained in the events barely a day old and swiftly took the Bench and the entire Court through the squirt of 174 cannon shells, the wounded, the flight engineer's heroic effort in repairing the devastated controls twice, his treatment of the wounded and his immediate award of a DFM, which he had been celebrating. I think I left the Bench at least with an impression that they had someone very special to deal with. I was, of course, all the time praying that no one for the police would ask for his Conduct Sheet, which they overlooked after making a dutiful response to the Bench, and I hurried away to be met outside the Court by Stewart, who at once asked me to lend him a pound.

'A pound' I shrieked, 'What do you want a pound for?'

'To buy the policeman I was fighting with last night a drink.'

There could be no answer to that, none that I could think of at the time. And sadly the first time he flew without me he perished, leaving Bob Pointer and myself wondering why events in our puny lives are so ordained and arranged as to inflict the maximum hurt at a time like that.

Victory when it came I found tasteless. I was ashamed to be envious of air crews who were able to turn up at reunions with a crew intact, and they still can even 40 years on, and relive those cruel yet wondrous days when the composition of a crew was as binding as the sanctity of marriage. Remember Maj Christie, our Norwegian Pathfinder, who wondered at how his crew just happened to appear as though from some mystique of chance; how Middleton said in effect 'my crew is the best in the Command . . . leave them be or I return to the Main Force'. I never had the opportunity to tell Christie of my method of making up crews. At Kinloss when I was chair-bound there for a short period, all too frequently I received complaints about the composition of crews. Normally a list was published at random and took no account of any previous personal arrangements arrived at by crew members. This unsettled all aircrew before they even started training at the Operational Training Unit. I was able to persuade my chief ground instructor to let the crews pick themselves. I placed the pilots' names on a blackboard with four spare slots for the rest of the crew. The pilots drew cards for their turn and, in less time than you would believe, crews were made up and never a complaint thereafter.

I had good cause to enjoy the many favours bestowed upon me by my inspector friend with the Cambridge police. It started with a piece of foolishness that could have got me into a deal of trouble had I not have had a wise check in time from the inspector. I was friendly with one of the local farmers, and I had in mind on one of our 'stand-downs' to run a small flock of sheep through the *Lion*. I would,

78

of course, be dressed in ancient drover gear and had no doubt that it would cause something of a riot at the *Lion*. In due course my friendly farmer, Cyril Young, delivered four sheep to Oakington and everything was set for a bit of a barny at the *Lion*. I changed in *The Bun Shop* and slipped through an alley to the *Lion* to be confronted by a police sergeant and two bobbies and there was no way that I and the sheep would put on our act at the *Lion*. The whole jape took on a rather serious complexion when the police refused to accept that it was all a joke. In the meantime, the sheep took off on cue and I could hear they had reached the *Lion* by the din coming from the main bar. I was put in a police van and off to the 'cop-shop'; when I took off my smock and the stupid hat there really was a frightened wing commander underneath. Happily my inspector friend was at hand. He opened the Chief Constable's hospitality cupboard, I had a dram and was told that they had been tipped off that afternoon about some Scot that would run some sheep through the *Lion*. He was a member of a Scottish organisation and he was known as Aberdeen Angus. After thanks and apologies all round I was driven back to the *Lion* to find that my borrowed sheep had been sold and had disappeared. I was to learn that one of my air gunners had sold the sheep, and he seemed to go into hiding. Shortly afterwards he went missing in the cauldron of the Ruhr. I only wanted to tell him he should have got more than 30 bob a piece for them. He was, of course, an Aussie.

An experience of which I am thoroughly ashamed, and thankfully at the time my crew never knew, came to pass one night early in 1943. It was my role to lead the squadron off and that night we were bound for somewhere in the Ruhr and we were on the short runway at Oakington. We had instilled in all of us a very strong sense of timing, which had to be to the second, and this had become a habit. So, as a rule, I would always get out of dispersal in plenty of time. I would get very testy if things weren't exactly right come the take-off time.

On this occasion something had delayed me and I was late. I was in command of a heavily laden Stirling which was renowned for the fact that on a cold night the engines took a long time, even with the grills closed, to warm up. The orders were very strict that one could not move off until the oil temperature was above the minimum and on this occasion I was quite determined to make up the time. I got out to the end of the runway first, applied my brakes and did my run-up and magneto checks, whilst waiting impatiently for the oil temperature to rise to the required degree. The flight engineer, who had been at Halton as an apprentice with me and had left and later returned to the Air Force, complained bitterly as I was making all the preparations for take-off, but I ignored him. The navigator was giving me the countdown; as soon as the needles on the oil-temperature gauge started moving I would be off, making sure I took-off on time as this would be vital for the rest of the squadron. I was very proud of the reputation I had earned for exactness on timing. Take-off time arrived and the oil temperatures were still somewhat below the criteria, but I opened the throttles and very shortly the tail was up and I was heading down the short runway into a brisk headwind, pointing straight for the little pub outside the camp that had become a second home for us. The wheels lifted off the runway, up came the undercarriage and, as it was the short runway, I left the flap down a little longer than usual. To my absolute horror I found that all my controls were completely frozen. I was quite certain I had seen the ground crew go round and remove all the external locks before I had climbed aboard.

We were climbing away at a very gentle angle and I could not understand why I could not move the controls. Fortunately the aircraft maintained a perfect climbing attitude while I tried to sort it out. I reached for the elevator trim wheel; one glance told me it was in the normal position. We were still climbing at full power and a touch of nose up trim enabled me to increase the rate of climb. As my hand came away from the trim wheel I touched the auto pilot control and, on looking down, I found to my horror that it was 'Engaged'; I had taken off with 'George' in control.

Being one of the most experienced pilots in Bomber Command and having done an instructional tour, meant nothing. In my hurry and in the conceit that is deep within many of us pilots, with our belief in our own infallibility, I hadn't done my pre-take off checks.

I was able to climb to about 1,200ft at which height I felt it was safe enough for me to control any sudden change of attitude when I disengaged the auto pilot. Fortunately, when I did we maintained a perfect climbing attitude. I completed my mission, during which I spent sometime thinking about the young airman who had done the daily inspection of the instruments, and had left the auto pilot engaged. However, I should have done the proper cockpit checks which I certainly did ever after. Fortune smiled on me that night, and what could have been a disaster was averted.

Despite my wealth of experience and my time as an instructor, I had become over confident in my own ability. My crew were never aware of my lapse and I am just as ashamed to tell this story today as I would had I told it 45 years ago. The lessons are of course, don't be distracted and DON'T ASSUME — CHECK.

Do you speak English?

Quite apart from my constant wonder at how crews withstood the enormous pressures about this period (and that was the early part of 1943 whilst we were learning our craft, or the art, of Pathfinding) was the great belief that crews had in themselves. Our losses in the first few months of 1943 were rather harmful, and would have been very damaging to morale; something happened about that time which affected me very deeply.

Despite the rigours of the time, whenever there was a stand-down aircrews — generally headed by Canadians — would get out on the airfield and they would mark out a pitch and play baseball. From somewhere they would suddenly turn up in all sorts of fancy gear, funny sorts of knickerbockers and sweatshirts with strange devices thereon, and also funny hats. I thought this was marvellous, good for the lads, and got us all out in the open air. However, I found the most frightful difficulty in persuading the various captains of these teams from one flight or the other to let me join in.

'No Boss,' they would say, 'you Scots are all very well at this and that, but this is baseball, this is quite different. You won't be any good at this'. Eventually I got very browned-off.

'Well if you don't let me play,' I said, 'you can't have my airfield!'

So they agreed to let me play and I asked them where they wanted me. 'Go out in the airfield and we will tell you, and field away out,' they said. I went away out to the most remarkable end until I was on the edge of the main runway. Now I could not hear what was going on and I was quite sure nobody could hit a ball, or whatever they use in baseball, away out where I was standing. However, they had got me out of the way and I felt at least with a following wind a big lad would hit the ball in my direction and I might be able to do something. Now it was whilst I was standing out there on my own — and really feeling very, very, browned-off — that I saw an aeroplane approach the airfield and make a quiet and dignified circuit. I just do not know what aircraft this was, I had never seen such a type before, but he made a very cautious circuit and then to my amazement an approach to land despite the red Very lights pooped off from the control tower. He landed down wind (not that there was much wind), but he landed very carefully and taxied with his tail up to where I was standing, roughly about halfway or a little more up the runway. Out popped a very strange gentleman from this aircraft that I noticed had American markings, but I still did not know what the aircraft was. I had a vague idea but I was not sure. This strange gentleman came round who was wearing a sort of baseball cap like all my Canadians were. He came towards me and stopped about 10 to 15 yards away, put his hand inside his bomber jacket and brought out a monster hand-held cannon which he pointed in my direction. It was the sort of weapon that you saw John Wayne wielding so well and twisting round his finger, but I did not like the idea of this thing which I was looking straight up the barrel of.

'Hi Bud' he called, 'do you speak English?'

'Well' I said, 'there is some considerable doubt about that: I am a Scotsman'.

'Oh . . . What is that town down there a piece?' he asked, pointing a thumb behind him towards Cambridge.

'That's Cambridge, the university city of Cambridge.' He paused for a moment.

'Oh, is that the same as Yale and Harvard?'

'Well' I said, 'there is even more doubt about that'.

At this stage a very smart young officer got out, immaculate in the rig of what I was to learn was the American Army Air Corps. He looked as if he had just stepped straight out of one of those bespoke tailors in Saville Row in London's West End.

'Everything all right, Hank?' he said to the gentleman who was holding this artillery piece in his hand.

'Yes, it seems alright,' he replied. Then the officer spoke to me:

'Tell me, sir, what are those aircraft?'

'They are Stirlings — Stirling bombers.'

I cannot remember if he asked if they were British or not, but there seemed to be some doubt as to whose side these bombers were on. Then the officer enquired:

'Tell me sir, are we far from Alconbury?'

By this time I was feeling very friendly towards them and I might have said something to the effect: 'If you will just mosey on down this trail (meaning the main road between Cambridge and Huntingdon) you will come to Alconbury, some 15 to 16 miles away.'

'Thank you very much,' and he saluted smartly.

I got some vague sort of signal from the gentleman with the artillery piece which he put away in his bomber jacket again, and they turned round and took off — this time into wind — and sped towards Alconbury. But the thing that I reflected on was here we were, into our third bombing year, and the mighty Eighth Air Force had come to our aid over thousands of miles of land and 2,000 miles plus of sea; and they can come down through the clouds and land almost within sight of the place they were making for, with no navigation aids at all. More especially, I wondered at their risk when I learnt that some of them had landed across the Channel and were astonished to find that the natives did not speak English. In fact they did not speak French either, they spoke a sort of fractured German. But this was a great feeling of what we had been used to over the years in watching American movies and, with our tongue in cheek and a bit of a giggle, seeing the adventures of the cavalry arriving. And for the first time in our years of combat I had a glow, a rosy glow, inside me and I knew and was certain for the very first time now we could not be beaten. It was a feeling that I never had until that nice little man with a funny hat and a big gun got out of a strange aeroplane and asked me: 'Do you speak English?'

Despite the pleasure it gave to my family, the advent of four gongs in one week of February 1943 produced certain embarrassing moments. One occurred whilst I was in the old Berkeley Bar in Piccadilly, awaiting my wife. I was standing at the bar with an ancient 'Whitehall warrior' lieutenant-colonel when a very attractive and well-upholstered blonde looked across the bar in the mirror and said in not too gentle a voice: 'What are those medals the airman is wearing?'

The Colonel quietly told her the first three, but he said 'I don't know what the last one is, so ask him'.

So after certain nudges and pushing her handbag nearer to my beer, nearer than I liked, she turned and said: 'Could you tell me, what is your last medal?' and I trotted out my favourite answer: 'I really have no idea, it was on the uniform when I bought it.'

The blonde said 'Thank you very much' and turned to the 'Whitehall warrior'. 'He doesn't know, it was on the uniform when he bought it,' whereupon the entire bar was convulsed and I made my escape.

Whilst waiting outside my wife happened to come along and said to me 'Isn't it open?'

82

Above:
Able-Oboe-Charlie — AVM D. C. T . Bennett AOC No 8 (PFF) Group. *Sqn Ldr H. Lees*

Above:
No 35 Squadron was one of the original Pathfinder squadrons in August 1942. This Halifax Mk II Srs 1 W7676-P went missing at the lowest point of my 'trough of despair' over Nuremberg on 28/29 August. *The Aeroplane*

Below:
Mosquito Mk IV DZ353 (seen in the markings of No 105 Squadron PFF) began life with the PFF during 1943 as an OBOE-equipped aircraft before passing to No 139 Squadron and finally to No 627 Squadron — one of the three hijacked by No 5 Group in April 1944. She failed to return from an attack on Rennes marshalling yards on 8/9 June 1944.
Real Photographs via Jonathan Falconer

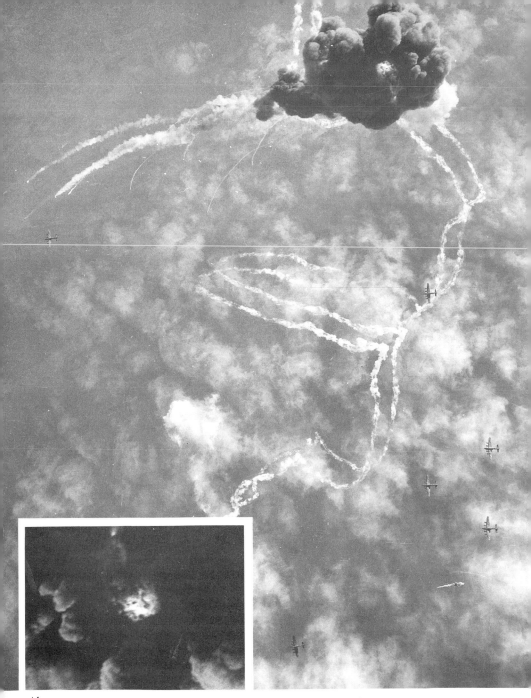

Above:
One of No 3 Group's Lancasters explodes in the bomber stream over Wesel on 19 February 1945, the victim of a direct hit by flak. The moment was captured by the starboard oblique camera of Flt Lt Bennett's high-flying PFF Mosquito. The enlarged portion of the photograph shows a likeness of Hitler at the seat of the explosion. *Sqn Ldr H. Lees*

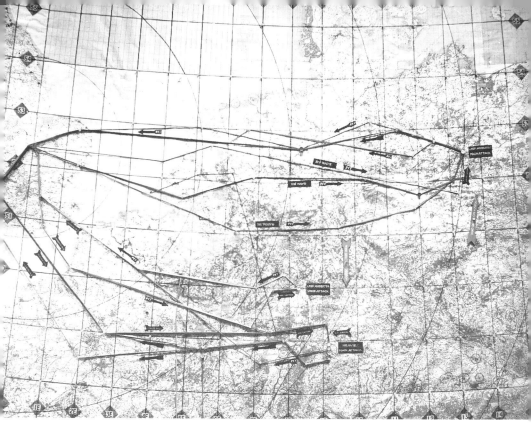

Above:
Target for Tonight: the map on the wall of HQ PFF Operations Room showing a typical routeing plan. *Sqn Ldr H. Lees*

Below:
Fraser Barron (second from right) with his No 7 Squadron crew at Oakington.

Above:
The irrepressible Tommy Blair with me at the Pathfinder Dinner held at RAF Wyton in May 1962. *RAF Wyton*

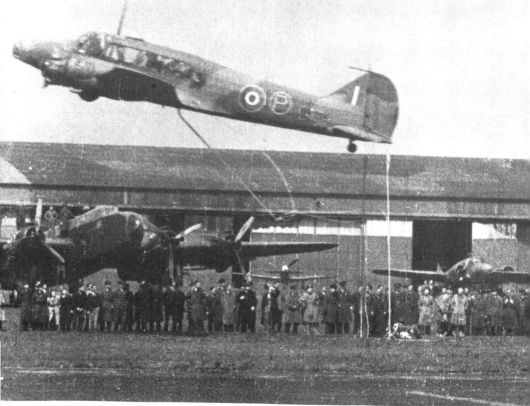

Top:
'Mad Doc' Winfield prepares to be plucked from the ground in his 'Robinson Jacket' . . .

Above:
. . . by an Avro Anson with a hook.   *Institute of Aviation Medicine*

Left:
Erik Hazelhoff-Roelfzema: he was ADC to Queen Wilhelmina before joining the Pathfinder Force. Here Erik and I are pictured together in his native Holland after the war. *P. Wierikx*

Below:
Second tour — No 7 Squadron: the original long and the short and the tall! *Crown Copyright*

Above:
Jimmy Marks: 'a brilliant pilot, a wonderfu leader and a man that this country could not afford to lose.' So spoke Bill Higgs, his flight engineer. *W. G. Higgs*

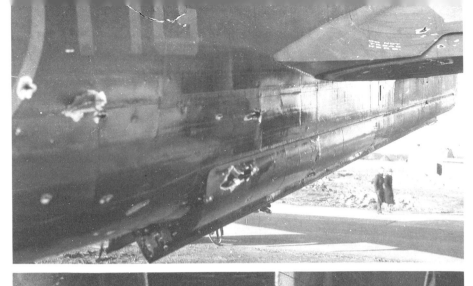

Above:
Round-the-clock bombing: a Mosquito takes off for a night raid as Flying Fortresses of the US 8th Air Force return from a daylight op. *Sqn Ldr H. Lees*

Left:
Two views of my Stirling 'C' for Collander after the Ju88 attack over Köln on 3 February 1943, which wounded four of my crew and hurt our pride. *Crown Copyright*

Below:
The 'Erks' with my Chiefie — 'A' Flight, Oakington, May 1943. *Crown Copyright*

Above:
With No 1 son and his mother at the Palace to collect four gongs in 1943.

Below:
With No 2 son at the Palace for the second AFC.   *London Evening News*

Above:
Hamish — Acting Squadron Commander of No 7 (PFF) Squadron, Oakington, 1942.
R. A. Thompson RA, courtesy of the RAF Museum, Hendon

Above:
Hamish — Station Commander, RAF Warboys, summer 1944 with his 'left and right hands'. Note that both my secretary and driver wore PFF badges. *Crown Copyright*

Top right:
Originally the Airmens' Dining Hall, the station theatre-cum-cinema at Warboys was redesigned and converted by Cpl Christian with the aid of salvaged seats from the Globe Theatre, Shaftesbury Avenue. It is seen here in December 1944. *Crown Copyright*

Bottom right:
The Sergeants' Mess, after treatment by Cpl Christian, was transformed into a sort of social club with a bit of a dance floor and a proscenium arch. *Crown Copyright*

Top:
Warboys' NAAFI Club, originally the Sergeants' Mess Lounge.   *Crown Copyright*

Above:
The Warboys 'Tiller Girls' presented by Davy Burnaby in 1944.

13 A Question of Morale and Moral Fibre

In my wanderings to the Staff Colleges and branches of the Royal Aeronautical Society all over the world, the USAF Academy, Colorado Springs, and also that incredible edifice of aeronautical and technical learning — the Smithsonian in Washington, the main question that always crops up and in almost entirely the same way is 'how was it possible to maintain morale?' How did it just happen that Harris could maintain his Offensive despite disastrous occasions like Nuremburg. We could not have sustained many Nuremburgs when we lost more aircrew in one night than was lost in the entire Battle of Britain (in several months). I am not drawing comparisons here, I am just making the point that 500-plus were lost in the Battle of Britain and nearly 700 were lost at Nuremburg on one raid.

By the same token the Americans, on their not entirely successful Schweinfurt ventures, lost a great number of aircraft. It is said — and I have never been able to verify this figure — 70%, and not all were shot down by the fighters, although the majority of aircraft were. Some reached the UK, crashed on landing and were written off; others fell into the sea.

When we look at these disasters we must again ask ourselves how it was that Harris and Eaker could sustain those losses and go time and again. We, of course, began to think — and think very seriously — what if our losses got beyond 10%? The Americans could take this a little further, but after Schweinfurt they had to stop and lick their wounds; and so this leads on to the inevitable topic when I am confronted with the audiences I meet in all those places. The question is simple and with some concern 'how was morale maintained?' And I fear I cannot answer that question to anyone's satisfaction.

First of all it comes from the top. I think all of us were in great sympathy with what Harris and the American generals had to do. Their brief was simple and straight: attack the morale of the enemy. That is just a simplification, but that is what it amounted to. So down at squadron level we had this very much in our minds when in time the orders came down through Group, through station, right to the people who had to do the carting and the bombing. I feel I should explain right at the outset that I can only view at the later stages of the war the state of morale as I saw it in the entire Pathfinder Force. Please to remember I had finished my own stint, and I had served a period on Bennett's staff as his 'horse-thief' — the recruiter and trainer. I was the Group training inspector. My function was to select and train the Pathfinders. I was given the choice of what I claim was the best and if I did not pick the best, I was the only one who could be charged with dereliction of duty. I judged who I thought was the best; I selected them and then took them to my station — Warboys — where they were trained as Pathfinders.

Now let me just add very quickly here, I am not going to tell you or anyone that I got the best out of Bomber Command. Whilst I did track down what I thought was the best, several of them, in fact quite a number of them, said 'no'. For one reason or another the loyalty of the squadron of some other loyalty said 'no, I won't join the Pathfinders, I want to stay where I am'. I know that many of you might doubt that, but I hope you will take my word for it. There were cases where chaps said 'I don't like leaving the WAAF'. Now they did not say 'the wife', they said 'the WAAF', and I said quite clearly 'she can come too'. It was no problem for me to post a crew, and I did, and many of you must know I did post WAAF at the same time.

Now I have been digressing and let me say quite clearly that I never knew the answer and I do not know it now, how the tremendously high level of morale was sustained, not just in the Pathfinders, but throughout the Command as a whole. Of course, if you want a particular example, certain squadrons like 617 had their own particular style of morale and nobody can say how that was acquired; I think in a way its success produced its own style of morale in any event, and in this case one has to look no further than Guy Gibson. After all Confucius he say: 'fish go rotten by the head', therefore the converse must apply.

But as I am reflecting now, let me just leave you with this thought about morale. As I said in the case of No 617 Squadron, their enormous success on the Dams raid and on some of the less spectacular sorties that they had flown, rubbed off on all 617's sorties thereafter. Years later, even, when 617 just happened to be in my Canberra Wing at Binbrook after the war, oddly enough both Nos 617 and 9 Squadrons found themselves together in my four-squadron wing. The enormous rivalry between those two squadrons started way back on 12 November 1944 when, together, they attacked and sank the *Tirpitz* in Tromsö fjord. No one would dare tell 9 that it was 617 that turned her over, and the reverse holds with 617.

To this day — and I have exhaustively researched that particular sortie led by Willie Tait — and, despite watching several 8mm films of the bombs falling, shot by the camera crew in a No 463 Squadron Lancaster, I still cannot say whose bomb did turn the *Tirpitz* over. But this is all good for morale; like the piece of the *Tirpitz* that I was able to secure for these two happy squadrons, encased in a large frame of good British oak, and displayed at Binbrook as a trophy of what Willie Tait and his gang of two — 617 and 9, or 9 and 617, the choice is yours — achieved.

However, with regard to the length of each operational tour of duty, it is obvious that there was a deal of confusion between the Commands. It is clear that each Command had a basis for judging tour length; for example, Bomber Command seemed to feature the number of sorties to establish this. Fighter and Coastal Commands felt that 200/300 hours of operational flying could embrace a tour. To resolve these differences a meeting was called by the Chief of the Air Staff, at which I was present, and the result for Bomber Command was as follows:

the first tour should consist of 30 sorties and the second tour should normally not exceed 20 sorties. The Pathfinder Force should be on a different basis and these should consist of 45 sorties, but crews could be withdrawn at any time after the completion of 30 sorties. This in effect meant that PFF actually did 45 sorties, but please to remember that few Pathfinder aircrew elected to opt out at the 45 mark and most carried on to the magic 60. And further take note that over 100 PFF aircrew managed the ton (100 sorties). Let me leave you there for the moment with my views of high morale as I saw it, and I saw a great deal of it during my constant circuit within the Command. In the last two years of the war I was in orbit visiting every station and squadron in my endless quest for Pathfinders. Thus, let me leave the Command and the Pathfinders and turn to the darker side of morale — the lack of moral fibre.

I never actually experienced the drama of dealing with any lack of moral fibre (LMF) cases, although I can imagine the difficulty faced by a CO who is trying to run a squadron in wartime if suddenly he was confronted with a case of LMF. It was obviously much easier during the Kaiser's war when a short sharp Court Martial was followed by the offender being shot the next morning. Happily, we lived in a much more enlightened time during World War 2. I never understood the treatment of LMF cases; it was something I could not understand as outlined in the Air Ministry Order, which was a very harsh document and did not give much leeway in the treatment of a chap if he felt he could not do any more. He was stigmatised, hounded and humiliated.

My sympathies, however, were very much with the wretched fellow who had the courage to own up that he could not face the prospect any longer of flying against a lethal enemy. Whether, of course, I would have taken this view were I to have had someone in my squadron who turned LMF is open to question. When I reflect on the young aircrew that I helped to train in 1940 at Kinloss, some 10

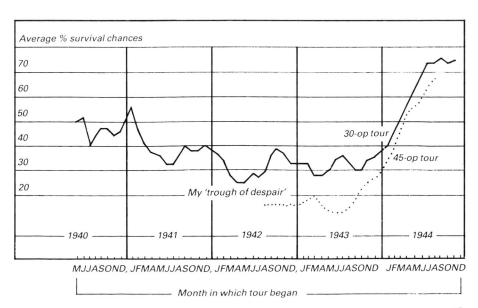

85

years younger than myself, I marvel that the conversion stage was the last stint before they were to confront a highly lethal opponent. I am still amazed that, despite our losses at the time — and they would worsen until well into 1942 — some would survive what I called my 'trough of despair'.

Don Bennett had always publicly — and to my embarrassment — told anyone who would listen, that I recruited 16,000 Pathfinders for our heavy bomber squadrons, the OBOE Mosquito squadrons and the Mosquitos of the Light Night Striking Force. Now I would say to you, without fear or favour, that the only people recruited in that period of my appointment that I would *not* have had in the Pathfinder Force were people that came in through some rather dubious trap-door. They were either brought in by Don Bennett himself, and there were very few of those that got through my fine mesh, or those who were somehow or other forced on us by agencies over which we had no control. So out of the 16,000 I personally recruited from the very first day of my appointment to the Pathfinder Force, to the last day of the war, I am not aware of one occasion on which a member of aircrew, whatever his category, was dealt with under the terms of the AMO. What I will tell you, and I will tell for the very first time, is that I personally dealt with people whose future may well have been considered under the terms of the AMO. A squadron commander would suggest to me that 'old so-and-so is getting a bit teased-out and perhaps he should be rested', or 'it might be convenient if he did not return after his next leave' — these leaves were quite frequent, something like six or seven days every six or seven weeks. And so in these circumstances I dealt with much speed and remarkably low Scottish cunning. So it would be futile to say that no more than three of four, or at the very most five, of these categories were dealt with during the whole of the period of the Pathfinder Force.

Now I personally felt that it would be quite inhuman to deal with someone who was somewhere near the magic 60 cut-off, for reasons that it would be impossible to examine with any clarity the reasons for this change of heart, and the strong will that he had shown during his previous operational record. I find now that I can take a little comfort for acting beyond my authority and without Don Bennett's knowledge of what I was doing. I also take some comfort from the fact that I have enormous pleasure in remembering that all those who I dealt with in this capacity returned to the Pathfinder Force before the end and wished sincerely to finish their Pathfinder tour. Sadly two of them perished before the end of the war and the two remaining, that I remember well, saw the end of the war. And as far as their consciences were concerned, they justified the colour under their brevets that they earned during the period when they were having grave doubts about their own efficiency.

None of these eternal operators faired very well when they had a posting to a training unit. They were not welcome, they grated on the conscience of many in these establishments who had no intention of operating. But I will say, and this is without criticism, they were doing a much better job instructing than they could possibly have done on operations. Very few of the most senior people at training establishments bedded down well within the operational theatre. Bomber Command also organised from the 'Petrified Forest' the operational training units through non-operational Groups, and it was very important after Harris's one-off when he stopped training to mount his 1,000-Plan, that some of the more senior and very experienced training instructors remained operational. It may sound impossible to many that a sergeant or a young junior officer coming straight from the Empire Training Scheme either in Canada or Rhodesia, was a far better prospect than shall we say a group captain or a wing commander, or even a squadron leader, who had spent the entire war in the training machine. It was my experience that seldom did the more senior of this element — and there were many of them — fit into the operational set-up, more especially as it got towards the end of the war. One of the things I do recall, Command in its wisdom used to send some of its very senior people to spend a period — not to fly mind you — but just to see and taste the scene at an operational station.

They would come, spend a night and then they would go through the entire paraphernalia. The orders came from Command right down to squadron level; the preparations started about mid-morning as soon as this vast sheet of paper from the teleprinter indicating every facet of the job ahead arrived. Each section would grab its particular portion of what was called the 'Y' Form, the gunners would be briefed and tactics would be discussed. Flight engineers would know how much fuel and its distribution. The navigators would disappear into their hideout and work out their courses and prepare their charts. The set operators — that is the navigator or observer who would operate the H_2S set — also had plenty of preparation, and the captain would be a sort of overseer who went round each section. He could glean from each category what was happening and, of course at a convenient time, he would test the aircraft itself and then put it on line so that the bombload could be installed before mid-afternoon or early evening. He would then have an aircrew meal and attend the final briefing.

Now these people who did come as visitors went through all of this, and then they would spend the rest of the evening in the Mess. The people that were left behind such as the section leaders — the gunnery leader, flight engineer leader, navigation leader and one or two people that were not on the battle order for that night, would meet these people and speak to them. We were always rather intrigued with their eagerness and how they all seemed to pick up and wallow in the atmosphere of this period when it was very trying for the squadron commander if he was not on that evening. His great worry was literally following in his mind's eye the squadron's contribution to the target that night and wondering how they were getting on. Then later when they started coming home his real concern was counting them in, and it was in this period that these pleasant and very charming visitors frequently wanted to get nearer to the operational scene. Some of the squadron commanders, and maybe the odd flight commander who again was not flying, invariably pointed out that they need not go back to their operational training unit, they could remain and we would send for their kit. I do not recall that offer ever being taken up seriously. But let me make it very clear that it probably was not the best place, a Pathfinder station, for anyone to get near to absorbing the incredible state of affairs.

As we made our way through 1944 the advancing Allied forces were able to give us more room — by that I mean there was more Allied occupied (and therefore less hostile) territory for us to fly over in order to get to our targets. Please to remember I was no longer actually the horse-thief, but I was now at Warboys with the Pathfinder Training Unit and so I was training replacements. It is probably prudent to suggest here that as the war progressed, especially after mid-1944 until the end, aircrew generally throughout the Command — and more especially in the Pathfinders — improved enormously. First of all starting in 1944 the loss factor was diminishing and once ground forces were proceeding to recapture and liberate large portions of Europe, the sortie value was debased and it was quite common for no one to bother to consider the 60 sorties as cut-off for a Pathfinder tour.

I would like, if I may, to give just one illustration of how this happened throughout the Pathfinders and to the same degree within the Main Force. I commend to you, therefore, a delightful little paperback entitled *Rear Gunner Pathfinder*. Here is a story of a very ordinary sort of chap who, when the cut-off time was 60, became a Gunnery Leader. That meant he carried on and when someone at the last moment dropped out, he dropped in; it was more or less par for the course that, by the end of 1944, a very large number of Pathfinders had notched up 70 or more sorties.

But now I shall leave you with one final anecdote which impinges on both issues of morale and moral fibre. The Commander-in-Chief in 1939 felt it necessary to review his 'troops'; and when he came to Driffield he obviously felt that the occasion was so important that he spoke to the officers in one corner of the hangar and spoke to the sergeant pilots in another. One idiot amongst the sergeants asked him 'How long, sir, do you think we will last?' And the great man looked very tense and thoughtful and answered: 'I think about two or maybe three sorties.' I can assure you that did less than nothing for my morale at the time.

14 *Staff Officer*

'Ground flight to ground skip,' intoned the flight engineer. And as though I was acknowledging some distant voice at the end of a long tunnel, I replied 'ground flight to ground Jock.'

The snap of the heavy switch plunged the whole aircraft into darkness and silence — well a sort of silence: the engines after the rundown and shut-off remained protesting. Following hours of running at something exceeding 1,100°C, the dissimilar metals cooling at different rates seemed to debate the wisdom of stopping as though they were good for at least the reserve fuel still in the tanks. But slowly the groans and the pops diminished. The glow from the exhaust ports was the first to go, like the duller end of a steel tempering chart. And the voices were also fading further away as I sat on in the cockpit until I became aware that I was not alone. Oddly enough, I was conscious of her scent first — it was not something expensive that came out of a bottle or a spray — it was that indefinable yet simple fragrance of a clean young woman, a bonny girl, so nice to be near. I saw a flash of white teeth in the gloom as she smiled and said: 'I've come for your 'chute sir.' At least, that is what I think she said because my sweat-dampened flying helmet was still on my head. Then the unfeeling voice of Tommy the navigator called: 'What's going on up there Skip?' in his best authoritative Metropolitan Police (Special Branch) manner. 'The coach is about to leave.' Reverie was complete, leaving me with a strange presentiment that I would not be climbing in or out of a Stirling for some time. I still had two trips to complete my Pathfinder tour, but in my heart and mind I felt that this phase was over for the time being.

At debriefing I was met by the station commander, Gp Capt Teddy Olsen RNZAF, with a casual 'Don Bennett wants to see you in his office at 1000hr tomorrow,' (meaning today). If I was expected to register surprise I did not — but I was disappointed that it had been Hamburg that night — not exactly finishing on double-top, but there had been compensations.

And so to No 8 Group on 20 March 1943 and to the Presence, where that morning I was told that whatever my squadron might think of me, my personal best *might just* be good enough, and I was now the Group training inspector and would be solely responsible for the selection and training of all future Pathfinders — just like that!

'Find yourself an office and collect your gear from Oakington later this evening.' From being a frightened operational type to a terrified staff officer under the direct gaze of DCT was a most trying experience to suffer within the span of only a few hours. Moreover, I returned to my squadron, packed, stayed the night and the next morning heard that my crew were missing. This only served to compound the hurt at the manner of my posting which lasted some considerable time, and only receded when I became aware of the desperate need to attract the right material to the Force. From that moment until the end of the war, my feet barely touched the ground. For the record, I still recall the short and simple brief from Able Oboe Charlie that morning: 'The Main Force groups have not maintained the early standard of replacement crews, we are now experiencing heavier losses than expected and the standard of our latest crews is on the downgrade. 'I want you to do something about it.'

There was no actual threat or an 'or else' actually uttered, but the tenor was ominous, followed by that sharp hard look that I came to know so well.

Here, for the first time, I saw Able-Oboe-Charlie at close quarters and, to say the least, it was impressive. But so, also, was the rest of the Group Staff. At station level, Group, Command and the Air Ministry were distant bodies which seemed to exist only to dispute the urgent need '. . . of these my most immediate and, of course, reasonable demands'. The normal short reply was just a bold 'NO' dressed up in two or three paragraphs. Our requests for action almost always received a flat refusal or immediate modification when they reached one or the other of these higher Command authorities. Naturally, this lower level viewpoint only prevailed until one was posted to one of the higher corridors of power. The general opinion held at operational level received a sharp rethink if a posting was threatened to the Air Ministry or the Ministry of Aircraft Production (MAP), and then a prisoner of war camp would be a haven compared with that possibility. MAP was usually referred to, up at the sharp end, as the Ministry of Accelerated Promotion.

Bennett immediately manned his Air Staff and Ops Room with selected tour-expired operators: I once counted a total of nearly 400 bomber sorties around the morning conference table when planning that evening's sortie. A lighter side of these 'morning prayers' was a gentle tussle between our genial civilian Met man, Tommy Thomas, and the AOC. Normally Bennett would produce a sixpence to support his Met view against the considered opinion of the Command forecast; after all, he was a Fellow of the Royal Meteorological Society.

From that moment until the war ended I was left entirely to my own devices. Perhaps I should remind the student of the air war during World War 2 that PFF was originally formed by the hiving off from each bomber group a squadron (see Chapter 10). The squadrons moved with their entire air and ground crews and a built-in logistic problem since each squadron operated a different type of aircraft. Thus the Commandant of the PFF had to plan and carry out an entirely new concept of bombing technique which had eluded the Command for the previous bombing years, and that was on the same night that the squadrons arrived from their parent groups. That was at the Command's insistence; small wonder that our first sortie was a disaster, due mainly to weather over the target. But our failure, I know, brought great joy to Bennett's distractors — not only within the Command, but on a broader level where there were many on high who never could understand why 'this bloody civilian should have been elevated to command this vital Group'. I shall take relative pleasure in explaining why D. C. T. Bennett was selected to develop the vast potential waiting in the wings to devastate Hitler's Third Reich. But, dear reader, it is my personal view that no one remotely of the calibre required for this task was obvious in our Air Force, or indeed in any other Air Force. And so, from a tatty hut outside the Headquarters at RAF Wyton, the PFF came into being.

Hopes were high as 1942 drew to its close, and the PFF and Prof R. M. Jones, the inventor of OBOE — were together able to develop the device on the job.* One of the biggest problems was fitting the black boxes in the limited space available. It is a story in itself how the OBOE gear was eventually squeezed into the Mossie, against all the clamour from the Air Ministry that the 'Wooden Wonder' was too vulnerable as a bomber. Mid-1943 saw the real start of the Bomber Offensive as we came to know it. H$_2$S was firmly established and OBOE was progressing well but navigation was still the name of the game and, with the full force of Bennett's total commitment to pure navigation, it soon became obvious that accuracy and timing was the be-all-and-end-all of Pathfinding.

He insisted that one minute was sufficient latitude to get to, say, Berlin. This meant approximately 10 seconds per hundred miles and although this seemed impossible, crews accepted the challenge and set their own criteria. For instance, a captain who asked his bomb aimer why he dropped the bombs 13 or 14 seconds *early* received the reply: 'Oh, I thought that was the time they had to arrive TOT.' (Time on Target)

Whilst Bennett did daily battle with the rest of the RAF and the Air Ministry, the Command itself during its first six months or so was beginning to see the shape of things to come. But after the first flush of good intentions by the Main Force groups in the matter of releasing their best crews as replacements, they even used posting to PFF as a means of disposing of crews who may even have qualified for Matlock (Aircrew Punishment Centre). Thus I found myself winkled out of my squadron overnight and appointed to the PFF Staff responsible for the seeking, selection and training of the future crews. A prospect as frightening as any sortie to the 'Big City' (Berlin), but even more so under the daily scrutiny of Able Oboe Charlie. I recall feeling, at first, rather helpless and more especially since my first task was to tour all the Main Force stations and lecture on the PFF techniques, and also to counter complaints about our less commendable marking. As it was, I happened to be highly placed to speak on two such embarrassing lapses. I figured prominently in the 'Saarlauten for Saarbrücken' mistake and later, in March 1943, the futile Hamburg H$_2$S attack.

Whilst I used these two examples to illustrate the difficulties of seeking and marking targets I made no excuses, but stressed how easy it was — more especially in those early days of PFF — to make mistakes. Unless all the plus factors were collated in our favour — ie the best equipment, the best crews and, of course, the weather. Although it was not said in as many words, the inference

---

*Another key figure in OBOE development was Gp Capt H. A. L. Bufton who commanded No 109 Squadron (Mosquitos), on the changeover from Wellingtons.

was clearly 'all right you chaps, come and see if you can do better' and, oddly enough, it not only quietened the critics but it had a positive effect on volunteers for PFF, too.

My constant orbit within the Command belied another purpose, but was never mentioned whilst lecturing. When the Command issued its bomb plot charts after every sortie, these were studied carefully and the Main Force crews who constantly got aiming point pictures were carefully noted. When I went to their station, I made a point of enquiring about these 'star' crews and I wanted to know why, with such consistency, they had not volunteered for PFF. These crews invariably claimed that they had volunteered, some said twice. They were then posted within the next few days to our Pathfinder Training Unit at Warboys. And so there was an end to the Pathfinders receiving rejected crews from the groups. Very sensibly, a Pathfinder Navigation Unit had been set up at RAF Warboys to initiate Main Force crews to Pathfinding techniques.

Nevertheless, despite this promise, Bennett was still permanently in orbit, dashing from the Air Ministry to Command and forever debating whether some new aspect of tactics should be abandoned or changed. One such example was his tussle with the Commander-in-Chief, Coastal Command, on the priority for the latest model of H$_2$S. It was left to Bennett to fight for what seemed to be a Pathfinder priority by right. He doubled the OBOE commitment by splitting the founder squadron — No 109 — thereby creating No 105 Squadron. A third Mosquito squadron was next on the list, No 139, hived from No 2 Group, which later became the marker squadron for the Light Night Striking Force.*

Bennett was the first to realise that the swift production of Mosquitos took little account of the negligible losses, so he splintered No 139 Squadron and formed yet another new squadron. Eventually, nine squadrons formed the Light Night Striking Force which became the 'hand maiden' to the Pathfinders. These squadrons were used primarily on 'spoof' targets. They would go to a target in advance of the main attack elsewhere and start the usual PFF preliminaries. These diversionary raids were usually most successful and helped the hard-pressed Main Force. Bennett started Planned Group Maintenance for Lancasters and Mosquitos and although this 'garage' system proved unpopular with the more elderly of the ground staff, it was more efficient and economic in manpower and, in effect, kept the number of aircraft available for operations at a higher level than any other group in the Command. All these innovations were his brain children alone. Everything seemed to be coming together by mid-July 1943 when the great 'firestorm' on Hamburg took place. Aided by a strong ground wind of nearly 90kt, the fearful heat created a vortex which took thick smoke and ash up to 30,000ft. The introduction of 'Window' on this occasion completely saturated the ground defences and made the raid just that much easier. Bennett never seemed to tire of acclaiming Hamburg (July 1943) as a great bomber victory since it was here that we, the Pathfinders (to put a finer edge to that sortie), had earlier made one of our classic blunders, one on which I was instructed to lecture

---

*At the same time, the strength of the OBOE squadrons was raised to three flights making 30 aircraft per OBOE squadron.

budding Pathfinders. Bennett told me that few people knew more about the earlier Hamburg debâcle than 'the Hamish did'.

The main body of the staff were by no means overshadowed by tour-expired Pathfinders. I have always maintained that Command thought long and hard about the appointment of the Senior Air Staff Officer (SASO) as DCT's right hand. Air Cdre C. D. C. Boyce — 'Bruin' to his friends — was, in my view, a perfect foil to match the abrasive approach used (more, I felt, defensively) by DCT in the earlier stages of the Force. Bruin was very popular because he made himself easily available to the aircrew and even I was never able to establish how many sorties he did with different crews. I have no record of his 'tour', but at a rough guess between 20 and 30. The very best of prewar Cranwell, and the last RAF officer to award me a 'Royal Rocket', and so well deserved.

Another popular figure was the Group medic, Wg Cdr J. C. McGown MD, ChB, DFC, a craggy West Highland Scot and a great character to boot; an ex-RFC pilot and a fugitive from Harley Street, W1 where he was an eye specialist. It was never officially established how many sorties he actually did, but based on the number of Pathfinders who claimed he had flown with them, 50 trips would seem conservative. He retired to the Isle of Ilay and settled amongst several thousand sheep, a distillery and, he maintained, what more could a man ask — all the good life, food, clothing and sustenance were close to hand.

Perhaps the hardest-worked staff officer was the 'chief plumber', Gp Capt C. F. Sarsby, officially known as the group engineer. He must have been on the receiving end of a deal of backlash from Command for the methods of servicing introduced by the AOC and the host of unofficial modifications. For example, the Mossie exhaust shrouds: he must have borne heavy retribution for that one. But that was DCT's *modus operandi*, although even he was hoist with his own petard when the High Master at High Wycombe told him, in turn, to fight for the priority he claimed his Force should have for the swiftly developing H$_2$S.

A splendid aide to Sarby was the Group equipment officer, no storekeeper but an absolute ferret where AOG (Aircraft on Ground) were concerned. I doubt whether any AOG signals ever reached DCT, Wg Cdr J. C. Rose, MBE, intercepted them and acted at once. The Group signals officer, Wg Cdr E. L. T. (Dick) Barton, reacted in like manner. Dick, with a vast and specialised background knowledge, used this incessantly to service the Force, and was perhaps better known to TRE and industry than to the rank and file within the PFF.

The Group armament officer, Wg Cdr 'Basil' Rathbone — known as 'The Reluctant Dragon' — was another in the same mould, individual and with the personality and energy to match the needs of DCT. The PFF tag 'press on regardless' could well have been originally styled for 'Basil', and I doubt if we will ever know his true worth save that it was whispered in the tap rooms that he could have been a Director of Brock's. I have always felt that the aircrew were served best, with immediate effect, by the Group photographic officer, a well established professional in his field — Howard Lees.

Indeed, every member of DCT's staff seemed to be besotted with the Bennett flair for getting on with the job in hand. The mood appeared to be 'tomorrow's too late'. That could have been the epitaph of the late Flt Lt A. J. Rogers MBE. I must disclose my personal interest here. Rogers was officially the Group's P4 (aircrew postings officer), and as such was more or less my assistant. Before I became the GTI, he bore the full brunt of the sharp practice of off-loading unsuitable crews by most of the Main Force groups. Happily he was a fugitive from a high street bank, and as such, had all the guile and craft of the average bank manager (or should that be above average?). With my unstinted support, he could do battle with all the other P4s in the Command, since he could now speak with the voice of his wing commander, and at times, he even spoke with great authority for DCT. We were a splendid team, I chained Jimmy to his desk and did all the outside calls; in fact, in our splendid liaison, I find I did over 200 flying hours throughout the UK and within the Command. Whilst this was almost entirely for body-snatching, it also involved talks on the PFF techniques used (and our shortcomings). When Rogers drew my attention to a particularly bad posting-in (generally a case for disciplinary action, or indeed, Court Martial), I would go to the group concerned. I remember in one case flying an errant captain back to his group and that succeeded in arresting the trash from that area. Rogers was one of the very best flight lieutenants I ever served under; and so from day one we were able to stem the flood tide of ropey crews coming to PFF, and may I add here that there were many crews that I badly wanted to entice to the Force, but evaded me — Len Cheshire in particular, and Dave Shannon, who I believe was actually u/t at Warboys and snatched in the dead of night by Guy Gibson (a legitimate reprisal for the Searby snatch).

These happenings were, of course, in the early days of my being the GTI and once the group's bad habits had been stamped out the PFF enjoyed a steady stream of trainable aircrew; but please to remember that by mid-1943 there were many second-tour crews returning to operations. These aspects were compounded by the excellent turnout from the Empire Air Training Scheme and experienced tour-expired senior staff from the home-based training establishments. But above all the stabilisation of the casualty rate, and in the final months the sharp decline in the rate which led to the increase in the tour length, merged into the final bombing phase, in tandem with the Eighth Air Force which heralded the end of Hitler's Third Reich.

My personal stint was made easier by my regular visits to Group HQs and in particular to No 5 Group. I had basked in Sir Ralph Cochrane's favour when in the early days PFF lodged with his No 3 Group; thus it was relatively simple to have direct access to the AOCs where it was prudent to do so. I speak generally because two of the AOCs would never see me, but this was an advantage as it turned out, because they were clueless about operations; happily their Senior Air Staff Officers were first class and were of enormous help.

The Pathfinders had their share of VCs despite the fact that Don Bennett announced early on after the formation of the Force that there would be no living VCs in the PFF — take for example Sqn Ldr Edwin Swales VC, DFC, SAAF, or indeed Sqn Ldr Robert Palmer VC, DFC, and Sqn Ldr Ian Bazalgette VC, DFC, RAF (but in fact a native of Winnipeg, Canada). The latter was one of the many tour-expired bomber pilots that seemed to rot in our OTUs. I have pitiful letters from him begging me to wangle him back into PFF which I did, and have always regretted because he may well have been alive today — but possibly without his VC.

16 Sycamore Grove
New Malden
Surrey

24th August 1943

Sir

I understand from my telephone conversation yesterday with Flt Lt Rogers that Air Cdre Kirkpatrick of No 3 Group requested that the PFF should not claim me, as there was a 'special job' for which I was required.

No 115 Squadron have informed me by letter that I am posted to Lossiemouth on a routine exchange for a Flight Commander from that station, with effect from the 1st September.

The actual position, as I see it (and writing very unofficially), is that No 3 Group cannot obtain the particular replacement for me they require without offering me in exchange. The upshot is that my application for the PPF is quietly squashed whilst I am on leave on the grounds of a 'special job'. The only work that I have heard of is either an OTU or a Stirling Conversion Unit.

The real point is where can I be of the greatest value, and I am convinced that a PFF tour does more good than a Flight Commander's job at an OTU.

My personal angle is that anyone missing ops this autumn and winter has 'had it'. I entreat you to rescue me before the 1st September if I can be of use to PFF.

Again, I must apologise for bothering you with my personal affairs, but the incentive is very strong.

I am, sir, yours faithfully

(Signed) Ian W. Bazalgette.

15 RAF Warboys

The advent of my getting command of Warboys on 24 July 1944 was after a short spell on the Staff, having been winkled out of my squadron just two sorties before I had completed a Pathfinder tour, but nevertheless my period on the Staff was extremely helpful. My function there was not by any means over, but the main reason for me being there was to arrest and reverse the habit of sending indifferent crews to the Pathfinder Force.

Warboys was a satellite of nearby Wyton and home to the PFF Navigation Training Unit which used Lancs and a handful of Mosquitos in its task. No 1655 Mosquito Conversion Unit was also in residence for a time, and was responsible for the conversion of crews to the Mosquito for Bomber Command, and also training them to use OBOE and H_2S. However, the MCU disbanded at the end of December 1944 and the navigation training commitments were passed on to the PFF NTU.

When I took command I relieved Gp Capt John Searby, of Peenemünde fame, who had been promoted to Air Commodore (he was a specialist in navigation) to take over the navigation post at Command. It was a particularly pleasant thing for me to take over from John who, as with everything else he did, ran a very tight ship and therefore it was comparatively easy for me to take this big jump from staff officer to group captain commanding a PFF station. It was also very pleasant to experience this second phase of my work: I began as what became known as 'Bennett's horse-thief', that is going round the Command and other places selecting and recruiting Pathfinders, then sending them to Warboys. Here I was now commanding the training establishment and seeing what happened to my produce once it got to the training ground. It was very comforting indeed to be able to check and find out whether the people I had selected were in fact worthy of the attention and training that they would get at the Navigation Training Unit. Therefore, first of all, I had to make myself very familiar with the whole training set up.

Warboys was a very large establishment. It had just under 100 aircraft, mostly Lancs and Halifaxes, but not all heavies. We had quite a number of Mosquitos used for OBOE training which was a very skilled business indeed (even taking into account that the people selected for OBOE had the biggest possible chop rate) because they wanted people who were experienced on Standard Beam Approach (SBA). They were highly skilled in this field, in the main most pilots had to have something in the order of nearly 1,000 hours on SBA. That was the first step to qualify, and then after that they underwent lengthy training at Warboys by expert instructors. The other crews on the heavies were trained on Lancasters and Halifaxes, because at that period No 35 Squadron had Halifaxes and the other two squadrons had Lancasters. No 7 Squadron still had Stirlings and had not yet received its Lancasters but this was to follow very soon. So therefore the training establishment was very interesting indeed and I went from one department to familiarise myself. This was something completely new for me to be right in amongst the training and witnessing as I did the new Pathfinders arriving. Each crew I personally interviewed (and I do not recall very often having to reject aircrew, save those who came complaining that they had not volunteered and did not wish to volunteer once they got to Warboys, but they were soon disposed of) and very very soon it was unusual to have crews that did not want to carry on a Pathfinder tour.

And so in a very short period of time I was able to absorb all the mystique of the pathfinder training and, indeed, even found time to do a little 'body-snatching' of my own where I knew there was a particular crew. I also scoured the bomb-plot charts that came out after each sortie to see if any of the better crews that ought to be coming through to me by rights had actually volunteered for PFF at their home base. This was easy to do because I had a choice of aircraft to jump into and go off to interview these possibilities. So I settled down to becoming the High Master of Warboys and together with my staff, whom I found extremely helpful, I was able to run the station and let those who were running the training establishment get on with their function, which was training Pathfinders to the standard that Don Bennett had laid down and insisted upon.

One of the first things I found rather pleasant about Warboys was the CMC of the Sergeants' Mess, a warrant officer, who had oddly enough been an apprentice with me many years before at Halton. As Chairman of the Mess Committee he invited me to the Sergeants' Mess for no other reason but to have a quiet drink at the bar and meet some of the Mess members that I probably would not have met in my daily round. It was my wont to go to one department of the station every morning once I had dispensed with justice and the petty sessions. I not only found this helpful, but oddly enough it became a thing I did very regularly. I do not know how it came about but after the second or third round it generally transpired that somebody began telling me a story about some aspect of station life that was not quite as it should be. Now this was not a blatant chap ratting on somebody and saying this was wrong, as indeed it was; it was just pointing out — probably he was trying to tell me in an off-the-record way — that somebody was not doing the job as well as he thought he was doing his. But I found these sessions absorbing. I just made a mental note, and probably not the very next day or the day after, but very soon after in my morning circuit round the camp I found myself in this particular section, and just wanting to see what was happening.

Almost without exception the 'something' I turned up would have been unnoticeable had it not been for the gentle steer in the right direction. We call this in Scotland 'being a klipe' — someone that, in the criminal world, rats on you. I never looked on it in that way; it was something that could not be said outright but was said in a very roundabout way that I picked up. That was one of the great features of my monthly visits to take a drink with the chairman of the Sergeants' Mess Committee. Very helpful for a CO, very helpful indeed, because there were many aspects of station life that of course I knew nothing about and I had to learn. I learned very fast because I found the excuses that airmen, and indeed WAAFs, came up with had not changed at all! In the previous 10 to 15 years, when I was an airman, indeed you could say that I was 'makee-learn on the job'. I made mistakes, I made some frightful mistakes.

One particular mistake that I made very early in my 'makee-learn' period was in respect of the station commander's benevolent fund. As many of you know a Station Commander has a Benevolent Fund, mine was a very wealthy one, and it had been accumulated over the years. I found particularly that people were very kind and there was always money coming in. One day I was confronted with one of my airmen who had come to me with a most impassioned plea. He wanted leave to go back and see if he could do something about his children who had been deserted by his wife, who had gone off with somebody else, and the children were staying with his mother. The mother was old and not very well and he just wanted a few days leave to sort this out, and could he also have an advance of his pay? I very soon found out that he had no pay coming to him, so the station commander's benevolent fund lobbed out £10. When I gave him the money I should have heard the warning bells: 'Twenty, sir, would be very much better. It will see me right through, and I will be able to do something about the children. And, sir, if I could also have 10 days instead of seven days.'

Now that I commend to all of you — there are danger signals that ring and lights that flash when such a person wants just a little more than you think is enough. It should have been a signal to me. It was not, but it was for evermore. The first indication that I had boobed in this case was when I called up my WAAF secretary. (I had a very good WAAF secretary called Irene Hunt who was the custodian of my fund. She kept it in her safe, on the box I used for communicating with my secretary.)

'I wonder, would you kindly bring in £20,' I asked. I knew when I saw her face that I had done the wrong thing. I have never seen a more boot-face on any WAAF, and she was not boot-faced normally in any way at all. However, he got his £20 and off he went. That evening, oddly enough, the publican in our local rang me up.

'I've got a very strange airman in here', he said. 'He's been here since we opened and there's hardly a person come into the pub that he hasn't bought drinks for. And he's telling everybody that the drinks are on that silly old sod up at the camp who gave him money to go home and look after his children, and instead he went to Newmarket.'

At that time there was racing occasionally at Newmarket. By all accounts he had won a packet and he had money bulging out of every pocket in his battledress. The landlord continued: 'He's just bought all the whisky I have available, a drop of gin, some sherry and a couple of crates of beer and he's taking it all back to the camp to have a bit of a "ding-dong".'

'Well just keep him there as long as you can', I replied. Then I got hold of my Flight Sergeant Policeman who was a good type and asked him how would he like to acquire two crates of beer, some whisky, gin and some sherry? Take a jeep and a couple of your lads, I told him, and go down and arrest Corporal so-an-so in the pub. 'I don't think I can do that, sir', he prevaricated. 'Well, by the time the *Daily Mirror* gets to hear about it I will have sorted it out in the morning. Go down, arrest this fellow and put him in one cell and all the grog in the other. If it works the way I think it's going to work out the grog is yours and I will deal with this lad in the morning.' Sure enough, in the morning the airman was presented to me, not on a charge because I could not charge him with anything I could lay my hands on in the Air Force Act, but I told him: 'I hear you've had a very good day at the races.' 'Yes, sir', he grinned. 'How much did you win?' From every pocket — battledress pockets, trouser pockets, back pockets — he pulled out great rolls of money and he put them on the table in front of me. 'I want my 20 quid back; the Benevolent Fund is there for desperate cases — airman or NCOs who must have money for some genuine reason or other. That's what its there for. So I want my 20 quid back!' He did not even bother to count. One of the rolls he put down, I do not know to this day how much was in there; he passed that over my desk and said: 'There's your money back sir.' 'I want, now, a donation to my benovolent fund', I demanded, 'because I have to deal with fellows — unlike you — who are very much in need of this immediate assistance that I can dole out'. He passed another bundle over to me — all this was happening in my office where there was no escort, no warrant officer or Adjutant or anybody else, just the two of us. Whether he was concealing more money, or whether he thought he might be able to sell the grog which was in another part of the guardroom, I do not know. But eventually I got all the money that he had spread out on the table counted and put into my benevolent fund. I could see no way that I could have charged him because it would, I am sure, have become one of the fabulous *Daily Mirror* occasions. But that is just one example of how a station commander has to learn, and if you are learning on the job it is sometimes very much harder.

Warboys was an unusual station in so far as it had originally been built as a one-squadron station. All the buildings — the living quarters and domestic quarters like the Airmens' Mess and all the various other sections — were constructed to a one-squadron scale. Warboys was now a training establishment with at least four times the number of aircraft one would have found on a one-squadron station; in fact it would be true to say it was nearly five times. However, all the buildings were of that scale: the Sergeants' Mess, the Officers' Mess, the Airmens' Mess, and all the other facilities were very small in size.

Eventually it became necessary to build a completely new establishment of quarters. So the older quarters were all abandoned and new quarters were put up very quickly, as indeed was the case with the Nissen. Everything, practically everything, was of the Nissen style — the Officers' Mess, the Sergeants' Mess and all the living quarters.

Thus, when I took command there was a great number of empty quarters. There was an empty Sergeants' Mess, and empty Officers' Mess and all the living quarters. Some were used for other purposes, and the rest of these other vast Nissens I used for my own purpose. For instance we built a dance hall out of the original Sergeants' Mess. Now you might think this was an impossible task — build a dance hall? Now with the strength of Warboys at the time standing at very nearly 2,500 people it was possible, taking into account the number of aircrew coming through regularly for training. There were the Mosquito crews that made a very large aircrew floating population, and we also had domestic and technical staffs to meet the needs of the training establishment. So I found, and quite by accident, a corporal who was very well qualified with City & Guilds examinations. He was in effect a master builder, but he had never had anything to master. Somehow I got him into the old Sergeants' Mess and suggested we could make this into a sort of social club, with a bit of a dance floor and a proscenium arch in the form of a shell where the band could play, and WAAFs, airmen and NCOs could dance. He said it would be no problem and he set about it.

The airmen's dining hall was a very pleasant Nissen hut that was made into a cinema-cum-theatre. We had so much building material about the place that I was able to start what I called the 'station commander's chain gang'. I would go to the Tannoy and I would rattle chains and call — at maybe 7.00 or 7.30pm — when everybody had time to go back to their billets after their evening meal: 'this is the station commander's chain gang. Work tonight will be in such and such an area.'

For instance when we were building the cinema and the theatre we had the ENSA concerts staged in the old Airmen's Dining Hall, where the floor had to be raked to get a nice incline, and seats had to be produced. On this occasion I heard from ENSA that the Globe Theatre in Shaftesbury Avenue had been bombed and ENSA had been offered the seats from the dress circle. They were covered in dust and had suffered from a soaking when they had been putting the fire out in the roof. I was able to get these seats from ENSA and we put them into our theatre-cum-cinema, all built by the airmen.

It is surprising how often a lad would come to me and say: 'Look, sir, I'm a surveyor', or 'I'm a qualified architect, I'd like to help on this project'. In no time at all you got the airmen — LACs, sometimes AC1s — who would come and say they were a qualified this or that and they would get down and design and show you how this sort of thing should be done. But it was all done under the total and absolute command of a corporal.

Cpl Christian with all his City & Guilds qualifications co-ordinated everything. He would come to me and say: 'Do you think, sir, I can have a load of sand?', or 'Could I have four or five bags of cement?' That aspect of it was relatively easy because, not very far away, at RAF Upwood they happened to be extending their runways and I can assure that there was plenty of sand and cement available.

I will touch on another aspect of our entertainment. One of the aircrew who was on the staff of the Pathfinder Training Unit — a young officer, who had finished his Pathfinder tour and was acting as navigation instructor — I appointed to be the Entertainments Officer. Now this fellow was absolutely mad keen on getting more and more entertainments for ourselves. I am going to tell you a little about how I got additional entertainment, such as arranging for a circus to come to Warboys, and getting more than my fair share of ENSA concert parties. Indeed, the first class shows being shown in the West End came to me through a contact I had in London, but that will come out a little later.

First of all we had to have one, or sometimes two, live plays or concerts from ENSA. I was very friendly with Col Bell, the number two to Basil Dean who ran ENSA. If he wanted to try something out and he was not sure of whether the troops would take to it, he would send it to me. Sometimes I would go down to

Drury Lane and vet something to see if it would be suitable, not that we wanted anything very dreary or off-beat. It meant that my people at Warboys got much better entertainment simply because I was able to offer this facility to ENSA. A lady you hear about, Elsie Byer, who was secretary to Binkie Beaumont who in turn was probably the greatest impressario in the London West End at the time, would select plays from the West End and come to Warboys. Probably the greatest of these was a play by America's greatest theatrical couple called the Lunts. They were in a play in London called *Love in Idleness*. This was probably our best show and they came up and stayed with us. I would send an aircrew bus down to the theatre (and please remember that in those days the theatres started in London at 6.30pm and finished at 8.30pm) so shortly after that the aircrew bus brought the entire cast up to Warboys. Here, with all the spare accommodation, we were able to run a sort of small motel, in which we looked after these people. The WAAF and the airmen were very good at this particular job and the cast were generally fed and watered in the Officers' Mess. After the show early on a Sunday they hared back to London and were able to start again in the West End on the Monday.

Shortly, you will hear about my circus and the elephant that was on the strength of Warboys for a short period. Now some 40-odd years afterwards I rather enjoy the look of absolute disbelief when I tell the story of the Warboys circus and, in particular, of my elephant. As I mentioned earlier I was particularly friendly with the hierarchy that ran ENSA from their headquarters in Drury Lane, and to that end Col Bell rang me and said, as I had accommodated all sorts of other experimental ENSA activities, what did I feel about a circus? I told him that I liked the idea and then we got on to the question of the elephant. Now apparently the elephant was quite small, seven or eight years old, and therefore not fully grown.

It was agreed that the elephant would be delivered to Little Staughton from where I would pick it up. Apparently, when you are an elephant, and you are only seven or eight, your pads, or feet (or whatever elephants have away down there) are very tender and therefore it could only make about a maximum of 13 or 14 miles a day on the hard tarmacadam roads. So the circus duly arrived at about midday; the ringmaster reported to me and told me that he was very pleased with all the facilities. And well he may have been, because I happened to take all the OBOE Mosquitos out of a specially heated hangar and put them outside in order to put my circus inside. Then he enquired about the elephant. 'It set off some time before us and we passed en route; it seemed to be doing very well.' He showed some surprise that it had not arrived before he had. 'That's alright', I answered, 'I'll go and have a look for it.' I rang up the Flights and said to the flight commander: 'Send me a Mossie pilot, I want to brief him.' In the fullness of time a very young flight lieutenant came in, and young flight lieutenants I might say here are very blasé young men, especially if they have got three or six months' seniority. Well, this character came in and said rather accusingly: 'You sent for me, sir?' He was obviously not quite sure why he had been sent for. 'Yes, get in a Mossie and fly down the Great North Road, until you get to the Bedford turn-off and see if you can find my elephant.' He did not turn a hair and he looked me straight in the eye and said: 'Of course, sir, what colour is your elephant?' And I could only think it was elephant colour. So he gave me another rather weary salute and off he went. 'Call me on the box', I said. We had a very ancient form of R/T in those days which was called a TR9. It was a most vile sort of instrument, it seldom worked, but on this occasion it did. So then I sent for the MT flight sergeant. Now if you think that young, brash, over-confident Flight Lieutenants are unshakeable, then here is something that is not only unshakeable — it is indestructible — the flight sergeant MT. He came in, a very different character indeed. He stood there very bright and awaited his briefing. 'Did I see a Queen Mary on the station this morning?' I enquired of him. 'Yes, sir, it's a visitor', he replied. 'Well, commandeer it and send it down the Great North Road and I will instruct you before you leave as to how far and where you should go.' So, about the same time, I got a call from my Mosquito friend: 'Zero One', he called over the R/T. 'I've found your elephant.' 'Good gracious', I exclaimed, 'surely that's what I sent you for.' 'Ah', he said, 'but it's in a pond and it's having a tremendous time with all the kids in the district. They're in the pond with the elephant and the elephant's squirting water everywhere. If any mum picks up her skirts and goes into the pond after any of her children the elephant resents this tremendously and puts out a squirt of water, then mum retires not only hurt but very wet.' The flight sergeant set off and just before he left I said: 'You'd better go to the NAAFI and get some elephant food.' Quite nonchalantly, he turned around and said: 'Why of course, sir, elephant food.' 'Perhaps one of those empty 90 or 100 gallon drums that you've got about the place. Fill it with water because the elephant's bound to want some water.' 'Elephant; water; sir; of course, sir', and off he went. After a lapse of time, perhaps an hour or so, the WAAF in the orderly room was looking out of the window when she saw an elephant pass just below. Now she did not see the lower part, with the elephant on the Queen Mary low-loader. As the saying goes, she rushed in: 'Chiefy, you'll never guess', and the Chiefy who was very busy, obviously preparing a return, did not even look up. 'It's a ****** elephant and it belongs to the CO — don't touch it.'

My own children learnt from somewhere that bread was a favourite with the elephant and it was quite impossible to get either of them to eat a crumb of bread. We used to find slices hidden under their pillows or in the bedclothes and when challenged would say that it was for the elephant.

Another great character at Warboys was Buddy Featherstone-Haugh, who had a successful band that I was able to base at the station; and so once the dance hall had been completed we had a resident band. We could also call on none other than Maj Glen Miller's Band, which was based at Alconbury only about 10 miles away. They would always come — when free — to Warboys, particularly in the first days of the month when the Officers' and Sergeants' Messes had a ration of whisky.

In more modern times Warboys has featured in the annual Pathfinder Dinner which in the past 10 years has been held in the Officers' Mess at RAF Wyton. This is followed the next morning by a Church Parade in Warboys; this is a standing-room only event in the main because, although the Dinner is a boys affair, the wives now attend and stay at the Bridge Hotel in Huntingdon and meet up with their husbands at the church the next morning. I understand that the Airmen NCOs are now having their own reunion and also attend the church parade. We all gather in the community hut and are entertained by the ladies of Warboys who lay out an amazing array of village goodies and provide coffee before we disperse in all directions.

One of the things that always intrigues me at this annual get-together is that some aspect of Warboys crops up which I have not heard of before. For instance, I had not heard of the Warboys ghost, but apparently several incidents occurred after aircraft were returning from raids.

An aircraft was returning after one such raid and was seen to make a good approach but after a certain distance along the runway it sudenly swerved off, with fatal results. Another aircraft was seen to do the same thing but fortunately the crew escaped injury and a little later on another aircraft did the same thing. Each time an aircraft made a safe landing, only suddenly to swerve off the runway at a certain point. After each incident the aircraft's undercarriage and braking system were checked, but in every case there was nothing found to be wrong. The pilots were questioned but they would not say what had made them swerve. Eventually one pilot was induced to say what happened. He said he had just made a perfect touch-down and was hurtling down the runway when suddenly what appeared to be a little girl walked across the runway and he had to swerve to avoid her. After hearing this strange explanation the other pilots were again questioned and at long last they all said the same thing — that a little girl had crossed the runway in front of them. Now there were no dwellings in the vicinity and the nearest village was a mile or two away; nobody could account for the strange apparition. However, a little while after this some people were walking beside the runway when they came upon the skeleton of a little girl, partially buried. The remains were never identified but they were taken away and buried in a nearby churchyard. From then on there were no more sightings of the apparition.

An amusing story was put about concerning Willie Tait after the Tirpitz *turned turtle. All the aircrews of Nos 9 and 617 Squadrons were invited to a cocktail party at the Admiralty. Whilst Tait and his crews were being lionised by many of the senior officers of the Royal Navy, it is claimed that Willie, on being congratulated by some Lord High Admiral, is alleged to have cracked 'I suppose all you seafaring gentlemen are now out of business'.*

Could this possibly have been the reason why Willie Tait DSO***, DFC, did not receive the VC?

16 Treble Mac Wing

It was a tremendous anti-climax when, after VE-Day, I found myself commanding nearly 3,000 people, of which 250 were WAAFs. I had heard many tales after the end of World War 1 about what the vast numbers of our excitable and unpredictable fellow warriors from the Empire and Commonwealth had said about the station — and indeed many of the officers and particular parts of the station that they did not like — and they went in for a deal of arson. So I asked my 'acker-basher' (that is the accountant) if he could get hold of enough money so that I could pay anybody who wanted to go on leave for seven days. 'Oh yes', he said, 'I will speak to Group and that is something that can be arranged in a very short time.' 'Well go ahead', I said, 'and let it be known that those who live locally, especially aircrew, can go off for seven days and can have any money that is due to them'.

The whole reason behind this was that I wanted to get rid of a very volatile type of character on the station, and whilst I said make this available to the aircrew, I really meant everybody. I wanted to get as many people off the base as possible. An awful lot of people, even if they had no money, would not want to go to Northern Ireland or indeed Scotland because they may not have a railway warrant. I could not extend this to railway warrants and so I reckoned I halved the overall establishment of Warboys overnight.

At the same time that I got rid of roughly half the strength on the base it also meant that I had double rations for that half left on the base, and so the various cooks at Warboys could lash-up just a little more fare.

At the same time as I did this my entertainments officer, who was ex-aircrew, laid on some interesting stuff to do on the station. We had a sports day for instance, and that was a great success; people were winning prizes. Although they were not very much in the way of prizes they had never won anything in the athletic arena in their lives before.

He also got on to ENSA and my friend Col Bell down in Drury Lane. We had ad hoc shows, and of course the Royal Air Force Cinema Corporation were excellent! They let me have special films just for the day and I gave them back the next day.

At the same time as all this was happening I had a very pleasant call from Transport Command. Some of you may remember that the Hon Sir Ralph Cochrane, who had relinquished command of No 5 Group, had become the

Commander-in-Chief of Transport Command. He told his Senior Personnel Staff Officer to get in touch with me and offer me a job, now that the war had finished, in Transport Command. Now this was a most delightful fellow who had been an oppo of mine for many years and his name was John Warrell — a group captain, Cranwell type. John Warrell rang me and said that the Commander-in-Chief wanted me to accept the station at Bassingbourn which was not very far away down towards London, only about 10 or 12 minutes by air. He told me the American 91st Bomb Group had occupied it for a couple of years but they had now moved out. So whilst all the preparations were afoot at Warboys, everybody that had any sense at all grabbed themselves their next week's wages and ran off in every direction. This was all quite unofficial; I had no authority to do this and I reckoned I could justify it if I was ever accused of doing something that was quite illegal (as indeed it was). But to me to cut the strength of the station by nearly half was something that I had to do; I was simply halving the risk of trouble arising.

So I jumped into an aeroplane and I flew to Bassingbourn, down the Great North Road; I landed there and to my absolute amazement and delight I was met by a civilian, the Mess manager. Now I could not remember this fellow's name except that I beg of you to believe that we called him Jeeves. He had the manner, the entire manner, of the perfect butler.

'I am so pleased to meet you again sir. You may remember I was the Mess manager in the Sergeants' Mess at Honington when you were a sergeant.' Of course I remembered; I could not think of his name but there he was standing there just like Jeeves of old. He said they had laid on a very nice lunch for us and was at pains to express how pleased he was that I was going to command the station. 'Well just hold on a minute', I said, 'I have come down to have a look, just have a sniff at it'. 'Well, first of all sir, we have laid on a very nice lunch all with American rations.' 'Really', I said. 'Yes, it will be a long time before we use up all the American rations.' 'What about the grog, the American grog?' I probed. 'Oh yes, we have got plenty of that,' he assured me.

By this time there was a Fortress running up on the edge of the tarmac and I was approched by a very young 'lootenant', in fact I could not possibly have made a guess at his age. I would have thought he was 12 or 13 and possibly in a year or two he would start to shave. He came up and gave me a typically American salute which I acknowledged in the Air Force style. He put at my feet two fire buckets painted red with 'FIRE' on the side, filled with keys of all shapes and sizes. 'There you are captain,' he said. (I was never able to persuade the US Army Air Force to address me as group captain and I never tried.) 'There you are sir, there is your station, would you sign here?' 'My dear chap' I began, 'we don't do that sort of thing in the RAF, it will take me the best part of a week to take over the station and I am certainly not signing for it here on the tarmac, with two buckets of keys'. 'Oh, please yourself', said the young 'lootenant', 'I'm going State-side', and he retreated to his Fortress, climbed in and took off pointing due west. And I presume he got State-side eventually.

By this time Jeeves had conducted me to the Mess where in those days there was always an RAF officer, either a squadron leader or a wing commander, who stayed on the base because it was still a Royal Air Force station despite the fact that the US Army Air Force was heavily engaged there.

'Perhaps you would just like to have a quick look round the Mess', Jeeves invited. I had a feeling that he really wanted me to see the Mess, but not for any particular or personal point of view. In those days (some of you may remember) in the living quarters on a station which originally was designed for two squadrons, a squadron leader would have a sitting room and a bedroom. In the middle was a bathroom and a toilet, and on the other side there was another sitting room, bedroom etc, so the two squadron leaders in effect lived together. He took me into the first one — in the sitting room there was a bevy of young ladies in various stages of undress, and the emphasis really was on undress. They were sitting there — some were sewing, some were reading — and they were all drinking Southern Comfort in some form or other. Now when I appeared they all gave me a 'hi-there-good-looking' — but they were obviously referring to Jeeves and not myself. 'We hear you have come to take us over', they called in unison. I backed out and Jeeves, who had also brought a little retinue with him, shunted back like a goods train. I removed myself and asked Jeeves who these ladies were.

'Well', he began, 'they've been in residence for a very long time and that big ginger one was the Base Commander's; if she had to go away for a haircut, or whatever they went away for, her sister took over and stood in, stood up or laid down — whatever the case might be — whilst the big sister was away'. 'You had better get rid of them', I ordered. 'Sir, I've tried for days and I've given up. I thought you would be able to do that.' So I went and had a very very nice lunch in the Mess on American rations then I rang up my friend John Warrell and said: 'John, did you say there was an alternative to Bassingbourn?' 'Yes, it's a wing, a transport wing in Germany belonging to Sir Ralph Cochrane', he said. 'He only put this down as a second or third choice for you; he was most anxious that you took Bassingbourn.'

'Well, I'll take No 111 Wing', I said. No 111 Wing provided all the air transport requirements in Germany and Occupied Europe between Oslo in the north, Brussels in the south, Holland in the west and Warsaw, Poland, in the east. The Wing had some 98 Dakotas, serviced and operational, controlled by a dear friend of mine, Gp Capt 'Shadey' Lane — or probably known to some as Reg Lane — a very well-known and distinguished Pathfinder and a Canadian to boot; the Dakotas were within a Canadian wing I believe centred at Benson or some place locally.

Apart from being Sir Ralph's transport adviser I was loaned to Air Chief Marshal Sholto Douglas as his transport adviser, too. He dealt with my Wing and all our internal affairs as my landlord, and I had several staging posts within all these countries. I think it was 11 in all and my brief was, whilst conducting daily transport within what was called the British Forces of Occupation in Germany and liberated Europe, I was also briefed to hand over every airfield as quickly as possible to the Nationals involved. This meant Holland, Belgium, Denmark, Norway and ultimately Poland.

With the Nationals involved I dealt with Governments. My AOC was Whitney Straight and his brief was very clear: get rid of the Nationals and their airports as quickly as possible. This was also Sholto Douglas's wish, and I did this in a remarkably short time. The Nationals were keen to get their airports back and we were equally keen to see that they got them. Please to remember that despite this fact many of these airfields were very badly blitzed, first of all by ourselves and then in a 'scorched earth' policy by the Germans leaving them. In fact the airport in Amsterdam — Schipol — was still smouldering when I got there.

Perhaps you can savour the taste of the times when I paid an official visit to the main Brussels airfield — badly blitzed, but serviceable — and the occasion was the delivery of a four-engined aircraft from the people of America to Queen Wilhelmina. It was flown by a famous Dutchman, possibly the most experienced transport pilot in the world. There was great excitement: the Queen and her Cabinet were present, a band had been produced as if by magic. However, at that time there was none of the modern gear associated with air traffic control today. The controller was one of my corporals in a jeep with a lash-up in the back that made contact with the Queen's gift. The thrill in the crowd could be felt as the giant aircraft appeared overhead. My corporal gave him a hail but received no reply. Again and again he repeated his call which, incidentally, was being broadcast to the assembled crowd in the immediate vicinity. Having made a circuit the aircraft lined up with the runway and, having regard to the many bomb craters just off the runway, it was quite obvious that he was going to land, but there was still no sign of his wheels coming down. My corporal gave me an appealing look: I told him to try once more and stress 'this is an order from my group captain, are you going to land?' Back came a reply at once, in a voice choked with emotion: 'Yes I am landing — I am Dutchman — landing Dutch aircraft — on Dutch soil for my Queen.' By this time the aircraft was about a half-a-mile from the threshold and my corporal, in an ice cold and very English voice, said: 'Roger, clear to land, BUT PUT YOUR ＊ ＊ ＊ ＊ ＊ ＊ ＊ DUTCH WHEELS DOWN!' I will never know how the pilot was able to abort and save the present for his Queen. The pilot was the famous Capt Parmentier, later of KLM. Sadly, he was killed near Prestwick some years later when attempting a landing in bad weather conditions. At the reception after the presentation Parmentier was being pressured by the Press about the low approach to the field. We were agreed, he and I, that he did not actually forget to put his wheels down. We said later that day that he was making a pass at the field with the permission of the Commander of No 111 Wing. The things we have done for England!

I had rather a dramatic introduction to my posting to command the Treble Mac Wing in June 1945 and I hope I can remember the names of the other two Macs. One was my wing commander — admin, and the other was a wing commander — operations. But the other aspect that I found quite exciting, if not a little frightening, was my introduction for the first time to my new Boss who was the Commander-in-Chief of the British Air Forces of Occupation in Germany — Sholto Douglas, and I found this vast and imposing figure more like Herman Goering than any Air Force officer I had hitherto come into contact with. When I was marched in to be introduced he sat there behind an enormous desk which appeared to be clear of anything other than a series of telephones and empty trays; he sat on what looked like a throne but it was a very large, heavily-carved Germanic chair with great wooden armrests. This very distinguished, and only recently removed from being Commander-in-Chief of Fighter Command, figure sat there and surveyed me coldly: 'Well, Mahaddie', he began, 'you come to me with a very fine record and a blessing from your Commander-in-Chief in England, the Hon Sir Ralph Cochrane. But let me warn you that if you get up to the antics of your predecessor, not only will you be sacked but, Mahaddie, I will break you. Good morning'. I do not remember leaving the office, I just seemed to crawl under the small gap between the bottom of the door and the heavy Germanic carpet that graced his office. I saw very little of my new Boss save that he had at the time as his PA none other than Wg Cdr Bob Wright, who for years had been the PA to Lord Dowding. No doubt Sholto Douglas had snatched him from Stanmore when his stint as Commander-in-Chief, Fighter Command, terminated and his posting to Germany coincided with the end of the war.

Now Bob Wright used to invite me to the Farmhouse which was a remarkable establishment. It was the Commander-in-Chief's residence and he entertained in the most lavish style, and I am sure quite on a par with the entertainment that Reichsmarshal Herman Goering was accustomed to. And so I would find myself dining quite frequently at the Farmhouse, rather as far removed from the salt as a lowly group captain and also a very acting wing commander would be permitted, and I can recall very many occasions when perhaps I became the butt of the Commander-in-Chief's keen wit. I would like to feel that I perhaps responded as I was expected to respond, having been invited there only to make up numbers or, indeed, for comic light relief. I never quite realised which.

I remember on one occasion Sholto Douglas once said to me with a certain glint in his eye: 'Why do you wear that brooch on your uniform?' 'That's a Pathfinder badge sir', I said. 'A Pathfinder badge, what did you get that for?' he enquired. 'It has no business to be there. Take it off, remove it.' 'I am very sorry sir, I can't, it is a Royal Warrant. It was made a Royal Warrant by His Majesty King George VI and I have a certificate which permits me to wear it.' But he continued: 'Nevertheless, I am going to order you to take it off. What will you do about that?' I pondered a short while and said: 'I am a very well brought up airman, sir, and I always obey the last order.' He looked a little astonished and exclaimed: 'Good gracious! You would remove it.' 'Oh yes sir', I said. He looked round the table for a little support and he got none. He then asked: 'But you would put it back?' 'No sir', I said, 'you gave me an order, only you could order me to put it back; but what I would do in the meantime, I would tear it off my pocket flap and I would repair that pocket flap with red wool and henceforth people would say "Hamish is a Pathfinder but Sholto Douglas ordered him to take his badge off".' I do not remember how the conversation went from then on but it seemed to lapse. I enjoyed very much working with and for Sholto Douglas who was every bit as large and famous in his own way as his counterpart was infamous.

Another interesting thing: Sholto Douglas noticed that I had been favoured by the Czechs and he asked me on this occasion how I got 'that Czech medal'. I answered him quite honestly and truthfully that I did not know. I had gone looking for Prague many years before to deliver some pamphlets telling them to hold on and eventually help would come; but we did not know how we were going to help them. 'That's remarkable', he said. 'I can tell you how I got mine.' And the story told to me by Bob Wright on this occasion and Sholto concurrred. He paraded himself shortly in Prague after the war in one of the imposing squares in the centre of the city, with full military pomp and circumstance. Dr Benes was to award him the Most Noble Order of the White Bear (or something like that) which was an enormous sash that looked resplendent on Sholto's ample figure. But apparently before he was invested with this great honour one of the President's staff noticed that Sholto did not possess a Czech Medal for Valour. There was a moment's hesitation when Dr Benes saw that the Staff Officer was wearing the Czech War Cross — he disinvested his Staff Officer, invested Sholto Douglas, and then turned to the Staff Officer and asked: 'Is it now alright for me to invest the Air Marshal?' That is how Sholto Douglas, like Lord Montgomery and many others, came to wear the Czech War Cross, or as it is sometimes called the Czech Military Cross.

I thoroughly enjoyed my period commanding No 111 Wing and all the many facets of running air transport; I was left entirely alone by Sholto and his Staff. This rather unique position of running a very small Group with an excellent Staff I enjoyed very much. And, of course, having at my command aircraft that went the length and breadth of my rather vast parish. I have difficulty now in recalling some of the great occasions we had in the early part of the peace. One of the things that did shock me, and it took a little swallowing, was the enormous destruction of urban Germany. In fact wherever you went there was a great deal of destruction, not always in built-up areas. I would estimate, and I am sure there are many who would claim that my guess is way out, but I would say half our bombs did a bit of farming — they ended up in fields nowhere near the target, but the other half that did find built-up Germany left their mark there for all to see.

It is just a minor thing I suppose, but I had my own establishment which was very comfortable — a beautiful flat in Buckeburg — which was near Sholto's headquarters, and where I had a sort of live-in batman who was an excellent fellow. There was a Mess which was quite handy where I could eat all my meals, and an excellent Wing Headquarters with all the paraphernalia of a Group, yet reduced in establishment. And, as I was trying to say, the rather minor things did impress me. It was odd to find there were no young men, only men of very advanced years. Remember that at that period of the war I had still to reach my middle 30s. There were no men about under 60 or 65, only women.

The currency at the time was cigarettes: you could have your hair cut and you could have all your washing done for a cigarette or two. You could have your shoes repaired beautifully for one cigarette and this was the order of the day, but please remember this was within a few days of the end of the war. The one thing that I found that nearly choked me was to see the children: despite the rigours of war the children, as indeed we found at home, seemed to flourish. There were very few infants about; they were all two, three, four or five years of age.

Every Friday, when I went to the Mess for lunch, we had a ration laid out on a table in the hall. We were given an issue of 200 cigarettes, some chocolate in bars and also some Mars Bars which came from the NAAFI originally but they were a free issue for the troops. We all got the same, which again was the order of the day. Now every Friday when I came back from lunch before starting the afternoon stint, all the little boys and girls there might have been in the three-storey block of flats (and I had the bottom flat) formed a guard of honour, some exquisite little girls with flaxen plaits; they would stand there and curtsy. I would hand out various sweeties to all of them and they would give me a very shy little smile, bob a curtsy and say 'Danke schön Herr Kapitän', and then rush away to their mums to show the spoils of peace.

Whilst there was a very strict 'no fraternisation' rule immediately after the war — not that it lasted very long amongst the troops — I saw very little of my neighbours, except when I had this 'Guard of Honour' of the children from the block that oddly enough seemed to grow each Friday. When I say it started off with maybe eight until we lost our sweet ration it grew steadily, and then I had my Batman explain because he did speak a little German, and so the 'Guard of Honour' came to an end and I was very sorry. But whenever I met any of the children they would all give me a quiet little curtsy, and I was always 'Herr Kapitän'.

One amusing episode that I remember occurred one morning at petty sessions when I had one of my own corporals up in front of me. There was a very strict curfew in Germany at this period and everybody had to be off the streets by 10.30 or 11.00pm. Sometime after midnight this corporal was found making his way back to his billet when he was accosted by our Service Police and when it was pointed out to him that it was well after curfew and what was he doing abroad at this time, the corporal replied that he had been dining with the Commander-in-Chief. The policeman who had accosted him asked which Commander-in-Chief? 'Marshal of the Royal Air Force Sir Sholto Douglas' he replied. It transpired that the corporal had been dining with him at the Schloss that Sholto Douglas inhabited in the middle of Buckeburg, a very imposing German castle. The policeman asked him 'what the occasion was', to which he replied that the Commander-in-Chief was entertaining the Sadlers Wells Ballet who were over performing for the troops. The two policemen obviously thought that the corporal was taking the 'rise' out of them so they told him he could explain that in the morning to the group captain.

So in the morning my corporal was in front of me and gave me the same yarn. I adjourned and when he had left the office I rang up Bob Wright, Sholto's PA, and told him that I had got a corporal here who said he had dined with the Commander-in-Chief last night. Bob Wright assured me that he probably could have done, since they entertained the Sadlers Wells Ballet on the previous evening. He told me there were some of my people at the dinner but they were all very famous ballet dancers. So I had the corporal back in and asked him if by any chance he was a member of Sadlers Wells. He assured me that he most certainly was and then gave me a name which I cannot remember, nor could I pronounce at the time. Apparently, the Corps de Ballet found out he was serving in Germany and they invited him to take part in the presentation to the Commander-in-Chief in the Schloss. So I had the very pleasant duty of dismissing the corporal and whenever I saw him after that I expected him to do one of the movements where he would leap into the air and come down on whatever ballet dancers come down on.

17 To the Cocos via Haifa

Having been selected and recommended for a Staff College course by my Commander-in-Chief, the Hon Sir Ralph Cochrane, I found myself posted to Haifa, Palestine in 1947. Aloft on Mount Carmel in fact, just above the coastal town of Haifa. Right at the very beginning I had a great feeling that things were not well for me here.

Please remember that I had had a fortunate war in a sense and I had received a great deal of reward for that period. I now found myself amongst some 60 selected, extremely able and highly decorated Air Force officers, and in an academic situation which certainly was not of my choosing. From the very beginning it turned out to be something of a complete disaster, and eclipse is the only word I can think of at the moment.

But Haifa was no Oakington, Warboys, or indeed No 111 Wing. One was left entirely to one's own devices and I never recovered from that initial shock in these short few months of the course.

This may of course have been one of the major aims of staff training. Whilst I did badly, by my efforts on the course, many years later in business I seemed to be able to implement the purpose of staff training at Haifa and was able to apply staff doctrine to the methods I used as an aerospace consultant; oddly it took some 10 years for this process to work through and be such a benefit to me in retirement from the RAF. Thus all was not lost.

I did, however, on occasions have difficulty in interpreting staff logic. For example we were asked on one occasion to write to a Civil Authority about placing some device on the roof of their building which could be used by aircraft for simulated bombing. This was an infra-red device which the aircraft could track over in the dead of night; there would be a trace on the camera by which your results could be assessed. So I just happened to suggest that I would put my infra-red device on the harbour master's office at a small harbour in the Firth of Forth near Edinburgh, called Granton. Not only was it very near my home when I was a lad and long before I joined the Air Force, but I felt that I could approach the harbour master, and indeed I did. I found no problem at all about getting this device placed on the roof of the harbour master's office in this tiny fishing port. All went well and I even quoted from memory as far as I could recall the sort of correspondence I had with the harbour master. I was completely shattered when I found that the remarks I received from the Directing Staff (I cannot remember who he was) couched rather in the terms that 'we should try and discuss these problems and the writing should not be imaginary', as if one was writing for one of the more hysterical newspapers, or indeed one was writing a novel. I found this not only shattering because I was dealing with an actual event, but also something I did whilst I was an Instructor at Kinloss teaching Whitley crews. I never quite recovered from this and there were several other instances when I failed to persuade the Directing Staff. But in no way did I blame the Directing Staff for, what I thought at the time, were quite cruel crits.

Now in retrospect I have not the slightest qualms about saying — within this great bevy of distinction and academy at the staff College — that I was certainly very much below average as an embryo Staff Officer. I was quite happy to be judged with anyone on my course, and indeed on the Directing Staff, but here for the first time my whole being was in question. I was taken right back to the early days at Halton where again the focus was on my lack of academy and the fact that I had left school at the age of 13.

Reading in recent times a report that had been published about the Staff College at Haifa, I was invited to comment. But I always felt so embarrassed about how poorly I had shown at Haifa, and I regret now that I did not contribute as indeed most of my contemporaries had done and made some excellent and interesting comments about the Course. It was a very difficult period to be in Palestine with the Hagana and all the other Jewish gangsters that were around at the time. One thing I do remember is that one had always to carry side-arms: you clambered down the hill from the summit of Mount Carmel to the beach and spent an afternoon looking rather odd in bathing trunks with side-arms, holster and ammunition. But the intrreresting thing about this period is that, to the best of my knowledge, no-one ever had to use their side-arms; but what is probably more important was the fact that none of our revolvers and ammunition were ever stolen, although there was plenty of opportunity.

But I must say there is, to some degree, a happy ending to this sad saga of my Staff education. Somehow or other all that I did seem to absorb at Haifa appears to have been stored away in some form of cerebral computer and from the moment I left the Air Force I found I had belatedly some feeling for Staff College doctrine. Ever since, in commerce and industry, I have been able to relate and communicate with people that I have been associated with whilst masquerading as a consultant, mainly in avionics. This is an echo from my pathfinding days when I was associated with the very earliest forms of avionics which were the hand-maiden of Don Bennett's pathfinding techniques. I find it gives me a great deal of reflected pleasure now, these many years later, when I learn that in my reports and particularly my letters I seem to reflect some of the techniques of that sad period.

Whilst I was in the Air Ministry on my first tour serving in Bomber Operations, I was tasked with making preparations for the UK-New Zealand Air Race. This was in 1953 and it was my firm intention and hope that I would command the New Zealand Air Race Flight, having inaugurated the English Electric Canberra at Binbrook in the first Canberra Bomber Wing. But this was not to be. Whilst I was serving in the Air Ministry I started to plan the New Zealand Air Race, and the only bit of comfort or cheer we had whilst serving in the Air Ministry was looking forward to the time, of course, when we got out of that fire trap.

The telephone rang one day and when I picked it up a very Scottish voice, that I thought was mimicking my own Scottish accent, said to me:

'Will you no be Hamish Mahaddie?' and I, of course, reverted to the basic Scottish and replied: 'Ay, I'm Hamish Mahaddie.' And the voice said: 'I am Hector MacPherson and I have a shop in Queen Street, Edinburgh; I make all the paraphernalia for the Highland Games and have made some 20 sporran that I would like you to take out to Singapore for me.'

How he knew I was going out with the Vice-Chief of the Air Staff to prove the route that the Air Force was taking for the New Zealand Air Race I know not. But what I can tell you was that I was going with the Vice-Chief down the route and we were going to land at the Cocos and someone was coming out from Singapore to meet us there, so it was quite feasible.

'Certainly', I said, 'I will be delighted to take your 20 sporrans out and see they get to the Singapore Pipe Band.'

Then I dashed out of the office and peered into several other offices on the same landing, quite sure that somebody was taking the mickey out of me, but they were all beavering away, or doing *The Times* crossword which was part of their daily duty.

However, we had a party. Believe it or not the Air Minister — 'Lord Delyle and Deadly' as we called him — came along, and the Chief of the Air Staff came to see the Vice-Chief off on this world tour right down to New Zealand. So it came to pass that we arrived at London Airport all very much in the aftermath of a nice hail and farewell party in the RAF Club at Piccadilly. They all passed through Customs with great glee and a lot of merriment until it was my turn. Being the wing commander I was the most junior person, a sort of batman of the party; when I got to the Customs there was a great carton waiting for me and the Customs officer tentatively enquired whether or not I was Wg Cdr Mahaddie. I replied that I certainly was. When he asked me if the sporrans in the box were mine I suddenly realised that this was not a hoax. It was a very real thing. Hector MacPherson, or whatever he was called, had really been ringing from Queen Street, Edinburgh, and here I was confronted with 20 sporrans for the Royal Air Force Pipe Band in Singapore.

The Customs officer asked me if I was exporting them. I told him that I was just taking them out to the RAF who have a Pipe Band. The Customs officer was plainly trying to ease the sporrans through Customs without somebody, certainly not me, being charged on the spot for exporting them.

'They are your personal property Sir?' 'Oh yes', I said, 'certainly'.

He then looked at me very kindly with just a trace of a smile on his face.

'Tell me sir, how do you wear 20 sporrans?'

Having been active in planning the UK-New Zealand Air Race, the Vice-Chief of the Air Staff invited me to fly down the route and, as he put it, 'to see what a mess I had made of it'. Our Air Marshals have a finely tuned sense of humour.

When I arrived at the Cocos Islands one of the first persons I met was one of my own airmen from my earlier Canberra days. He came up to me and suggested that I should have a look at both ends of the runway. We got into a jeep and there, at an unmarked threshold of the runway, was some 200 yards of very rough surface. The Cocos runway is what you might call a 'living area' and spikes of coral grow up some two or three inches proud if left untreated. The runway was under the control of the Australians and every morning they sent a skimmer, followed by a roller up and down the runway to roll the overnight growth into the surface, followed by a dusting of sand. This made a superb surface but the extremities of the runway were left untreated. I asked the Aussie Flying Controller why these bad areas were not marked. He told me that he was going to do this tomorrow. I suggested that he did it that very afternoon, and this was done. I also warned the RAF Engineering Officer in charge of handling our aircraft to make doubly sure that these areas were clearly marked before our aircraft landed.

This splendid performance of the Australian team was rather ironic, being first at every touchdown. When they arrived at the Cocos led by my very good friend Jel Cumming RAAF, the Australian team had decided to land from opposite ends of this very long runway. The leader chose to land facing his refuelling point (which was downwind) and then raced towards the refuelling team, braked rather fiercely, burst a tyre and ended up off the runway. The second aircraft, piloted by Bob Raw, heard of his leader's mishap and also turned around and raced up to the refuelling point. Once again, he too braked rather heavily and shed some one-and-a-half inches off his nosewheel tyre, but it did not burst.

Raw quickly refuelled and was off in short order and, unhappily, his nosewheel tyre burst on landing at Woomera, which I believe cost Bob Raw and Australia the Air Race.

Another aspect which may well have contributed to the Australian defeat I heard about whilst I was on the Cocos. The Australians had positioned a couple of frigates across the Tasman Sea to act in an air/sea rescue capacity and assist any of the aircraft that might be in trouble over this area of water. I left a strict message at the Cocos for the RAF team that they were not, under any circumstances, to answer R/T calls from the Tasman vessels and therefore to ignore any requests to transmit their position. I also believe that this was another feature that assisted the RAF entry winning the race.

It was indeed a most pleasurable moment when, in typical monsoon conditions — heavy rain and low cloud — Monty Burton, one of my own, my very own original Canberra pilots at Binbrook, crossed the line for a RAF win; and also to be able to greet him when he wearily got out of his Canberra after a little under 24 hours of elapsed time from Heathrow, London.

Whilst at the Staff College at Haifa, Palestine, the course was being lectured by none other than Adm Sir James Somerville of Taranto fame. At question time Willie Tait stood up and said:

'Sir, we on this course, in keeping with others on former courses, are coming to the view that our present formation of army, navy and air force organisations could well be improved by having one integrated defence staff. What are your views?'

The Admiral, who had been prowling the stage on courses east to west and reciprocal as he would the bridge of his flagship, stopped as if struck by a cannon ball, glared down at Willie and said:

'Sir, if we ever have a single integrated command you will all wear navy blue.'
Willie stood his ground and very quietly said:

'Sir, in view of the entirely unsatisfactory reply to my first question, what are your views about the simple fact that airborne devices — rockets, bombs and aerial mines etc, sank more surface tonnage than the combined weights of the Allied navies?'

On this occasion the Admiral glared at Willie: 'What bloody fool said that?' and then looked for support from his 'Flags' (the Navy have the most unique gentlemen that are a fine trawl from the deep; they are what the Air Force would call a very personal assistant to the Air-Marshal), and 'Flags' replied to the question:

'I fear it was you, Sir, in Volume XX of The War at Sea.'

I cannot remember any further comment on that issue save that the College encumbents — half Air Force, half Army — seemed to collapse with much glee.

18 On the Beach

I will not deny that when I was retired from the RAF on 24 March 1958, somewhat shaken after 30 years, I was determined that I would make a complete break from aviation — 'but where?' I asked myself. It was unfortunate that I had a motor accident in Germany and never felt that I would get my flying category back so I decided to leave the RAF, although I did recover to AIB rating in a few months.

Happily after some months of being on extended leave I found that there were people who seemed to want me to work for them. The first was a senior Air Chief Marshal for whom I had worked in the Arthur Marshall (Air Ministry) years before and who was now retired and 'something in the City', with a host of directorships and chairman of several large concerns including a merchant bank (all gleaned from an advertisement in *The Times*). He suggested that I could relieve him of half-a-dozen technical directorship chores and overnight I had a ready-made consultancy, all with the full backing of Sir, who loved to introduce me to his cronies as 'one of my naughty boys who generally introduces me to his friends as 'Sir'. Just fancy — twice a Knight at his age . . .' And thus I embarked on the rather dicey role of persuading total strangers to consider some aspect of the desperate needs of the Services, against the general background of the constant financial restrictions that are the stock-in-trade of Governmental thinking *vis à vis* Procurement. This situation is best summed up in the (I believe) true story of one RAF Commander-in-Chief who wrote direct to the Air Minister to this effect: 'These are my minimum demands without which I cannot continue to carry out my commitments, and if you reject my pleas . . . I will retire from the RAF.' The Minister, very brave fellow — in fact the bravest of the brave — wrote back by return and said briefly: 'Would 1 April suit you for your retirement . . .?'

Although I was particularly sad at leaving, I had not enjoyed the Service in the years after the war, more especially after the Staff College episode. I did enjoy the short period I had in Germany in the early days of peace, when my brief from Whitney Straight was painfully short — 'you have some 16 airfields in your parish; the Nationals are keen to get them back; get rid of them overnight', which I set out to do and it so happened that I was destined for the Staff College shortly. Those airfields in Norway and Denmark were easy, almost a formality. Those in Holland and Belgium followed as a matter of routine. The one in Poland I left to an excellent Air Attaché we had there and I am sure he coped with that. Thus before I left, those in Germany — including the Tempelhof Airport — were off-loaded to Sholto Douglas's Staff, and the liquidation was completed ere I removed myself to Haifa.

Having taken deep draughts of Laddie Lucas's heavy water Luck/Fate, I am now confronted with his next stage, Destiny; and here Luck, Fate and Chance deserted me and I felt that my entire future was in some melting pot. At Halton I had at least three years to adjust and find a lever, at Staff College time was short and the whole process was designed to take due measure of embryo Staff Officers. Possibly for the first time I realised how much help I had received from my oppos in the billet.

I dearly wanted to do well, but somehow I was always struggling; I was never able to lift my morale until I left the Service and had to fend for myself in business. And then, oddly enough, I found I was able to draw on the lessons that should have been so obvious to me on the course. So all was not lost.

I found the transition from being a sad Service type to that of a consultant to several highly respected concerns, more especially under the banner of my 'Twice Nightly Guru', very easy and pleasant to take. I was given sanctuary of an office just off Park Lane where I shared half a girl (I chose the half with fingers) and slowly let myself into the deep end of industry and commerce. My first aim was to strive to maintain my family in the style we had enjoyed in the Service, but I quickly realised this was not to be until, out of the blue, I was offered the oportunity to act as Technical Adviser on a movie called *633 Squadron*. The offer came as a sort of echo from one of the auditors that we thought we had tricked whilst we were Don Bennett's clueless station commanders in the final days of the war. This fellow was now doing a stint with Director of Public Relations in the Ministry and heard someone ask where could they find someone with Mossie experience, and from that tiny acorn I became involved in 15 full feature movies.

Some I go out of my way to deny that I had anything to do with, some I really enjoyed like *The Battle of Britain, Operation 'Crossbow'* and *A Bridge Too Far* which I was unhappy about because history had been treated in an extremely lax fashion, although it was a good box office success. I may have offended Attenborough by not claiming a credit, which I understand is a sacrilegious thing in the movie business. The main reason was that it was British history being lampooned and I was unhappy about the treatment of Gen 'Boy' Browning in the movie. *General Patton* followed and I wished that I had visited these battle sites before, and not many years after, my function as Technical Adviser.

I thoroughly enjoyed *The Battle of Britain*, it was such a challenge. I had been involved with Harry Saltzman and 'Cubby' Broccoli on a couple of Bond movies which were great fun because the more outrageous you can get the better it seems to be. There is no question of sticking to the strict parameters of history — they are essentially fun movies — and you just do not even ask how you squirt say 5,000 gallons of foam out of the back of a car with a 20-gallon tank, or how the Wallis Autogyro fires rapid cannon shells at the baddies. This neither impinges on what is strict aviation history, nor on the ingenuity of the movie man's special effects expert.

The main reason I enjoyed the making of the *The Battle of Britain* was the two principals — Harry Saltzman and Ben Fisz (himself a Spitfire pilot) — insisted on the stark reality throughout. This was somewhat difficult nearly 20 years after the

Battle, even more so when I understood that only one Spitfire existed to fly down the Mall as a tribute to 'The Few' each year. However, the MoD gave me six teams of surveyors who inspected dozens of Spitfires and Hurricanes on gate duty throughout the UK and reported that there were about 100 Spitfires and less than a dozen Hurricanes that could be moved and then, after a thorough stripped down inspection, established how many could be made to fly. This total also included some held in private hands.

Finally, I found that within the scope of acceptable outlay — even by movie standards — I could mount 12 Spitfires to fly, but only six Hurricanes with only four that would fly. That accounted for the RAF side of the Battle. The Luftwaffe came from Spain. The Air Attaché in Madrid at the time warned me that a mass of Me109s were coming up for auction soon so, with the producers' agreement and a fortune in Bank of England Notes of Credit, I raced to Seville in time for a subasta; that heart-stopping drama is best recalled in Leonard Mosley's *The Battle of Britain — The Making of a Film*. He describes the event of the Spanish auction faithfully and under the heading of 'The Leprachaun in the Bowler Hat', and much better than I would dare without offending many. The Spanish Air Force also had several hundred Heinkel He111s and both these and the fighters were home-made — built under license in Spain — but all with Roll-Royce Merlin 500/45 series engines.

The Spanish Air Ministry loaned me 30 of the bombers for free, save that we had to paint them for the battle sequences and then repaint them back into Spanish Air Force colours. The fighters were bought outright for my client, and sold after production. None of the actual aircraft during production were destroyed; those seen to be destroyed were full-scale glassfibre models, generally with a motorcycle engine and a balsa wood propeller.

My main problem was to keep aircraft serviceable in a lengthy shooting period and, since I started without any spares backing (save what the Spaniards provided for 'their' Luftwaffe), I had to scratch around for our fighter spares. Happpily, so far as the engines were concerned, these came from Jersey Aviation, St Helier, CI, but in the field of movie making you find that nothing is impossible. I did not have a single spare radiator so if an aircraft came in spewing glycol from a leak in the evening, that radiator was off the aircraft, down to Delaney Galley, north London, and would be back repaired and on the line ready for call next morning. The Battle of Britain spirit seemed to affect the entire production and, whilst the budget was alarmingly overshot, the movie was made and well received — except in France and the States — as a faithful document of history if perhaps over-dramatised.

I would, of course, be guilty of crass deceit if I claimed that I was not enamoured with the film I was involved in featuring Sophia Loren — *Operation 'Crossbow'* — a fictional story but with the Peenemünde background. It was indeed a tremendous experience to witness this great artiste in person and in action. A delightful woman with a delicious sense of humour which seemed to explode frequently. I remember once when the camera crew were having a bit of a lark with George Peppard — her leading man — she connived with the crew to give Peppard a rough time. Now Sophia is so professional that she normally is known as a 'one-take' girl, and occasionally by grace and favour will allow an extra for a favourite director. The script called for a fight in a hotel bedroom, where Peppard turns up doubling as her husband (who has been killed in a air-raid). A fight starts in the bedroom and to help the crew Sophia kept asking 'can we have another take' as she was enjoying the battle. But not so Peppard, and after at least six such phoney takes he crawled off the set shouting for his stand-in, and Sophia collapsed on the bed hysterical with laughter.

I fear I was guilty on several occasions of making frightful boobs during my relatively short period on the perimeter of the movies. When the director wants a shot but wishes to conceal the camera he builds a 'hide' rather like the gamekeeper at a large estate shoot. On one such occasion the hide, hastily erected, fell down, but the situation had been delicately arranged with an aircraft, carrying the bare minimum of fuel because it was supposed to crash in front of the camera. I went forward to the hide to assist the fellows rebuilding and the result was pandemonium. I was accosted by a huge shop steward who not only stopped the entire movie, but insisted that I be removed before the production could continue. Union über Alles.

I think the worst thing I ever did was to follow a chap who was squirting airmens' tunic buttons with a form of dust to dull the shine. I, in my ignorance, removed the dust not knowing that the shine would give an unwanted reflection on the camera. In the field of TV production I found an entirely different standard and attitude towards detail; there was a positive 'that will do' sort of feeling. On one series that I am ashamed of, I worked on two episodes at the same time with separate directors and two separate camera crews, and I know that the most desperate blunders were shot simply because I happened to be on the set next door.

Despite all the trials and doubts I suffered during this brief excursion into the field of fantasy and mayhem, it was exciting — in fact exhilarating — and above all, to me, educational. Not so much at the time because there was not the opportunity to make a deep study of the historical background — except in the case of *The Battle of Britain* when experts such as Bob Stanford Tuck, who advised on the tactical aspect of the Battle, and 'Ginger' Lacey who was the director's assistant, and many others advised the producers on the state of the art at the time — but I am the first to admit that this is a case of 'you can't win 'em all'. I was only reminded on a recent visit to Canada when an ex-Battle of Britain pilot, an immigrant farmer, reminded me that in the early 1940s 'we didn't burn straw', which oddly was the only fault he found with the picture.

What I will be eternally grateful for is that few, if any, of the 'cheats' I have entered into with the special effects and the art departments in the movies I have given technical help to have rated any of the criticism they deserved, only because of the skill and dedication of the expertise in those departments. One of the better 'cheats' was substituting four Me109s cleverly disguised as Mustangs when Gen Patton demanded that his Padré got down on his 'God-damned knees' to pray for a break in the weather during the Ardennes breakthrough when Hitler, it was said, personally directed the Battle of the Bulge. The Germans were streaming through the Eifel region and the Allies had no air cover; Patton got very temporary air cover but it was not Mustangs but Spanish-built 109s with a glassfibre pregnancy bolted underneath. And I doubt whether many cinema buffs were any the wiser.

19 Reflections

There is so much I feel I should be reflecting on but for the first time I regret that, like my dear friend Air Cdre Banks, 'I kept no diary'. I find however that I spend so much time in orbit that a great deal of the past seems to come around again; this is, however, a double-edged sword. I am constantly reminded at great occasions like Winnipeg and the more family-type reunions in Adelaide or Sydney, and I tend to question some of the 'do you remembers . . .?'

I deeply regret the passing of the High Master — Harris, and the Master Airman — Don Bennett. As I indicated earlier in these chapters I saw nothing of Arthur Harris during his stint from 1942 to 1945 at Bomber Command, but I saw a great deal of Don Bennett, and at very close quarters, when he was my AOC No 8 Group. Both of these great leaders left questions unanswered. I enjoyed many pleasant hours in the company of the Chief after the war, but only had one person to person conversation with him on the telephone during the period I was at RAF Oakington. It was not until the postwar years that we used to meet in such convivial circumstances at reunions, or I was entertained at his home beside the River Thames. I tried, and failed miserably, to open Sir Arthur up about the Nuremburg raid, — or rather the Nuremburg débâcle — when we lost 97 aircraft, but the obvious distress that seemed to engulf him brought a great sadness to his eyes; all he would do was shake his head and I would back off hurriedly.

A great deal of my reflections emerge from the reactions I get from my audiences, whether they be branches of the Royal Aeronautical Society worldwide, RAF Association meetings or, perhaps most sincerely from the boys and girls of the Air Training Corps (out of the mouths of babes and sucklings). I cannot think why I should have been surprised to have been harangued by a woman in Australia, clearly one who was a 'new' Australian (of German origin), who berated me after my *Bombing Years* lecture about the killing of thousands of women and children in German cities during the Bomber Offensive. Before I could make my own personal counter, a 'fair dinkum' Aussie pointed out that the British government took considerable pains to remove women and children from vulnerable areas and send them as far afield as Devon and Cornwall during the blitz period; I could only remind my tormentor that was it six, seven or maybe eight million Jews that had been herded through the gas chambers? There was a period of quiet and then a very obvious Aussie reaction; there were also no further questions from the 'new' Australian.

120

I believe that the final voice has yet to be heard on the subject of the Allied Bomber Offensive, and sadly this voice may never be heard; indeed will it ever come to print? In my researches covering the lectures I peddle around the world, I can only hazard a guess as to the two possible sources, and both may well opt to leave this arena to the historian who has not yet completed the saga of the Offensive.

I trust that in this saga some of my 'why, why, oh why(s)' will be explained. Why for instance was so much time wasted in debate about the desperate need for some form of target finding/marking force? The latter-day historian will find much to digest in this area during his researches. Why also does one get a positive feeling that Radio Counter Measures (RCM) seemed to have to prove itself — not only in the early days of No 90 Wing, but also later as a strong and valuable asset in the guise of No 100 Group — before it was finally married to the Offensive? I personally felt that the Group's activities were always considered too secret for the Carter Pattersons to be briefed on much of the worth that was kept under wraps over this period.

My saddest reflection concerns my own crew — and please permit me to repeat myself — when I attend reunions and I see how happy crews come together, even after 40 years, can meet and let the years roll away. I am in deep envy of these happy people and this is only compounded when I consider my misery at how I was pitchforked from my squadron and crew to become a Staff Officer at Bennett's headquarters. It is of little importance to me now to be told, and I accept it really, that the Staff period I spent at Headquarters and later at Warboys was, in fact, a much more important aspect of my war effort. I did not think so at the time and I have even more difficulty in accepting it now. The saddest aspect of this period is that it never occurred to me at the time to question the wisdom of my posting, more especially since in retrospect my Staff and Warboys postings could have been assessed at a higher level than I had personally assessed my value as a Pathfinder. It is strange now as a Scot — and we are, if nothing else, self-analysts — that I could do better for Bennett on his Staff or as one of his station commanders.

I would like to leave you with something which has always been an embarassment to me. I may not have made it very clear but I got a certain amount of notoriety or infamous publicity about receiving four gongs in one week. Now I feel many of my Pathfinder colleagues, and I was extremely saddened by this, just happened to relate my personal activities within the Pathfinder Force as an operator with the arrival of these four gongs. I think it should be put on record that the first gong I received was a DSO which oddly enough came from the AOC of No 3 Group. The Pathfinders at the time were only a lodger unit on No 3 Group; 'Cockie' Cochrane was my AOC and I just happened to be something of a blue-eyed boy as far as he was concerned. Let us just accept that without question. So the DSO came along first. The next day the Czechoslovakian Military Cross, for which I cannot even remember being told about the citation. I did go to Czechoslovakia sometime in 1939 and left a great mass of pamphlets telling the Czechs we were very sorry for them; we were praying for them and were burning candles for them, but there was nothing we could do to help their present plight and would not be able to do so for the next four or five years. The next gong came along on the following day and was an Air Force Cross that I had received from Kinloss, for apparently doing more instructional flying than any other instructor on the base during that period. The last one was an immediate gong which I understand, and I could be wrong, was arranged by Command after the squirt that Stirling 'C' for Colander got from a Ju88 over Köln with 174 cannon shells. Now each one of those gongs I do not associate as having been originated within the Headquarters of No 8 Group. I would be very relieved, very interested, and educated, if someone could tell me if that is a correct and true feeling. I know that Bennett gave me one of my Mentions in Despatches, but as far as I am concerned my Pathfinder tour merited one — and only one — Mention in Despatches.

Another reflection that, sadly, is beyond research but has always chafed in my mind, is why it was necessary for such an important element of the PFF to be amputated overnight and sent to No 5 Group. Two Lancaster squadrons — Nos 83 and 97, and one Mosquito squadron — No 627, were removed from the PFF in April 1944 ostensibly to support No 5 Group's low-level (Cheshire) type of marking, as indeed was always so well demonstrated by Leonard Cheshire himself. I have always maintained, and I have not been in very much disagreement about this, that in the main the low-level technique was at its best on a lightly defended or undefended target. To put such a technique into practice on any of the averagely defended German targets would have ended in disaster. I have no need to go further than the sad demise of Guy Gibson to exemplify this.

I still feel that it was unnecessary to remove those two highly-trained heavy squadrons, and the Mosquito squadron, when within the confines of No 5 Group there was plenty of material that could have been made available to the Group for its special activities. Indeed, it still had all the facilities of my station, Warboys, at its disposal to train whoever they wanted; and I might add at this stage that the very moment the Pathfinder element was accepted into No 5 Group it marked the end of the rather dubious crews that would come to me on any pretence at all, most of whom I returned to No 5 Group as not worthy of training at my Pathfinder unit. But I got excellent crews from the very day that it had its own Pathfinder element. I then forgot about even interviewing crews that came from No 5 Group, they were outstanding and I reflect now on why, oh why, could that not have been the normal practice on previous occasions?

Above:
Binbrook 1951: the Canberra crew that introduced the type into Bomber Command service. Navigators Plt Off Brownlow (later AVM) and Flt Lt Barlow (pictured) were responsible for all the Service testing after the type's release by A&AEE Boscombe Down and Farnborough. *Crown Copyright*

Top:
UK-New Zealand Air Race 1953: the leading
RAAF Canberra piloted by Wg Cdr Jell
Cumming which burst a tyre on the Cocos
Islands. *Ron Swain*

Above:
Flown by Flt Lt Monty Burton, the winning
machine is seen here refuelling at the Cocos.
Ron Swain

Right:
Apparently this notice was put up by the
Aussies before the race was won. Happily,
when the result of the race was announced,
our lads managed to get hold of this notice
board and repaint it in the style you see.
But why were the Aussies so sure they were
going to win the race? *Ron Swain*

Left:
In the driving seat of a
Lancaster mock-up at
Pinewood Studios which was
used for close-up shots in the
ITV series *The Pathfinders*,
screened during the early
1970s.

Below:
One of several radio-
controlled model Lancs used
in the same series is seen here
at West Malling airfield in
May 1971. *Dolphin Studio*

NO PRIVATE
VEHICLES
BEYOND THIS POINT

STOP!
LOOK OUT FOR AIRCRAFT
REPORT TO CONTROL TOWER

Above:
The Queen Mother with the Patron of the PFF Association, the late AVM Don Bennett, and myself (the President), on the occasion of her visit to the Pathfinder Club in Mount Street, Mayfair W1. *Keystone Press Agency Ltd*

Above:
Leading the ANZAC Day Parade in Sydney during 1982 with the New South Wales Pathfinders.

Above right:
Hamish with his second wife Georgina.

Below:
Having lost my own crew on the first night they flew without me when I was hijacked to Don Bennett's HQ, I was asked postwar to find a 'crew' to take to Germany to meet former Luftwaffe fighter and flak crews for an Anglia Television documentary.

Above:
Sixty years on: some of the apprentices from the 17th Entry at Halton meet at Wendover railway station for a reunion in 1988. *Bucks & Herts Newspapers Ltd*

No 8 Group — Roll of Honour

In memory of those members of No 8 Group Royal Air Force who flew on operational missions against the enemy from bases around Ely and did not return.

Rank	Name	Squadron	Date
F/Lt	AALBORG. K. L.	7	13.09.44
F/O	ABBOT. A. F.	83	22.01.44
W/C	ABERCROMBY. W.. DFC '	83	02.01.44
Sgt	ABERY. F. J.	405(Ca)	24.02.44
F/Lt	ACKLAND. L. J.. DFC	109	26.03.44
W/O2	ACORN. G. W.	405	04.12.43
W/O1	ADAIR. L. J.	156	03.01.44
F/Sgt	ADAM. D. D.. DFM	635	05.03.45
P/O	ADAM. J. P. H.	405	19.03.45
F/O	ADAM. T. J. S.	128	14.01.45
Sgt	ADAMS. K. C. C.	156	25.06.43
F/Sgt	ADAMS. R. A.. DFM	83	20.01.44
F/O	ADAMSON. R. H.	83	27.01.44
F/Sgt	ADDIS. H. W.	1409 Flt	03.12.43
Sgt	ADGER. A. S.	97	02.03.43
P/O	AFFLECK. W. R.	156	08.03.43
Sgt	AGATE. G. E.	405(Ca)	06.09.43
F/O	AGNEW. J. T.. DFC	1655 CU	20.04.44
F/O	AINSWORTH. G.	83	23.11.43
F/O	AIRS. W.	7	29.06.44
F/Lt	ALBERTSON. A. I.. AFC	Warboys	02.03.45
F/Lt	ALCOCK. S. H.. DFC	83	27.01.44
F/O	ALDERSON-HILLER. J.	83	26.11.43
S/L	ALEXANDER. E. S.. DFC, DFM	156	14.01.44
P/O	ALEXANDER. F. N.. DFM	97	04.10.43
P/O	ALEXANDER. J. M.. CGM	7	15.02.44
F/Sgt	ALEXANDER. R. L.	635	30.08.44
Sgt	ALEXANDER. W. E.	97	25.04.44
F/O	ALEY. H. C.	97	26.11.43
F/O	ALFORD. R. W.	1655 MTU	08.11.44
F/O	ALLAN. G. I.. DFC	142	22.01.45
F/O	ALLAN. I. G.	83	03.01.44
F/O	ALLAN. J.	405	07.01.45
F/Lt	ALLAN. W. C.	405	28.12.43
F/O	ALLCROFT. F. C.. DFC	83	03.01.44
F/O	ALLEN. C. R.	578	19.03.44
P/O	ALLEN. E. A.	7	11.04.43
W/O	ALLEN. H. E.	83	24.08.43
F/Lt	ALLEN. L. A.. DFC	405	28.04.44
Sgt	ALLEN. R. W.	83	02.01.44
P/O	ALLFORD. F. C.	7	19.08.44
F/O	ALLINSON. J.. DFM	635	04.08.44
F/O	ALLISON. F.. DFM	97	29.01.44
F/O	ALLISTON. E. A.	35	04.12.43
F/Lt	ALLPORT. V.. DFC	1655 MTU	26.03.44
F/Sgt	ALLSO. G. W.	35	02.12.43
F/Lt	ALLUM. J.. DFM	7	24.11.43
W/O	ALSBURY. W. T.	156	13.08.44
Sgt	ALSOP. E. B.	156	05.03.43
LAC	ALSTON. W. A. G.	582	23.09.44
Sgt	AMBRIDGE. E. E. A.	156	26.07.43
F/Sgt	AMES. R. H.	582	16.06.44
P/O	ANNASTASSIADES. M. C.	156	16.04.43
P/O	ANDERSEN. H. R.. DFC	156	17.04.43
F/O	ANDERSON. D. J.	35	30.07.43
F/O	ANDERSON. E.	83	20.01.44
F/Sgt	ANDERSON. F. R. W.	405(Ca)	07.04.43
F/Sgt	ANDERSON. J.	405	03.01.44
P/O	ANDERSON. J.	405	04.12.43
P/O	ANDERSON. W.. DFC	156	23.11.43
Sgt	ANDERSON. W.	83	22.06.43
Sgt	ANDERTON. J. J.	83	12.06.43
S/L	ANDREW. C. F.. DFC	35	30.07.43
F/Lt	ANDREW. E. M.	7	24.06.44
P/O	ANDREWS. J. W.	35	22.06.43
W/O	ANDREWS. R. J.	156	01.06.44
F/Lt	ANDREWS. R. J.	7	20.01.44
S/L	ANEKSTEIN. C.. DFC	7	31.08.43
Sgt	ANGELL. D. W.	97	20.10.43
P/O	ANGELL. L. A. C.	83	22.06.43
F/Sgt	ANGUS. D. C. B.	405(Ca)	18.06.43
W/O2	ANNIS. L. D.	405	14.01.44
S/L	ANSET. D. C.. DFC	156	22.11.43
F/O	ANSTEE. J.	97	06.01.44
F/Sgt	ANTCLIFFE. K.	156	31.03.45
F/Lt	APPLEBY. R. R. G.. DFC	35	06.01.44
Sgt	ARCHER. D. W.	35	03.08.43
Sgt	ARCHER. W. F.	57	16.07.41
Sgt	ARCHIBALD. J.	156	13.07.43
F/Sgt	ARCHIBALD. K.	582	13.08.44
Sgt	ARMER. G. W.	15	02.03.43
F/O	ARMITT. J.	405	14.02.45
F/O	ARMSTRONG. A. T.	405	11.06.44
F/Lt	ARMSTRONG. C. A.	139	12.06.44
P/O	ARMSTRONG. G. W.	97	23.06.43
S/L	ARMSTRONG. J. D.	128	07.03.45
P/O	ARMSTRONG. T. A.	1655 MTU	13.09.44
F/Sgt	ARNOLD. L. W. J.	83	09.05.44

123

Rank	Name	Squadron	Date
F/Sgt	ARTER, A. E.	35	24.08.43
F/Lt	ASH, C. J. K.	635	12.06.44
Sgt	ASHCROFT, B. P.	156	27.04.43
F/O	ASHFORD, A. H.	405	30.01.44
Sgt	ASHLEY, W. G.	1655 MTU	25.07.44
F/O	ASHMAN, G. L.	106	02.12.43
F/Lt	ASHMAN, H. L.	7	25.05.44
Sgt	ASHWORTH, D.	7	26.11.43
Sgt	ASHWORTH, L.	83	23.06.43
F/Sgt	ASHWORTH, T.	635	08.03.45
Sgt	ASKHAM, C.	156	13.05.43
P/O	ASLETT, P. R.	7	23.04.44
W/O	ASPEY, W., DFM	7	08.08.44
F/Sgt	ASPIN, V. E.	635	31.03.44
Sgt	ASPINALL, K.	156	03.01.44
F/Lt	ASTBURY, J. W.	405	14.01.44
P/O	ASTLE, A., DFC	156	24.09.44
Sgt	ASTON, J. C.	83	03.04.43
Sgt	ATHEY, R. W.	7	11.06.44
Sgt	ATKINSON, D. J.	156	28.08.43
F/Lt	ATKINSON, H. P.	405(Ca)	01.05.43
P/O	ATKINSON, J. L.	635	31.03.44
F/Sgt	ATTREE, V. E.	156	24.08.43
F/Lt	AUBERT, C. O., DFM	156	16.12.43
F/Lt	AUNGIERS, G. R.	582	20.07.44
F/Sgt	AUSTIN, J. W.	582	29.06.44
P/O	AUSTIN, K. H.	582	23.12.44
F/O	AUSTIN, L. W. C.	582	07.03.45
Sgt	AXUP, G. A.	97	18.01.43
F/O	AYLIEFF, J. M., DFC	35	07.03.45
F/Sgt	AYRE, G. F.	692	15.01.45
F/Sgt	AYRES, R. J.	35	28.05.43
Sgt	BACON, J. E.	97	20.10.43
F/O	BACON, L. P.	7	20.03.45
S/L	BAGGULEY, R. B., DFC	139	09.03.43
Sgt	BAGNALL, G.	35	16.03.44
F/O	BAGOT, E. C.	156	14.01.44
F/O	BAHT, R. E.	97	09.10.43
LACW	BAILEY, D. F. J.	692	14.05.44
Sgt	BAILEY, D.	83	28.08.43
AC2	BAILEY, F. J.	83	26.11.43
F/Sgt	BAILEY, R. C.	35	22.01.44
F/Sgt	BAILEY, R. C., DFM	83	22.06.44
F/O	BAIN, D. P., DFC	7	25.03.44
F/Sgt	BAINBRIDGE, T. J.	7	12.06.43
W/O	BAINES, A. P.	582	29.07.44
Sgt	BAINES, C.	83	02.06.42
Sgt	BAKER, A. R.	156	04.04.43
W/O1	BAKER, C. G.	7	31.08.43
F/Lt	BAKER, E. T.	35	18.11.43
F/Lt	BAKER, H. W.	582	08.09.44
S/L	BAKER, J., DSO, DFC	7	20.05.44
W/O	BAKER, R. C. W. G.	97	23.05.44
W/O2	BAKER, R. M.	405	19.03.45
F/Sgt	BAKER, R. M.	156	02.03.44
P/O	BAKER, V.	97	11.08.43
W/O	BAKER, W. C., DFM	83	24.08.43
P/O	BALCOMBE, A. A.	7	15.08.43
F/O	BALDWIN, A. J., DFM	571	17.05.44
Sgt	BALDWIN, J.	156	31.03.44
F/O	BALDWIN, J. M	97	25.03.44
F/O	BALDWIN, S. A.	35	18.08.43
S/L	BALDWIN, W. H.	405	24.08.43
W/O2	BALDWINSON, W. B.	83	25.04.44
Sgt	BALE, A. H.	7	04.12.43
F/O	BALES, P. R.	35	21.01.44
Sgt	BALL, E. F.	97	29.03.43
Sgt	BALL, F.	97	24.08.43
F/Sgt	BALL, K. R.	156	30.01.44
S/L	BALL, W. A. C., DFC	156	09.03.43
F/L	BALLANTYNE, R. R. S., DFM	7	15.02.44
Sgt	BALSON, R. C.	156	17.06.43
W/O2	BANCESCU, G.	405	24.05.43
F/Sgt	BANGS, E. C.	156	21.02.45
F/Sgt	BANKS, E. W., DFM	156	13.05.43
Sgt	BANKS, J.	83	03.01.44
F/Lt	BANKS, R. J. L.	7	12.09.44
F/Sgt	BANNAN, J. B.	635	10.04.44
F/Lt	BANNON, J.	7	24.11.43
Sgt	BARBER, G. W.	15	04.07.43
F/Sgt	BARK, E. W.	7	25.05.44
F/O	BARKER, A.	7	22.11.43
Sgt	BARLEY, F. N.	7	11.04.43
Sgt	BARLOW, A. T.	156	25.06.43
Sgt	BARNARD, F. V.	35	22.06.43
F/Sgt	BARNES, A. D.	156	03.01.44
F/Lt	BARNES, R. L., DFC	7	15.02.44
F/Sgt	BARNES, S. J.	7	25.06.43
F/Sgt	BARNETT, R. F.	582	06.03.45
Sgt	BARNSLEY, P.	7	04.09.43
F/Sgt	BARR, A. C.	35	08.04.45
Sgt	BARRACLOUGH, O.	97	26.07.42
Sgt	BARRATT, T.	7	16.06.44
F/Sgt	BARRELL, E. R. N.	635	20.04.44
W/C	BARRELL, R. G., DSO, DFC	7	25.06.43
S/L	BARRETT, C. R., DFC	608	13.09.44
Sgt	BARRIE, J. I.	35	22.06.43
W/C	BARRON, J. F., DSO, DFC, DFM	7	20.05.44
P/O	BARROWMAN, A. McA., DFC	97	15.03.44
F/Sgt	BARRY, G.	156	02.01.44
W/O	BARRY, G. D.	35	25.04.45
Sgt	BARTHOLOMEW, E. F.	7	27.01.44
P/O	BARTHOLOMEW, J. A., DFC	97	21.02.44
W/O2	BARTMAN, L. W.	7	15.04.43
Sgt	BARTON, D. E.	156	02.03.44
Sgt	BATES, C. F.	7	05.01.45
Sgt	BATES, J. E.	156	31.03.44
F/Sgt	BATTERBEE, E. A.	7	19.08.44
F/Sgt	BATTLE, E. J.	97	16.12.43
Sgt	BAUMAN, D. C.	156	12.06.43
F/Sgt	BAXENDALE, R.	635	30.08.44
W/O	BAXTER, J. C., DFM	156	31.03.44
P/O	BAXTER, W. S.	7	27.08.44
Sgt	BAYLISS, E. P. G.	156	19.02.43
S/L	BAZALGETTE, I. W., VC, DFC	635	04.08.44
Sgt	BEARD, L. T.	97	13.06.43
F/Sgt	BEATON, A. C.	571	05.04.45
Sgt	BEATTIE, A.	156	27.04.44
F/O	BEATTIE, H. D.	405(Ca)	14.05.43
Sgt	BEATTIE, J. E.	156	30.01.44
W/O	BEATTY, W. S.	405(Ca)	04.04.43
F/O	BEAUMONT, G. A.	7	26.11.43
F/Sgt	BEAVEN, R., DFM	83	17.04.43
P/O	BEAVO, W. E.	405(Ca)	16.08.43
Sgt	BEBENSEE, D. G., DFM	405	14.07.43
F/Lt	BECKLEY, R. J.	1655 MTU	11.10.44
Sgt	BEDDOE, A. C.	35	11.04.43
F/Sgt	BEDWARD, A. A. C.	35	03.08.43
Sgt	BEE, R.	83	03.04.43
Sgt	BEECH, F. R.	35	05.05.43
F/Sgt	BEECROFT, J.	582	08.09.44
Sgt	BEESON, W. J.	635	16.06.44
Sgt	BEEVER, J.	156	17.12.43
F/Lt	BELCHER, G.	405	04.12.43
Sgt	BELDON, E. N. N.	7	31.08.43
Sgt	BELL, A. W.	83	03.01.44
Sgt	BELL, E.	35	30.05.43
W/O2	BELL, F. G.	35	12.11.43
Sgt	BELL, G.	7	09.03.43
P/O	BELL, J.	97	22.03.44

124

Rank	Name	Squadron	Date	Rank	Name	Squadron	Date
P/O	BELL. S. J.	83	21.10.43	S/L	BODDINGTON, R. A.,	635	14.02.45
Sgt	BELLAMY, C. E.	97	02.03.43		DFC *		
F/O	BELLINGHAM, K. G.	105	22.06.44	P/O	BOILEAU, J. P. R.	405	30.01.44
Sgt	BELTON, J.	635	22.04.44	F/O	BOLGER, T. J.	692	26.09.44
Sgt	BEMBRIDGE, J. W.	156	23.06.43	F/Sgt	BOLLAND, G. E., DFM	405	21.02.45
Sgt	BENEY, E. T.	7	08.03.43	F/O	BOLSOVER, A. R.	156	02.01.44
S/L.	BENNETT, G., DSO, DFC	405	25.05.44	F/O	BOLT, W. T.	7	26.08.44
Sgt	BENNETT, P. J.	97	14.01.44	F/Sgt	BOLTON, R. J.	608	12.10.44
F/Sgt	BENNETT, R. S., DFM	97	22.11.43	Sgt	BONAR, C. N.	156	27.04.43
F/O	BENNINGTON, I. C.	7	05.05.44	P/O	BOND, G. P. R., DFC	156	02.01.44
F/Lt	BENSON, H., DFC	156	31.05.45	Cpl	BOND, T. J.	83	18.06.43
W/O2	BENTINCK, G. H.	97	25.02.44	P/O	BONESS, H. P.	7	18.10.43
F/Sgt	BENTLEY, R. W.	35	05.01.45	P/O	BONNETT, H. J.	7	11.06.44
W/O2	BENTLEY, T. L.	405	27.04.43	Sgt	BOOKER, D. R.	156	29.09.43
Sgt	BERESFORD, D. H.	635	06.07.44	Sgt	BOONE, R. H.	35	12.06.43
P/O	BERKEY, G. R.	405	23.04.44	Sgt	BOOTH, R.	35	20.02.44
F/Lt	BERRIGAN, L. T., DFC	7	25.03.44	P/O	BOOTH, R. A.	405	28.04.44
F/Lt	BERRISFORD, N. C., DFC *	139	24.03.45	F/O	BORDISS, R. J.	35	10.04.44
F/Sgt	BERRY, W. S.	7	13.03.43	P/O	BORDYCOTT, K. W.	156	17.04.43
F/Lt	BERTELSEN, F. C.	582	04.05.44		DFC, DFM		
F/O	BERTENSHAW, C.	105	19.10.44	Sgt	BOREHAM, E. R.	156	09.10.43
F/O	BERTHIAUME, J. F. E. G.	7	26.05.43	P/O	BORLAND, J., DFC	156	03.01.44
Sgt	BESSENT, H. R.	405	17.12.43	P/O	BORROW, H. E., DFM	83	20.01.44
Sgt	BEST, A. E.	83	24.08.43	P/O	BORROWES, R. D., DFC	405	07.05.44
P/O	BESZANT, P. T.	83	24.08.43	F/Sgt	BORROWMAN, W. T.	1655 MTU	11.10.44
P/O	BETT, R. C.	7	15.02.44	F/Lt	BORTHWICK, G. W. S.,		29.01.44
Sgt	BETTANEY, L.	156	22.11.43		DFC		
P/O	BEVERIDGE, G. T.	35	29.06.43	F/O	BOSTON, B. J.	635	26.08.44
F/Lt	BEVERIDGE, R. W., DFC	635	04.08.44	Sgt	BOSWORTH, S.	405(Ca)	23.04.44
F/Sgt	BEVIN, A.	35	28.10.44	F/Lt	BOTKIN, R. T.	405	09.10.43
P/O	BIGORAY, W. W., DFM	7	28.04.44	F/Sgt	BOTT, J. W.	7	23.04.44
P/O	BILLINGSLEY, F. D.	405	17.08.44	F/Sgt	BOTTERILL, H., DFM	635	14.02.45
Sgt	BILLINGTON, C. L.	83	03.04.43	F/Sgt	BOUCH, A., DFM	582	15.06.44
Sgt	BILLINGTON, W.	83	03.04.43	Sgt	BOULGER, K.	7	24.06.44
F/O	BILSON, F. W.	405	09.10.43	F/O	BOULTON, C. A.	405	15.03.45
F/O	BINGHAM, R. B.	1655 MTU	21.08.44	F/Sgt	BOURNE, C.	35	16.04.43
F/Lt	BINGHAM, W. N.	156	30.12.44	Sgt	BOURNE, G. V.	Tilstock	31.01.44
Sgt	BIRD, H. J.	83	21.10.43	F/Sgt	BOURNS, D. B.	83	13.05.43
S/L	BIRD, W. D. W.	692	26.08.44	F/Sgt	BOUTTELL, R. L.	7	24.06.44
Sgt	BIRKS, F. R.	83	26.11.43	Sgt	BOWDEN, W. W.	105	06.10.44
F/Sgt	BIRTLES, R. J.	635	12.05.44	Sgt	BOWEN, J. A.	35	27.08.44
F/Sgt	BIRTWHISTLE, F. R.	97	29.03.43	P/O	BOWEN, R. J.	156	02.01.44
P/O	BISHOP, C. A.	105	27.04.44	F/Sgt	BOWER, T. C.	582	20.07.44
F/Sgt	BISHOP, T. D.	35	24.08.43	Sgt	BOWERMAN, R. V. T.	97	30.01.44
Sgt	BLACK, D. A.	40(Ca)	10.08.43	Sgt	BOWKER, A. P.	35	10.08.43
F/O	BLACK, G. J.	156	03.04.43	Sgt	BOWLES, T. P.	97	09.01.43
F/O	BLACKBAND, N. C., AFC	35	18.11.44	P/O	BOWLING, T. J.	405	18.08.43
P/O	BLACKBURN, R. G.	635	19.08.44	P/O	BOWMAN, E. A.	156	22.06.43
F/O	BLACKHURST, S.	97	23.06.43	F/Sgt	BOWN, T.	635	12.12.44
S/L	BLAIR, J. E., DFC, DFM	156	22.05.44	F/O	BOWRING, N. H.	405	04.12.43
S/L	BLAKE, W. A.	7	21.4.43	F/O	BOWRING, R. A. H.	35	04.07.43
Sgt	BLAKELY, W. J.	405	03.01.44	Sgt	BOWYER, R. M.	7	30.07.43
F/O	BLAKEMAN, A. W., DFC	83	03.01.44	F/Lt	BOXALL, C. F.	105	22.03.44
P/O	BLANCHETTE, C. E.	156	02.01.44	Sgt	BOYD, J.	156	16.04.44
F/Sgt	BLANKS, E. H.	7	24.11.43	F/O	BOYLE, S., DFM	83	22.06.44
P/O	BLATCHFORD, B. F.	7	19.08.44	F/Lt	BOYLSON, W. W., DFC *	139	25.06.44
F/O	BLAYDON, R. W., DFM	582	08.08.44	F/O	BRACE, A. R.	35	22.10.43
S/L	BLENKINSOP, E. W., DFC	405	23.01.45	P/O	BRAD, H. A.	105	27.04.44
S/L	BLESSING, W. W.,	105	07.07.44	F/O	BRADBURN, G.	35	11.09.44
	DSO, DFC			F/Lt	BRADFORD, C. S.	692	27.05.44
W/O	BLISS, O. L., DFC	35	28.08.44	P/O	BRADFORD, J. D., DFC	97	23.09.43
F/Lt	BLOCKEY, R. C.	156	03.01.44	F/Sgt	BRADFORD, M. A. E.	35	15.04.43
F/Sgt	BLOOMER, J. E.	635	25.04.44	F/O	BRADLEY, G. R., DFM	582	29.08.44
Sgt	BLOOMFIELD, D. B.	156	31.03.44	Sgt	BRADLEY, I. H.	156	25.06.43
F/Sgt	BLUNDELL, C. L.	35	24.12.44	F/Sgt	BRADLEY, J. S.	405	28.04.44
F/Sgt	BLUNDELL, C. F.	35	15.02.44	F/Lt	BRADY, T. S.	635	30.08.44
P/O	BLUNDERFIELD, W. E.	405	09.02.45	F/Sgt	BRAMLEY, G. W.	156	14.01.44
P/O	BLYTH, C. J.	405	29.07.44	F/Sgt	BRANCH, A. C., DFM	83	20.10.43
Sgt	BOAK, R.	Graveley	25.11.43	F/O	BRANDWOOD, F. B.	571	16.04.44
F/Sgt	BOAM, A. G.	35	09.05.44	Sgt	BREAKS, R.	156	26.01.45
Sgt	BOAR, A. J.	83	22.06.43	Sgt	BREAR, B.	156	24.08.43
Sgt	BOARDMAN, E. J.	83	21.10.43	F/Sgt	BREMNER, W. S.	7	22.03.44
Sgt	BOARDMAN, G. M.	7	09.04.43	F/O	BRENNAN, L. J.	692	26.09.44

125

Rank	Name	Squadron	Date
Sgt	BRENNEN, D.	83	03.04.43
P/O	BRENTON, L. A.	7	25.04.44
Sgt	BRETT, J.	97	23.09.43
P/O	BREWER, T. J.	156	20.02.44
W/O	BREWINGTON, R. A.	35	24.03.44
Lt	BRIEVIK, P. E. R.	PFF, NTU	07.04.45
F/Sgt	BRIGHT, R. F. J.	35	20.10.44
F/Lt	BRILL, D. J.	97	16.12.43
F/Sgt	BRIMICOMBE, R. A. J.	635	12.09.44
Sgt	BRINE, F. R.	7	09.10.43
Sgt	BRINTON, E. A.	7	09.10.43
F/Sgt	BRITCHFORD, A. T.	35	11.09.44
Sgt	BRITTAIN, J. C.	97	18.01.43
Sgt	BRITTAN, D. W.	128	07.11.44
F/Sgt	BRITTON, F. J.	7	15.04.43
P/O	BRITTS, A. J.	405	21.07.44
F/Sgt	BROAD, J. T.	582	13.08.44
F/O	BROADBENT, A. R.	7	14.01.44
Sgt	BROADHEAD, E.	7	26.05.43
P/O	BROCKWAY, G. W.	7	31.03.44
W/O2	BRODERICK, L. J. M.	405	06.09.43
F/Sgt	BROMHAM, C. G.	35	06.01.44
Sgt	BROMLEY, R.	97	13.06.43
F/Lt	BROOK, R., DFC	405	16.09.44
Sgt	BROOK, S.	35	25.07.44
F/Lt	BROOKER, B. C., DFC*	156	11.03.45
F/O	BROOKER, G. R.	139	24.11.43
P/O	BROOKS, J. A.	156	11.09.44
Sgt	BROOKS, W. S.	156	25.06.43
F/O	BROSNAHAN, F. T.	7	04.09.43
Sgt	BROTHERTON, A.	7	26.05.43
Sgt	BROUGHAM-FADDY, P. L.	156	17.04.43
Sgt	BROUGHTON, J. W.	7	22.05.44
W/O	BROWN, A., DFM	156	03.02.45
P/O	BROWN, A. J. E.	83	24.08.43
F/Lt	BROWN, C. M.	97	26.11.43
F/Sgt	BROWN, D. H.	405	07.01.45
P/O	BROWN, E. J.	35	31.08.43
F/Sgt	BROWN, F. G. C.	635	01.08.44
Sgt	BROWN, G. W.	156	22.06.43
F/O	BROWN, J. H.	35	09.03.43
Sgt	BROWN, J. H.	97	08.10.43
F/O	BROWN, J. T.	97	17.12.43
F/Lt	BROWN, K., DFM	97	04.10.43
P/O	BROWN, L. F. J.	156	24.06.43
F/Lt	BROWN, N.	3	23.12.44
Sgt	BROWN, R.	1409 Flt	16.04.43
Sgt	BROWN, R.	156	25.06.43
Sgt	BROWN, R. G.	7	29.01.44
S/L	BROWN, R. W., DFC	7	24.06.44
F/O	BROWN, R. W., DFC	35	19.10.44
Sgt	BROWN, S. C.	156	27.04.43
F/Lt	BROWN, S. W.	582	28.05.44
P/O	BROWN, T. H.	7	27.03.43
W/O	BROWN, W. D.	7	20.01.44
P/O	BROWN, W. G. L.	35	22.06.43
Sgt	BROWNLESS, T.	405(Ca)	03.08.43
F/O	BRUCE, J. G., DFM	105	28.03.43
F/Lt	BRUCE, J. S..	405(Ca)	17.08.44
P/O	BRUGGEMAN, J. A.	405	16.01.45
LAC	BRUNDELL, J. H.	83	26.11.43
W/O2	BRUNET, E. C.	405	20.10.43
Sgt	BRUNNING, W. H.	97	31.01.43
Sgt	BRUNSDON, E. R.	7	06.09.44
F/Lt	BRUNT, S. P.	692	17.12.44
Sgt	BRUNTON, A. C.	405	06.09.43
S/L	BRYAN SMITH, M., DFC*	97	06.06.44
Sgt	BRYANT, L. D.	35	26.05.43
F/O	BRYANT, R. M.	156	12.06.43
Sgt	BUCHAN, F.	35	21.01.44
F/Sgt	BUCHANAN, A. K., DFM	7	15.02.44
F/Sgt	BUCKLE, R. O.	156	22.11.43
F/Sgt	BUCKLEY, J. M.	405	09.05.44
W/O2	BUDD, H. E.	7	15.04.43
Sgt	BUGG, B. S. G.	7	11.04.43
Sgt	BULLAMORE, S.	83	27.01.44
Sgt	BULLIVANT, A. E.	7	22.03.44
F/O	BULPITT, A. N.	139(Ja)	03.03.43
F/Sgt	BUNDLE, J. T., DFM	97	18.10.43
Sgt	BUNDY, F. W.	405	20.10.43
Sgt	BUNTAIN, W. R.	7	16.12.43
P/O	BUNTING, W. F., DFM	582	29.07.44
F/Lt	BURBRIDGE, F. P., DFC	97	22.11.43
F/O	BURCH, G. J.	582	23.09.44
Sgt	BURDEN, J. W. S.	35	16.03.44
F/Lt	BURGER, T., DFC	7	29.01.44
P/O	BURGESS, J.	1409 Met. Flt.	05.12.43
F/Sgt	BURKE, D.	35	24.08.43
W/O	BURKE, J. Y.	692	18.03.44
F/Lt	BURLEY, P. K., DFC	692	08.07.44
P/O	BURNABY, M. A.	405(Ca)	04.05.44
F/O	BURNHAM-RICHARDS, S. G.	7	09.10.43
Sgt	BURNELL, W.	7	04.09.43
P/O	BURNETT, D. M. T.	692	13.05.44
W/O	BURNSIDE, H.	7	11.06.44
F/Sgt	BURR, W. C.	97	12.03.43
Sgt	BURROUGHS, J.	156	26.07.43
LAC	BURROWES, B. E.	139	09.09.44
F/Sgt	BURT, P.	635	26.08.44
F/Lt	BURT, P. R., DFC	35	05.07.44
F/Sgt	BURTENSHAW, D. F.	156	03.01.44
F/Sgt	BURTON, R. G.	156	01.06.44
Sgt	BURY, S. W.	7	14.01.44
P/O	BUSBY, D. C. C., CGM	156	17.06.43
F/Lt	BUSH, C., DFC	7	20.02.44
F/O	BUSH, K. S.	105	27.05.43
Sgt	BUSHELL, H. B.	7	16.12.43
Sgt	BUTLER, C.	156	02.12.43
Sgt	BUTLER, C. A.	35	04.02.45
Sgt	BUTLER, J. J.	35	24.08.43
Sgt	BUTSON, C.	7	24.03.44
P/O	BUTSON, J. F.	7	27.08.44
F/Sgt	BUTTERWORTH, J.	7	16.12.43
F/O	BUTTERWORTH, R. S.	405	19.03.43
F/Lt	BUTTON, D. G.	35	12.11.43
F/Sgt	BYASS, R. A.	156	03.04.43
F/O	BYWATER, A. H., DFC	7	11.03.43
F/Lt	CADMAN, A. R., DFM	97	31.03.44
F/Lt	CADMAN, P. E., DFC	105	10.04.44
F/Sgt	CADMAN, R.	635	26.08.44
Sgt	CAHILL, E. J.	156	28.07.43
F/O	CAIRNS, C. G., DFM	156	03.01.44
F/Sgt	CAIRNS, T. R.	83	13.05.43
F/Lt	CALDER, J. P. S.	571	21.07.44
Sgt	CALEY, A. A.	7	25.06.43
F/Lt	CALHOUN, M. B., DFC	405	17.08.44
P/O	CALLAN, N. J.	97	25.03.44
P/O	CALVERT, C. D., DFM	83	03.04.43
F/Sgt	CAMERON, B. C.	405	02.01.44
Sgt	CAMERON, D.	97	09.07.43
F/Sgt	CAMERON, N. D.	97	02.01.44
F/O	CAMPBELL, A. P.	405	02.01.44
F/O	CAMPBELL, D.	31	12.09.44
F/Sgt	CAMPBELL, E.	7	15.02.44
P/O	CAMPBELL, F. W.	582	23.12.44
Sgt	CAMPBELL, G. L.	156	27.07.43
Sgt	CAMPBELL, I.	156	08.06.44
Sgt	CAMPBELL, K. A. J.	35	06.01.44
Sgt	CAMPBELL, R. A.	97	23.11.43
Sgt	CAMPBELL, R. G.	582	08.08.44
P/O	CAMPBELL, S. S.	608	21.04.45
F/Sgt	CAMPEY, W.	692	31.03.45
S/L	CAMPLING, R. D., DSO, DFC	7	15.02.44

Rank	Name	Squadron	Date
F/O	CANDLIN, G. W. C., DFC, DFM	Upwood	25.01.44
F/Lt	CANDLISH, J. M.	35	12.11.43
F/O	CANDY, A. R.	635	11.04.44
F/Lt	CANE, M. J. T., DFM	571	13.04.45
F/Lt	CANN, L. N. B., DFC	156	17.12.44
W/O	CANTWELL, R. P.	582	15.03.45
F/O	CAPON, R. B.	35	22.06.43
Sgt	CAREY, L. E.	35	29.06.43
P/O	CARNEY, R. A.	405	16.08.43
F/Lt	CARPENTER, E. C.	109	23.12.44
F/O	CARPENTER, E. J. L.	97	30.01.44
F/O	CARR, K. S.	7	19.08.44
F/Sgt	CARR, T. S.	156	21.02.45
F/Sgt	CARRELL, G., DFM	35	20.02.44
Sgt	CARROLL, B.	156	02.12.43
Sgt	CARROTT, D. C.	405	29.07.44
F/Sgt	CARSON, A. L. B., DFM	7	05.05.44
S/L	CARTER, A. L., DFC	582	23.12.44
P/O	CARTER, D. A.	7	15.03.44
Sgt	CARTER, E.	7	21.10.43
P/O	CARTER, J. W.	405	17.08.44
F/O	CARTER, N. H.	156	07.09.43
F/O	CARTER, R. D.	97	25.04.44
Sgt	CARTER, S. C.	—	25.06.43
F/Sgt	CASSJUANA, R. D.	635	22.04.44
P/O	CASE, T. E.	156	19.02.43
F/Sgt	CASEY, A. J.	128	14.01.45
P/O	CASS, R.	83	30.01.44
Sgt	CASSIDY, P.	97	08.10.43
F/Sgt	CASSINGHAM, E.	35	12.06.43
F/Sgt	CATCHPOLE, W. J.	156	15.02.44
F/O	CATERER, J.	635	16.06.44
F/Lt	CATTLE, A. E. H.	16 5CU	13.05.44
Sgt	CAVILL, E.	35	28.05.43
F/Sgt	CAWDERY, V. N.	156	14.01.44
F/Lt	CAWTHORNE, P. E., DFC	635	04.04.45
P/O	CEELEY, A. F.	571	19.03.45
Sgt	CHADWICK, C.	156	24.08.43
Sgt	CHADWICK, T. N.	105	28.03.45
F/Sgt	CHAMBERS, W. O. E.	156	07.09.43
F/Sgt	CHANT, L.	35	02.12.44
F/Sgt	CHAPMAN, F. L.	7	22.11.43
Sgt	CHAPMAN, G. C.	83	23.06.43
W/O2	CHAPMAN, J. R., DFC	97	10.05.44
F/Sgt	CHAPMAN, K. S. J.	156	03.01.44
F/Lt	CHAPMAN, R.	35	07.03.45
F/Sgt	CHAPMAN, W.	97	25.03.44
Sgt	CHAPMAN, W. S.	635	12.06.44
Sgt	CHAPPELL, H.	97	16.12.43
Sgt	CHAPPELL, L. A.	635	31.03.44
P/O	CHAREST, J. M. A. L.	405	30.01.44
Sgt	CHARLES, E. A.	7	30.07.43
Sgt	CHARLES, R. T.	97	16.02.44
F/O	CHARLES, T. E.	97	30.01.44
P/O	CHASE, D. J.	156	23.04.44
F/Lt	CHASE, W. McL.	405	09.05.44
F/O	CHAUNDY, G. R. P., DFM	692	15.01.45
Sgt	CHELU, R. W.	582	29.06.44
F/Sgt	CHENOWETH, E.	635	31.03.45
Sgt	CHERRY, A. J.	7	26.08.44
Sgt	CHESHIRE, H. W.	83	18.06.43
S/L	CHESTERMAN, H. W. A., AFC	7	11.04.43
P/O	CHILD, R. J., DFC	35	67.01.44
Sgt	CHIPCHASE, K. W.	83	11.03.43
S/L	CHISHOLM, A. F., DFC	83	23.11.43
S/L	CHOPPING, R. C., DFC	7	26.08.44
F/Sgt	CHRISTIANSON, C. S. R.	7	09.10.43
LACW	CHURCH, D.	HQ 8 Gp Huntingdon	13.12.45
Sgt	CHURCH, I. M.	156	30.07.43
F/Lt	CHURCHILL, H. D., DFC	156	07.05.44

Rank	Name	Squadron	Date
LACW	CHURCHILL, J.	Upwood	22.03.44
F/Lt	CLAMPITT, R. W.	1655 MTU	08.11.44
F/Sgt	CLARK, A. J.	156	27.09.43
F/O	CLARK, C. P.	156	03.02.45
F/O	CLARK, C. T.	405	24.11.43
F/O	CLARK, H. A.	83	28.08.43
Cpl	CLARK, J. G.	7	23.09.43
F/Sgt	CLARK, K. G.	635	31.05.45
F/Lt	CLARK, W. A. G.	156	22.11.43
Sgt	CLARK, W. H.	156	05.03.43
F/Sgt	CLARK, W. L. J.	405	02.01.44
W/O	CLARKE, A. B.	571	05.04.45
F/Lt	CLARKE, D. A. W.	1655 MTU	30.08.44
F/O	CLARKE, H. T.	405	24.11.43
P/O	CLARKE, J. A. C., DFC	35	20.10.44
F/Sgt	CLARKE, J. D.	405	03.01.44
F/O	CLARKE, M. W. P.	35	22.06.43
F/O	CLARKE, R.	139	15.07.43
P/O	CLARKE, R. J.	35	23.12.44
F/Lt	CLARKE, R. M., DFC	635	07.01.45
W/O2	CLARKE, W. R.	16	02.12.43
LAC	CLAY, J.	9035 SE	20.04.44
Sgt	CLAY, T. S.	83	26.08.44
W/O	CLAYDEN, D. J.	405	19.04.45
F/Lt	CLAYES, N., DFC	105	13.05.44
P/O	CLAYTON, F., DFM	1409 Flt	14.11.43
Sgt	CLEASBY, F. J.	83	05.05.43
Sgt	CLEAVER, F. C.	35	28.05.43
F/O	CLEMENT, G. B.	156	07.09.43
Sgt	CLEMINSON, J. H.	Warboys	10.04.44
P/O	CLENAHAN, R. L., DFC	582	15.06.44
C/O	CLIFFORD, N. H.	405	28.04.44
F/Sgt	CLIFT, A., DFM	7	11.03.43
F/Sgt	CLIFT, J. E.	7	02.05.44
F/Sgt	CLIFTON, C. T.	83	28.02.43
Sgt	CLOUD, A.	156	28.07.43
F/Lt	CLOUTIER, W. B. B., DFC	405	14.01.44
F/Sgt	CLYNE, G. A.	582	04.05.44
P/O	COATES, W. D., DFM	97	25.03.44
F/Lt	COBB, H. W.	35	08.04.45
P/O	COBB, I. A. G.	35	05.05.43
F/Lt	COBB, N. A., DFC	35	29.06.43
Sgt	COBLEY, P.	7	18.10.43
S/L	COCHRANE, A. G. A., DFC	83	20.10.43
Sgt	COCHRANE, J. H. F.	7	04.12.43
W/O2	COGHILL, C. M. McG.	83	03.04.43
Sgt	COHEN, S. G.	7	29.01.44
F/O	COKER, H.	156	15.07.44
F/O	COLBERT, S., DFC	156	14.01.44
F/Sgt	COLBERT, S. R.	97	09.01.44
S/L	COLDREY, G. E.	405	03.06.44
S/L	COLDWELL, P. R., DSO, DFM	7	20.05.44
F/O	COLDWELL, W. F.	83	30.03.43
F/Sgt	COLE, F. W. R., DFM	7	08.03.43
F/O	COLE, K. A.	405	15.03.44
F/O	COLEBATCH, N. H.	156	03.01.44
P/O	COLEMAN, A. J.	97	04.12.43
F/O	COLES, S. A.	35	05.05.43
F/Lt	COLLEDGE, M. W.	139	14.09.43
F/Sgt	COLLENS, R. J.	156	03.01.44
S/L	COLLETT, A. L., AFC	83	27.04.44
F/O	COLLIER, C. M.	405	16.12.43
Sgt	COLLINGE, J. D.	35	05.05.43
F/O	COLLINS, G. B.	128	11.12.44
Sgt	COLLINS, H. W.	582	23.04.44
P/O	COLLINS, J. C.	156	03.09.43
Sgt	COLLINS, R. N.	35	27.08.44
W/O	COLLINSON, G. T.	692	23.08.44
Sgt	COLLOTON, W.	405(Ca)	24.07.42
F/Lt	COLSON, W. A., DFM	97	17.12.43
P/O	COLVIN, A., DFC	156	25.02.44

Rank	Name	Squadron	Date
P/O	COLVIN, J.	7	25.05.44
F/Sgt	COMBE, G. E.	7	15.02.44
Sgt	COMPTON, F. C., DFM	35	29.06.43
F/Lt	CONLEY, R. J., DFC	97	06.06.44
F/Lt	CONLON, W. M., DFC	156	08.06.44
F/O	CONNOLLY, E. W.	405	14.02.45
W/O	CONNOR, W. C.	7	18.11.43
Sgt	CONUEL, R. W.	7	05.05.43
P/O	CONVEY, L. J.	109(Ca)	28.03.42
Sgt	COOCH, C. W.	7	05.05.44
S/L	COOK, A. S., DFC, DFM	156	04.10.43
Sgt	COOK, D. H. W.	97	14.01.44
P/O	COOK, G.	139(Ja)	12.03.43
Sgt	COOK, H.	571	01.01.45
F/O	COOKE, A. S. (USA)	139	18.08.43
Sgt	COOKE, H. W.	405(Ca)	18.08.43
F/Lt	COOKE, J. G.	35	05.07.44
Sgt	COOLE, D. A. F.	582	29.06.44
P/O	COOLES, D. R.	7	16.06.44
Sgt	COOMBS, G. E. W.	97	24.08.43
F/Sgt	COON, G. A.	582	04.05.44
F/Sgt	COOPER, A. J. McF.	156	30.12.44
Sgt	COOPER, E. G.	35	24.08.43
Sgt	COOPER, G. S.	156	19.04.43
P/O	COOPER, H. B.	7	23.04.44
F/Sgt	COOTE, A. W.	83	20.01.44
P/O	COPELAND, D. J.	405	09.05.44
S/L	CORBET, W. H., DFC	Warboys	07.05.45
F/Sgt	CORLEY, L. E.	156	16.04.43
F/Lt	CORNELL, N. I., DFC	83	22.06.44
F/Sgt	CORNISH, E.	7	24.06.44
F/O	CORNISH, O. M.	83	05.05.43
Sgt	CORNWALL, J. A.	7	20.03.45
Sgt	CORNWELL, H. L.	405	17.12.43
Sgt	CORRIE, G. H.	83	28.02.43
Sgt	CORRIGAN, W.	405	17.12.43
F/Sgt	COTTERELL, C. H. W.	156	20.12.43
F/Sgt	COTTRELL, G. V.	582	15.06.44
Sgt	COULSON, J. F.	635	11.04.44
Sgt	COULSON, K.	156	19.04.43
F/Lt	COULTER, F. T.	97	22.03.44
F/O	COULTON, H.	35	04.02.45
W/C	COUSENS, A. G. S., DSO, DFC	635	22.04.44
Sgt	COUSINS, A.	83	24.08.43
F/Sgt	COUSINS, A. H.	35	24.12.44
F/Lt	COWDEN, J. D. F., DFC	635	14.02.45
Sgt	COWEN, J.	218	29.07.42
F/O	COWLEY, J. A., DFM	156	12.06.43
F/Sgt	COX, A., DFM	405	08.04.43
Sgt	COX, A. G.	35	04.07.43
F/Sgt	COX, A. W.	35	23.05.44
F/Sgt	COX, G. H.	7	25.06.43
F/O	COX, L. A., DFC	156	31.03.45
P/O	COX, R.	405(Ca)	02.08.41
F/Sgt	COX, S. T.	7	22.06.43
Sgt	COX, W. A.	156	02.12.43
P/O	COYLE, M. J., DFC	156	04.10.43
Sgt	CRABBE, E. S.	156	28.07.43
Sgt	CRABTREE, J. D.	635	06.10.44
Sgt	CRABTREE, T. J.	635	12.09.44
P/O	CRADDOCK, T. E.	35	23.12.44
P/O	CRADDOCK, W. J.	97	06.01.44
F/Sgt	CRAGGS, D.	582	29.07.44
Sgt	CRAIG, D. G.	156	02.12.43
P/O	CRAIG, W. D., DFM	35	24.08.43
Sgt	CRAIGIE, D. H.	83	26.11.43
F/Lt	CRAIK, J. G., DFC	635	14.02.45
Sgt	CRAIL, W. D.	692	12.10.44
F/O	CRAMPTON, L. R.	156	27.07.43
LAC	CRANE, C.	Graveley	25.11.43
Sgt	CRANK, A. A.	83	22.06.43
S/L	CRANSWICK, A. P., DSO, DFC	35	05.07.44
F/O	CRAWFORD, C. N. C.	7	15.10.44
S/L	CRAWFORD, N., DFC	405	02.01.45
F/O	CRAWFORD, V.	405	12.09.44
Sgt	CRAWFORD, W. E.	35	27.04.44
F/Sgt	CRAWLEY, J. S. F. V.	156	23.06.43
F/Lt	CREASE, R., DFC	7	14.01.44
F/Lt	CREBBIN, J. P., DFC	83	23.11.43
Sgt	CREEDE, J. D.	405(Ca)	27.07.42
F/Lt	CREW, G. C., DFC	7	25.05.44
Sgt	CRITCHLOW, R. N. P.	405	24.11.43
P/O	CROCKATT, D. E.	405	27.04.43
F/Lt	CROCKETT, E. G.	97	28.08.43
Sgt	CROCKETT, R. C.	156	30.01.44
F/O	CROCKFORD, A.	7	04.09.43
Sgt	CROCKFORD, W. S.	83	20.02.44
Sgt	CROFT, D. E.	97	30.07.43
F/O	CROFT, L. F.	582	29.10.44
Sgt	CROFT, M. W.	405(Ca)	20.12.42
F/Sgt	CROMAR, D., DFM	83	03.01.44
P/O	CROMARTY, J. D. R.	156	03.01.44
Sgt	CROOKS, S. E.	156	03.04.43
P/O	CROSBY, V. B., DFM	582	15.06.44
W/O	CROSS, D. H. J.	83	09.05.44
F/Sgt	CROSS, G., DFM	35	06.03.45
P/O	CROSS, W. H.	7	31.08.43
P/O	CROSSGROVE, R., DFM	97	17.12.43
Sgt	CROUCH, E. W.	156	17.12.43
W/O	CROWE, M.	1655 MTU	21.08.44
F/O	CROWLEY, J. W.	156	27.07.43
F/O	CROXFORD, R. J. C.	7	14.01.44
F/Sgt	CROZIER, W. J.	405	03.08.43
F/Sgt	CRUICKSHANK, J. M.	35	29.11.44
F/O	CRUMBLEY, W. M.	405	16.06.44
Sgt	CRUMP, J. C.	405(Ca)	24.07.41
F/O	CRUWYS, G. H., CROIX DE GUERRE	635	20.04.44
P/O	CUBBAGE, B. S., DFM	7	15.02.44
Sgt	CUBITT, T.	83	22.11.43
Sgt	CUDLIPP, L. W.	582	28.05.44
Sgt	CUGLEY, S.	405(Ca)	24.08.43
F/O	CULFF, E. R.	196	30.03.43
Sgt	CULLUM, J. F. W.	156	13.07.43
F/O	CUMMER, F. H.	405	28.01.45
Sgt	CUMMING, J.	97	30.07.43
P/O	CUMMINGS, M. K.	83	18.06.43
Sgt	CUMMINS, R. C. L.	90	23.09.43
P/O	CUNLIFFE, B. R.	405	16.01.45
P/O	CUNNINGHAM, F. L.	405(Ca)	01.10.42
F/O	CUNNINGHAM, P. S.	90	28.09.43
Sgt	CURLING, E. D.	196	29.04.43
P/O	CURRIE, D. R.	35	23.12.44
F/O	CURRIE, E. J.	97	31.03.44
P/O	CURRIE, W., DFC	7	03.01.44
F/Sgt	CURRY, J., DFM	97	04.10.43
Sgt	CURSITER, J. R.	35	23.05.44
P/O	CURTIS, B. A., DFM	196	29.04.43
P/O	CURTIS, D. D., DFC	156	07.09.43
Sgt	CURTIS, J. R.	156	12.06.43
Sgt	CURZON, E. W.	83	20.02.44
Sgt	CUTHILL, F. J.	156	17.04.45
P/O	DAGENAIS, J. J. G.	405	11.06.44
Sgt	DALE, H.	35	09.05.44
Sgt	DALEY, E.	35	28.10.44
F/Sgt	DALEY, J.	83	20.02.44
F/O	DALGARNO, W.	582	23.12.44
Sgt	DALLIMORE, L. W.	156	13.07.43
F/Sgt	DALTON, A. C.	156	07.09.43
Sgt	DALZIEL, J. R.	7	15.02.44
Sgt	DAMMS, R. A.	405(Ca)	05.04.43
P/O	DANAHY, S., DFC	83	28.02.43
F/Sgt	DANIEL, R. N. V.	156	24.12.43
P/O	DANIEL, W. N.	582	08.09.44
F/Sgt	DANIELS, N.	635	12.12.44

Rank	Name	Squadron	Date	Rank	Name	Squadron	Date
F/Sgt	DANIELS. R. D.	405(Ca)	09.05.44	F/O	DE VILLIERS. P.	97	30.07.43
Sgt	DANIELS. R. V. M.	35	15.02.44	Sgt	DEVINE. E. J.	97	21.01.44
F/Sgt	DAOUST. R. H. J.	405	06.01.44	P/O	DEVITT. J. F.	405	22.12.44
F/Sgt	DARBY. A. W. C.	7	25.04.44	Sgt	DICERBO. P.	582	25.07.44
F/Lt	DARBY. C. E.. DFM	608	28.08.44	Sgt	DICK. A. MacD.	7	18.10.43
Sgt	DARBYSHIRE. E.	405(Ca)	03.08.43	Sgt	DICKENS. F. D.	156	29.09.43
F/Lt	DARE. H. W. J.	405	03.08.43	P/O	DICKIE. R. J.	97	21.02.44
Sgt	DARROCH. J. W.	97	25.06.43	Sgt	DICKINS. T. E.	156	13.07.43
F/O	DARVALL. J. W. C.	156	27.04.44	F/Lt	DICKINSON. A.	7	31.03.44
F/Sgt	DATSON. J.	635	06.07.44	F/Lt	DIEMER. A. C.	PFF NTU Warboys	11.03.45
F/Sgt	DAVENPORT. J. J.	—	03.01.44	F/Sgt	DIGGLE. L.	97	10.05.44
Sgt	DAVENPORT. T.	405	21.07.44	Sgt	DILLON. G. W.	97	12.03.43
Sgt	DAVEY. P. J.	97	31.01.43	W/O2	DILLOW. W. E. C.	35	29.12.43
WO/2	DAVID. J. J. B. S. P. H.	97	23.06.43	Sgt	DIMOND. F. J.	35	04.12.43
F/Sgt	DAVIDSON. A. C.	—	06.10.44	Sgt	DINEEN. C. J.	35	24.03.44
Sgt	DAVIDSON. F. H.	35	12.09.44	P/O	DIXON. C. B.	405	27.04.43
F/O	DAVIDSON. G. R.. DFM	35	29.12.43	F/O	DIXON. D.	635	30.03.45
F/Lt	DAVIDSON. J. S.	635	14.02.45	Sgt	DIXON. D. A. H.	139	18.08.43
F/Sgt	DAVIE. A.	97	11.08.43	F/Sgt	DMYTRUK. P.	405(Ca)	09.12.43
F/O	DAVIES. C. H.	156	04.04.43	P/O	DOBBYN. R. J.	83	09.05.44
P/O	DAVIES. D. M.	156	14.01.44	F/Sgt	DOBSON. R. A. F.	156	17.06.43
F/Sgt	DAVIES. E. A.	83	23.05.44	W/O2	DOBSON. W. L.	405	17.12.43
F/Sgt	DAVIES. E. McH.	35	05.07.44	F/O	DOCHERTY. T.	156	02.01.44
F/Sgt	DAVIES. G. S.	97	22.03.44	P/O	DODDS. D. L.	156	03.09.43
F/O	DAVIES. J. C. H.	83	22.01.44	F/O	DODDS. G. H.	139	10.12.44
F/Sgt	DAVIES. J. M.	7	12.06.43	F/Lt	DODDS. J. R.. DFC	156	28.04.44
Sgt	DAVIES. J. W. T.	405(Ca)	29.08.41	P/O	DODDS. V. F.	405	21.07.44
Sgt	DAVIES. L. A.	7	10.11.42	F/O	DODSON. H. L. G.. DFM	83	20.01.44
Sgt	DAVIES. R. C.	35	03.08.43	S/L	DODWELL. T. E.. DFC*	571	19.07.44
Sgt	DAVIES. T. J. G.	83	20.02.44	F/Lt	DOHERTY. R. A. A.. DFC	608	23.02.45
F/O	DAVIES. W. C.	405	16.06.43	P/O	DOLBY. E. G.. DFC	97	01.09.43
Sgt	DAVIES. W. J.	—	24.11.43	S/L	DON. R. S.. DFC	142	22.01.45
F/O	DAVIS. A. J.	—	25.06.43	F/O	DONAHUE. C. J.. DFM	7	02.01.44
F/O	DAVIS. B. O.	571	06.02.45	F/O	DONALD. J. R.	635	06.01.45
F/Sgt	DAVIS. G. A.. DFM	405	04.12.43	Sgt	DONALDSON. D. S.	7	22.06.43
F/O	DAVIS. H. S.	635	24.12.44	Sgt	DONNELLY. H. McL.	156	31.03.44
W/O1	DAVIS. K. G.. DFM	83	26.11.43	F/O	DONNELLY. T. H.. DFM	405	02.01.44
S/L	DAVIS. K. G.	7	20.02.44	F/Lt	DONNER. W. J.. DFM	156	20.02.44
F/Sgt	DAVIS. S. J.	83	23.11.43	F/O	DONOHUE. J. R. C.. DFC	635	14.02.45
W/O	DAVIS. V. A.. DFM	582	11.09.44	F/O	DONOVAN. W. S.. DFM	1655 MTU	27.06.44
F/O	DAVY. H. D.	405	22.12.44	F/O	DORAN.P. B.	692	07.02.45
W/O1	DAVY. H. W.. DFC	156	24.06.44	P/O	DORRELL. S. G.	7	23.11.43
F/Sgt	DAWDY. L. D.	405	02.09.42	F/Sgt	DORSETT. J. W. A.	156	08.03.43
Sgt	DAWE. J. A. G.	156	17.06.43	F/Sgt	DOUGHERTY. G. S.	7	04.09.43
F/Lt	DAWES. J. E.. DFC	139	03.04.45	Sgt	DOVATSON. L.	405	16.03.45
F/Lt	DAWSON. J. S.. DFC	582	29.10.44	F/Sgt	DOVEY. C. W.	7	29.06.44
Sgt	DAWSON. J. F. B.	405	15.08.41	S/L	DOW. T. R. A.. DFC	139	04.04.45
Sgt	DAY. M. J.	35	02.12.43	F/Lt	DOWNEY. J.. DFM	571	11.06.44
F/Lt	DAY. R. O.. DFC	139	24.03.45	Sgt	DOWSE. B. J.	35	22.06.43
W/C	DEACON. J. W.	105	27.02.43	F/Lt	DOYLE. K. P. C.. DFC	156	24.09.44
Sgt	DEACON. T.	97	20.10.43	Sgt	DOYLE. W. E.	97	13.06.43
F/O	DEAN. G. E.	139	27.05.43	F/O	DRAKE. A. R. S.	163	22.03.45
Sgt	DEAN. J. G. K.	156	16.04.43	Sgt	DRAKE. W. J.	156	12.06.43
Sgt	DEARLOVE. L. N.	405	30.06.42	F/Lt	DRANE. P. J.. DFC	139	15.01.45
Sgt	DEARNLEY. H.	405	25.07.41	F/O	DRAWBRIDGE. H. J.	97	21.04.44
Sgt	DEAVIN. F. E.	7	23.11.43	F/O	DREW. W. P.	405	29.07.44
F/O	DEBROCK. F. C. G.. DFC	156	15.07.44	F/Lt	DREWER. C. H.	7	24.06.44
F/O	DEED. L. L.. DFC	156	13.08.44	F/Sgt	DRIES. P. W.	97	23.11.43
F/O	DEIGHTON. F. E.	105	13.05.44	F/O	DRIMMIE. G. R.. DFC	405	14.01.44
F/Sgt	DELANEY. C.	635	31.03.45	F/O	DRYER. H. R.	405	29.12.44
P/O	DE MEILLAC. G. M. M. L.	7	9.04.43	F/Sgt	DUBE. J. P. H.	405	17.11.43
P/O	DEMPSEY. J. H.	405	15.03.44	Sgt	DUCHENE. E. A..	156	23.06.43
W/O2	DEMPSTER. W. J.. DFM	7	02.02.43	F/O	DUDLEY. L. C.	7	22.05.44
Sgt	DENBIGH. A.	582	06.03.45	Sgt	DUFFY. M. H.	97	04.05.44
Sgt	DENBY. J. W.	156	19.02.43	W/O	DUGAN. J. H.	7	15.08.43
S/L	DENNIS. J. M.. DSO. DFC	7	20.05.44	F/Lt	DUKE. E. C.. DFM	405	02.01.45
F/Lt	DENNIS. S. L.. DFC	156	13.08.44	Sgt	DUKES. F. J. B.	7	22.06.43
F/Lt	DENNY. P. F.	83	11.04.44	F/Sgt	DULIEU. H. E. M.	83	22.11.43
P/O	DENYER. N. H.	156	03.09.43	W/O2	DUNAE. A.	97	23.05.44
S/L	DEVERILL. E. A.. DFC, AFC*, DFM	97	17.12.43	F/Sgt	DUNBAR. J. A.	97	30.07.43
P/O	DEVESON. E. O.	635	25.03.44	F/Lt	DUNCAN. G. R. P.	105	28.01.45
F/O	DEVILLE. E. P.	7	12.06.43	F/Sgt	DUNCAN. W. G.	97	21.02.44

Rank	Name	Squadron	Date
F/O	DUNHAM, D. W.	156	13.08.44
Sgt	DUNLOP, J. Mc.I.	83	03.01.44
S/L	DUNN, A. R., DFC	83	22.06.44
F/O	DUNN, J., DFC. DFM	139	27.07.44
P/O	DUNNE, J. P.	405	02.01.44
W/O2	DUNNET, H. N.	97	06.01.44
P/O	DUNNING, G. E., DFM	97	06.06.44
F/Sgt	DURN, M.	97	23.06.44
Sgt	DURRANT, K. M. C.	582	16.09.44
Sgt	DUSHMAN, D.	97	22.03.44
F/O	DUTTA, R. C.	97	09.07.43
F/O	DUTTON, J. A.	7	06.01.44
F/Sgt	DUTTON, T. R.	156	15.02.44
P/O	DYELLE, G. R.	405	12.09.44
F/O	DYKE, W. H.	83	03.01.44
Sgt	DYKES, R. E.	156	09.10.43
Sgt	DYNES, G. C.	35	27.03.43
Sgt	DYSON, J. H.	405(Ca)	26.02.42
P/O	EADES, A. H.	139(Ja)	13.05.43
W/O	EARDLEY, L. J.	635	19.08.44
Sgt	EARL, H. J.	156	29.07.43
Sgt	EARNSHAW, F.	83	20.10.43
P/O	EASTHAM, D. J.	405	24.02.44
P/O	EASTHOPE, H.	7	12.09.44
Sgt	EASTON, C.	156	25.06.43
Sgt	EASTON, R. H.	83	21.01.44
G/C	EATON, E. C., DFC	156	28.04.44
Sgt	EATON, H.	156	24.02.44
Sgt	EATON, H. A.	7	04.09.43
F/Sgt	EATON, R. J.	Warboys	02.03.45
F/O	EATON, W.	97	21.04.44
F/Sgt	EATON, W. B.	7	09.10.43
Sgt	EDDINGTON, W.	196	13.05.43
Sgt	EDE, A. J.	156	26.07.43
P/O	EDE, R., DFC	7	26.08.44
W/O	EDGAR, F.	128	29.11.44
F/O	EDGE, B. F.	7	04.09.43
W/O	EDINBURGH, W. H.	156	24.09.44
F/Sgt	EDMONDS, N. J.	156	02.12.43
W/O	EDMONDS, R. M.	7	18.10.43
P/O	EDMONDSON, N. T.	156	31.03.44
Sgt	EDWARDS, D. R.	156	19.04.43
F/Sgt	EDWARDS, F.	97	02.12.43
Sgt	EDWARDS, G. A. P.	156	22.06.43
P/O	EDWARDS, G. J., DFC	405	16.09.44
P/O	EDWARDS, I. P.,	7	11.06.44
F/O	EDWARDS, J. H.	405	07.04.43
P/O	EDWARDS, S. A.	97	10.05.44
F/Sgt	EDWARDS, S. L.	635	12.06.44
F/Sgt	EDWARDS, T. W.	83	22.01.44
Sgt	EGGLESTON, D.	582	06.07.44
F/Lt	EICHLER, B. (Czech)	142	05.01.45
P/O	EINARSSON, S.	405	30.01.44
F/Sgt	ELDER, T. W.	97	29.01.44
Sgt	ELEY, A. K.	156	19.04.43
Sgt	ELLENOR, W.	N.T.U. Upwood	25.01.44
Sgt	ELLICOTT, D. A. G.	635	06.07.44
F/O	ELLIOTT, D. J.	405	03.01.44
P/O	ELLIOTT, H. W.	156	17.04.45
S/L	ELLIOTT, P. C., DFC	35	02.03.43
F/O	ELLIS, A. J.	83	04.10.43
F/Sgt	ELLIS, H. W.	7	05.03.45
AC1	ELLIS, J.	156	09.09.44
F/Lt	ELLIS, I. L.	128	07.11.44
P/O	ELLIS, R. O.	405	16.06.44
F/O	ELLSMERE, R. O.	97	04.05.44
F/Sgt	ELLWOOD, R.	83	03.01.44
F/O	ELMY, G.	156	31.03.44
F/O	ELSON, F. R.	635	12.12.44
P/O	ELTON, C.	35	04.05.44
P/O	EMANS, A. E.	156	28.08.43
F/Lt	EMERSON, R. S.	97	21.02.44
P/O	EMERSON, T. H. N., DFM	405	14.07.43
F/O	EMERY, J. C.	405	11.06.44
Sgt	EMMS, A. E.	7	01.05.43
F/Lt	ENDERBY, P., DFC	105	04.04.45
F/Lt	ENDERSBY, J. S.	139	04.04.45
Sgt	ERICKSON, C.	35	05.07.44
Sgt	ERRINGTON, J. B.	405(Ca)	17.11.43
Sgt	ERRINGTON, S. A.	7	25.06.43
F/O	ESPY, H.	35	27.03.43
F/Sgt	EVANS, A. E.	83	20.10.43
F/O	EVANS, D. A. N.	35	24.05.43
Sgt	EVANS, D. C.	582	23.09.44
F/Sgt	EVANS, E. E.	582	12.12.44
F/O	EVANS, F. K., DFM	627	08.01.44
F/Sgt	EVANS, G. R.	405	03.01.44
Sgt	EVANS, G. W.	156	24.08.45
F/O	EVANS, H. T.	7	04.04.45
Sgt	EVANS, J. H.	405(Ca)	10.08.43
P/O	EVANS, J. K.	1655 MTU	16.09.44
F/Lt	EVANS, J. V.	109	05.03.45
P/O	EVANS, M.	635	06.07.44
F/Sgt	EVANS, N. R. J.	156	14.01.44
Sgt	EVANS, P. C.	97	30.07.43
F/Sgt	EVANS, P. E.	635	26.08.44
F/Sgt	EVANS, R. R.	7	20.03.45
F/Lt	EVANS, S.	7	31.03.44
F/O	EVANS, W. J.	7	14.01.44
F/O	EVERETT, A. C., DFM	635	24.12.44
S/L	EVERETT, D. B., DFC **	35	07.03.45
F/O	EWING, P. H.	83	03.01.44
F/O	FAHEY, F. F., AFM	1655 MTU	06.01.44
Sgt	FAIRLESS, A.	405(Ca)	01.10.42
P/O	FAIRLIE, K.	97	24.08.43
W/C	FALCONER, D. B., DFC. AFC	156	30.12.44
F/Sgt	FALLOON, H. R.	582	23.04.44
Sgt	FARLEY, D. C.	7	21.04.43
F/Sgt	FARMELO, K. E. L.	83	20.01.44
Sgt	FARMER, W. W.	Warboys	10.04.44
F/Sgt	FARR, F. R.	97	17.12.43
Sgt	FARRALL, D.	635	16.06.44
F/Sgt	FAARRANT, D. J.	635	10.04.44
S/L	FARRINGTON, A. L.	582	29.08.44
F/Lt	FARROW, L. R.	7	22.09.43
F/O	FATHERS, R. T.	97	23.11.43
Sgt	FAULKNER, A.	405	16.06.43
F/Lt	FAULKNER, J. G.	35	23.12.44
Sgt	FAULKNER, R. J.	156	24.03.44
S/L	FAWCETT, R. E., DFC	156	02.01.44
Sgt	FAWKES, J. A.	405(Ca)	24.07.41
F/Sgt	FAZACKERLEY, F.	7	25.06.43
Sgt	FEAKINS, F. J.	35	11.09.44
Sgt	FEARN, B. H.	405(Ca)	29.12.43
LACW	FEARON, D.	9635 SE	29.09.44
Sgt	FEATHER, E.	7	02.05.44
F/Sgt	FEAVER, T. E.	7	15.10.44
F/Lt	FEELEY, A., DFC	582	06.06.44
Sgt	FELL, H.	83	05.03.43
Sgt	FENSON, R.	635	12.09.44
Sgt	FENTIMAN, D. C.	97	30.07.43
F/Sgt	FENTON, D.	156	29.07.42
Sgt	FENTON, J. T.	35	04.05.44
P/O	FERGUSON, J. H.	35	04.05.44
P/O	FERGUSON, N.	156	08.04.43
Sgt	FERGUSON, R.	97	06.01.44
F/O	FERRIER, J. S.	7	31.03.44
F/Lt	FETHERSTON, W. H.	405	04.04.42
S/L	FEW, E. S., DFC. AFC	608	21.04.45
P/O	FEW, G. F. W.	7	06.01.44
Sgt	FIDDLER, J.	35	11.08.43
Sgt	FIDLER, E. G.	35	22.03.44
F/O	FIELD, D. A.	105	11.12.44
F/O	FIELD, T. B.	83	20.02.44

Rank	Name	Squadron	Date	Rank	Name	Squadron	Date
F/Sgt	FIELD, W. E. N.	405(Ca)	27.06.42	F/O	FRANKLIN, K. G., DFC	156	28.04.44
F/Sgt	FIELDHOUSE, L.	83	03.04.43	Sgt	FRASER, A. R.	7	04.09.43
F/O	FILLINGHAM, T. A.	405	12.06.43	Sgt	FRASER, W.	7	29.01.44
Sgt	FINCH, H. T.	97	08.10.43	F/O	FRAZER, R., DFC	83	27.04.44
Sgt	FINK, H. R.	35	22.06.43	F/O	FREBERG, P. G., DFC	7	11.04.43
Sgt	FISH, R. S.	156	29.07.43	F/Lt	FREDMAN, N. H., DFC	109	06.05.44
Sgt	FISHER, A. L.	7	26.05.43	W/O2	FREELAND, W. W.	7	09.05.43
F/O	FISHER, C. H., DFC	405	17.08.44	F/Lt	FREEMAN, J. H.	156	29.01.45
Sgt	FISHER, C. H.	35	05.05.43	F/O	FREEMAN, W. J.	35	13.02.43
P/O	FISHER, D. R.	7	27.08.44	F/O	FREER, K. B.	35	12.09.44
Sgt	FISHER, L. W.	156	02.12.43	F/Sgt	FREEZE, W. F.	83	28.08.43
P/O	FISHER, R. V., DFM	156	17.12.44	Sgt	FRENCH, G. F.	83	25.04.44
F/Sgt	FISHER, W. S.	156	16.12.43	F/Lt	FRENCH, K. H.	156	03.02.43
Sgt	FISHPOOL, R. V.	582	16.09.44	F/O	FRENCH, R. A.	405	14.02.45
F/O	FISHWICK, K.	635	13.05.44	F/Lt	FRENCH, R. O., DFC	7	04.09.43
Sgt	FISK, L. C. A.	97	29.03.43	Sgt	FRENCH, V. R.	405(Ca)	10.09.42
W/O2	FITZGERALD, R. C.	405	27.06.42	Sgt	FRENCH, W. D.	97	16.02.44
S/L	FITZGERALD, R. I., DFC	35	24.03.44	Sgt	FRESHWATER, J. M.	83	05.03.43
P/O	FITZHENRY, S. H.	405	02.01.45	F/Sgt	FRETWELL, A.	582	06.07.44
F/Sgt	FLAATEN, O. L.	35	28.10.44	Sgt	FREW, H. Mc.A.	97	02.03.43
F/O	FLACK, V. S.	97	06.01.44	F/Sgt	FREWER, J. H.	7	27.09.43
F/O	FLEET, A. G.	105	23.11.43	F/O	FREWIN, L. W. A.	405	16.06.43
F/Sgt	FLEISCH-FRESSER, C. A.	7	04.09.43	P/O	FREY, F. J. A.	405	26.09.44
Sgt	FLEMING, A. S.	35	23.12.44	F/O	FRIEDRICH, L. T.	7	05.01.45
P/O	FLEMING, G. H.	405	15.08.41	W/O	FRIENDLY, J., DFM	139	21.05.43
F/Sgt	FLEMING, J.	405	09.06.42	F/O	FRIZELL, J. C.	97	28.08.43
P/O	FLETCHER, A. G.	83	13.06.43	Sgt	FROST, A. H.	7	15.10.44
Sgt	FLETCHER, C. H.	405(Ca)	18.09.41	F/O	FROST, H. C.	156	31.03.44
F/Sgt	FLETCHER, D. W. C.	83	22.06.43	Sgt	FROUD, P.	35	12.09.44
Sgt	FLETCHER, E.	156	27.04.44	Sgt	FUGERE, M. W.	405(Ca)	20.12.42
Sgt	FLETCHER, E. J.	83	27.04.44	Sgt	FULLER, F. T.	7	31.03.44
P/O	FLETCHER, J., DFM	156	07.09.43	F/Sgt	FULLER, M. O'D.	35	26.05.43
F/Lt	FLETCHER, M. S., DFC	156	02.01.44	Sgt	FULTON, R. O.	83	05.03.43
P/O	FLETCHER, R. C.	156	31.03.45	Sgt	FUNNELL, R. E.	156	27.04.43
W/O	FLETT, A. H., DFM	109	14.01.44	F/Lt	FYFE, A. B.	405	15.03.44
F/Sgt	FLETT, R. H.	156	08.04.43	F/O	GABBOTT, W., DFM	635	14.02.45
F/O	FLINT, C. S.	635	13.05.44	Sgt	GADSBY, A. E.	97	08.10.43
Sgt	FLOOD, P. E. C.	7	05.05.43	F/Sgt	GADSBY, W. C.	97	14.01.44
P/O	FLOREN, H. A.	405	14.01.44	Sgt	GADSDEN, D.	7	23.11.43
S/L	FLOWER, F. J.	83	03.04.43	F/O	GAINS, F. G.	156	02.03.44
P/O	FLYNN, D., DFC	582	15.06.44	F/Sgt	GAINSBOROUGH-ALLEN, J. H.	83	20.01.44
F/Lt	FLYNN, J. P.	582	25.05.44				
F/Sgt	FLYNN, P.	35	09.03.43	P/O	GALBRAITH, B. E.	405	15.03.44
Sgt	FODEN, F. F.	83	23.06.43	P/O	GALBRAITH, D. I.	405	15.03.45
F/O	FODERINGHAM, C., DFC	156	03.09.43	Sgt	GALBRAITH, G. M.	35	26.07.43
F/O	FOGDEN, E. S.	608	13.09.44	F/O	GAMSBY, A. G.	405	16.06.44
F/Sgt	FOLEY, W. J.	405(Ca)	05.04.43	F/O	GANT, M. G.	571	27.03.45
Sgt	FOOT, J. E. T.	405	30.06.42	W/O	GARCIA-WEBB, J.	109	16.11.44
F/O	FORBES, A. L.	7	30.07.43	Sgt	GARDINER, K.	156	31.03.44
W/O	FORBES, J. F.	7	08.08.44	Sgt	GARDINER, H.	405(Ca)	03.08.43
W/O2	FORDYCE, G. W.	156	23.11.43	F/Lt	GARDINER, R. A., DFC	405	23.11.43
F/Sgt	FORMAN, G.	35	20.02.44	F/Lt	GARDNER, R. G.	608	09.10.44
S/L	FORREST, J. N., DSO, DFC	97	24.08.43	W/O	GARDNER, V., DFM	156	31.03.44
Sgt	FORSTER, F.	635	06.12.44	S/L	GARLICK, J. M., DFC*	97	02.12.43
Sgt	FORSTER, W.	156	12.06.43	F/Sgt	GARNER, C. H.	35	30.05.43
F/Sgt	FORSYTH, A. V., DFM	35	28.09.43	Sgt	GARNER, E.	35	26.05.43
F/Sgt	FORSYTH, T. K.	139(Ja)	20.10.43	W/O	GAUGHRAN, W.	582	08.08.44
F/Sgt	FORTIN, J. M. W.	405	02.06.42	P/O	GAVIN, T. D.	405	02.01.44
LAC	FOSTER, A. W.	2731	22.12.44	F/Sgt	GAY, J. C.	7	19.08.44
F/Sgt	FOSTER, C. W.	83	20.10.43	F/Lt	GEARY, G. V. J.	83	12.06.43
F/O	FOSTER, D. A.	35	12.09.44	AC2	GEE, R.	Molesworth	20.04.42
F/O	FOSTER, J. D., DFC	156	07.05.44	F/O	GEEVES, G. E., DFC	405	02.01.45
S/L	FOSTER, K. J., DFC*	97	23.09.43	Sgt	GEEVES, J.	582	06.07.44
P/O	FOSTER, L. A.	405	28.04.44	P/O	GENESIS, R. H., DFM	7	11.04.43
P/O	FOULKES, G. G.	35	28.04.44	F/Sgt	GERICKE, P. K. R., DFM	15	29.01.44
S/L	FOULSHAM, J., DFC, AFC	109	20.07.44	W/O	GIBB, J. W., DFC	156	20.02.44
Sgt	FOWLER, M.	156	23.04.44	Sgt	GIBBONS, A. N.	97	30.07.43
Sgt	FOX, C. E. R.	635	31.03.44	Sgt	GIBBS, F.	105	23.03.43
Sgt	FOX, E. C.	35	30.07.43	F/Sgt	GIBBS, L. E.	156	08.06.44
F/O	FOX, G. G.	405	29.12.44	P/O	GIBBS, W. L.	83	13.05.43
P/O	FOX, J. E., DFC	105	10.07.44	S/L	GIBSON, A., DFC	7	16.12.43
F/O	FRAAS, R. J.	405(Ca)	07.07.41	F/O	GIBSON, C.	156	02.02.44
Sgt	FRANCIS, K. G.	7	31.09.44	Sgt	GIBSON, R. C.	405	30.01.44

131

Rank	Name	Squadron	Date
Sgt	GILBERT, J. W.	156	25.02.44
Sgt	GILBERT, P. N.	405	21.07.44
Sgt	GILBERT, R.	156	25.06.43
F/Sgt	GILBERTSON, J. B.	83	30.01.44
F/O	GILBEY, J. F.	405	14.01.44
P/O	GILES, F., DFM	156	13.05.43
F/Sgt	GILES, W. H.	7	22.05.44
F/Sgt	GILL, J. T.	405	09.05.44
P/O	GILL, L. F.	156	02.01.44
Cpl	GILL, W. E.	9156	09.09.44
		Servicing Echelon	
Sgt	GILLAM, R. A. F.	83	27.11.43
F/Lt	GILLIAT, C. D.	156	09.03.43
F/Sgt	GILLESPIE, A. E.	163	08.03.45
Sgt	GILLHAM, R. W. P.	635	06.07.44
F/O	GILLIS, H. D., DFM	156	08.06.44
W/C	GILLMAN, J. R.	83	05.05.43
P/O	GILMORE, J. H.	7	22.09.43
F/Sgt	GIMBY, W. E.	405	18.08.43
F/O	GIRRBACH, K.	156	04.04.43
F/O	GISBY, M.	582	12.12.44
F/O	GLADWELL, W. J.	15	06.07.44
Sgt	GLANVILL, J. E.	97	25.02.44
Sgt	GLASS, R.	635	16.06.44
S/L	GLASSPOOL, L. H., DFC	156	28.04.44
F/Sgt	GLAUS, L. G.	7	15.02.44
F/O	GLOSSOP, C. H.	7	21.01.44
W/O2	GLOVER, C. G.	83	06.09.43
Sgt	GLOVER, H. R.	7	25.06.43
F/O	GLUCK, M.	405(Ca)	24.05.43
Sgt	GODDARD, J.	7	09.03.43
F/Lt	GODDARD, J. E., DFC	582	08.09.44
F/Sgt	GODDARD, J. H.	50	05.01.45
F/Sgt	GODDARD, R.	635	30.03.45
F/O	GODDARD, R. S.	635	05.03.45
F/Lt	GODDARD, W.	405	26.09.44
F/Sgt	GODFRAY, M. G., DFM	7	27.08.44
F/Lt	GODFREY, S. C. P., DFC	156	04.10.43
P/O	GODIN, J. J. R. T.	35	06.01.44
F/O	GOLDEN, B. W., DFC	35	21.02.45
Sgt	GOLDING, R. C. S.	97	04.07.43
F/Lt	GOLDINGAY, L. D., DFC	7	28.04.44
F/Sgt	GOLDNEY, R. E.	405	05.04.43
Sgt	GOLDSBURY, R.	156	31.03.45
W/O	GOLDSPINK, W. E.	405	28.09.43
F/Sgt	GOMERSALL, J.	97	19.03.44
P/O	GONCE, H. B.	156	16.04.43
Sgt	GOOCH, R. W.	97	14.01.44
AC1	GOOD, D. J.	4270 AA Flg	14.06.43
Sgt	GOOD, W.	405	21.01.44
F/Sgt	GOODBODY, W. J.	635	08.03.45
Sgt	GOODING, B. H.	156	17.04.43
F/Lt	GOODLEY, L. G., DFC	156	09.03.43
Sgt	GOODWIN, F. A.	156	25.02.44
F/O	GOODWIN, R. E., DFC	156	30.07.43
Sgt	GOODWIN, W. J.	582	15.03.45
Sgt	GORDON, A. D.	405(Ca)	07.04.43
F/O	GORDON, F. M.	405	14.02.45
F/Lt	GORDON, J., DFC	105	05.11.43
W/O	GORDON, J. R., DFM	635	19.08.44
F/O	GORDON, W. C., DFC	156	03.09.43
Sgt	GORDON, W. H.	156	23.06.43
F/Sgt	GORE, K.	7	21.10.43
W/O2	GORING, C. A.	405	01.09.43
P/O	GOSPER, L. G., DFC	7	08.03.43
Sgt	GOSS, J. E.	405	24.11.43
F/Sgt	GOTTO, P. G.	156	02.03.44
F/O	GOUGH, C. D., DFC	156	20.02.44
F/O	GOUGH, K. A.	7	15.08.45
F/Sgt	GOULBURN, J. W.	156	25.02.44
F/O	GOULD, J. C.	582	06.03.45
F/Sgt	GOULDING, A. L.	7	11.06.44

Rank	Name	Squadron	Date
Sgt	GOVER, H. P.	405(Ca)	10.08.42
F/Sgt	GOWDEY, A. W.	405	16.09.44
Sgt	GOWDY, W. J.	35	21.01.44
F/Sgt	GRACE, J. P. M.	156	08.04.43
Sgt	GRAHAM, J.	97	23.11.43
F/O	GRAHAM, J. P.	35	25.07.44
Sgt	GRAHAM, L. T.	15	03.10.43
LAC	GRAHAM, T. E. H.	156	09.09.44
W/O	GRANGE, A., DFM	7	21.02.44
F/O	GRANGE, A. H.	582	06.06.44
F/Lt	GRANGER, P. C.	35	12.09.44
P/O	GRANT, A. C. W.	7	16.06.44
Sgt	GRANT, A. H.	7	05.01.45
F/Sgt	GRANT, H.	97	10.05.44
F/O	GRANT, L. K. A.	97	17.12.43
F/Sgt	GRANT, R. H.	7	22.05.44
F/O	GRAY, C.	405	29.07.44
F/Lt	GRAY, E. McL., DFC	156	05.05.43
P/O	GRAY, H.	35	22.03.44
F/Lt	GRAY, K. MacG.	405	10.08.43
F/Sgt	GRAY, W. D.	35	30.05.43
P/O	GRAYLAND, G. J.	156	22.11.42
Sgt	GREAVISON, H. E.	83	06.09.43
Sgt	GREEN, A.	156	13.08.44
F/Sgt	GREEN, D. K.	156	24.09.44
W/O	GREEN, E. W.	83	27.04.44
Sgt	GREEN, J. A.	156	24.03.44
W/C	GREEN, J. D.	Warboys	10.04.44
Sgt	GREEN, K. F.	97	29.03.43
S/L	GREEN, R. J. G., DFC *	139	15.01.45
F/Sgt	GREENFIELD, R. E.	7	31.03.44
F/Sgt	GREENWOOD, E. W.	83	25.04.44
F/Sgt	GREENWOOD, F. J.	35	12.06.43
Sgt	GREENWOOD, N.	83	12.06.43
Sgt	GREGORY, A. F.	405	03.08.43
Sgt	GRESTY, J.	582	20.07.44
Sgt	GREY, F. B.	97	02.01.44
Sgt	GRIER, J.	83	11.04.44
F/Sgt	GRIFFIN, J. R.	35	31.08.43
Sgt	GRIFFITH, T.	83	05.05.43
F/Sgt	GRIFFITHS, D.	635	16.06.44
P/O	GRIFFITHS, G.	1409 Flt	16.04.43
F/O	GRIFFITHS, G.	156	03.01.44
W/O	GRIFFITHS, H. E. L.	139	01.07.44
F/O	GRIFFITHS, R. W.	35	17.08.43
Sgt	GRIGG, G. E.	35	21.01.44
F/Lt	GRILLAGE, F. G.	582	03.12.44
F/Sgt	GRIMES, G. L.	7	25.03.44
S/L	GRIMSTON, B., The Hon., DFC	156	04.04.43
Sgt	GRIMWOOD, P. J. W.	156	04.04.43
F/Sgt	GRINDLEY, J.	98	10.06.43
Sgt	GRIVELL, M. S.	156	24.08.43
P/O	GRODECKI, J.	405	23.04.44
Sgt	GROOM, S.	35	24.05.43
Sgt	GROUT, D.	156	06.09.43
F/O	GROVE, E. G.	156	23.06.43
Sgt	GRUNDY, G.	97	17.12.43
F/O	GUEST, C. H.	139	15.11.43
F/O	GUTTON, E. S.	405	30.01.44
F/Sgt	GURTON, J. L., DFM	156	15.02.44
Sgt	GUTHRIE, J. C.	635	31.03.44
Sgt	GUY, F.	196	29.04.43
P/O	GYNTHER, C. L.	156	02.01.44
Sgt	HAAGENSEN, F.	35	28.10.44
Sgt	HABBERSHAW, F.	156	30.01.44
F/O	HACKETT, D., DFC	405	30.01.44
F/Sgt	HADDEN, E. B.	156	18.03.43
F/Sgt	HADLAND, D. F.	35	04.02.45
S/L	HADLEY, R., DFC	156	16.12.43
Sgt	HADLOW, H. A.	156	17.12.43
F/Sgt	HAGEMAN, R.	35	28.05.43
S/L	HAGGARTY, P. A., DFC	35	17.08.43

132

Rank	Name	Squadron	Date
F/Lt	HAIGH, F., DFM	35	22.03.44
P/O	HAINES, F. J.	7	25.06.43
W/O	HAINSWORTH, R. W., DFM	405(Ca)	07.03.45
F/O	HALBERT, T. D., DFC	83	27.04.44
F/Lt	HALCRO, J. A. F.	139	12.09.44
Sgt	HALDEMAN, W. C.	156	04.04.43
P/O	HALEY, A. W.	405	29.12.44
F/Lt	HALEY, V. G., MM	PFF, NTU	19.02.45
W/O2	HALIKOWSKI, J. W.	405(Ca)	03.04.43
F/Lt	HALKYARD, R. C., DFC	7	04.04.43
F/Sgt	HALL, M. T. T.	156	29.07.43
W/O	HALL, S. G. W.	83	21.10.43
F/Sgt	HALL, S. J., DFM	83	23.05.44
P/O	HALLDING, E. C.	7	01.05.43
F/O	HALLETT, P. T. L., DFC	1655 MTU	05.11.43
Sgt	HALLIWELL, E.	405	17.12.43
W/O2	HALLORAN, W. R.	83	02.01.44
Sgt	HALLS, V. M. B.	35	05.01.45
P/O	HALPERIN, R., DFC	156	21.02.44
F/Sgt	HAMBLIN, R.	35	11.08.43
F/Sgt	HAMBLING, E., DFM	635	20.04.44
W/O2	HAMBROOK, M. D. W.	83	26.02.43
F/Sgt	HAMILTON, G. E.	—	22.03.44
Sgt	HAMILTON-FOX, R. S.	—	09.04.43
F/O	HAMLIN, A. R.	139(Ja)	05.05.44
F/O	HAMMOND, G. N.	97	30.07.43
W/O	HANCOCK, E. A.	Bourn	18.11.43
P/O	HANDLEY, C. D., DFM	139(Ja)	21.04.43
P/O	HANDLEY, C. M., DFC	156	02.01.44
F/Lt	HANDLEY, R. E., DFM	97	16.12.43
F/Sgt	HANNA, J.	405(Ca)	10.08.43
F/Sgt	HANNAH, A. J.	7	21.01.44
F/O	HANNAH, H. A., CROIX DE GUERRE	405	27.01.45
F/O	HANNAH, W., DFC	97	21.07.44
F/O	HANRAHAN, J. F.	7	25.06.43
W/O	HANSON, J. R.	635	20.04.44
F/O	HARALAMBIDES, S. C., DFC	7	05.04.45
Sgt	HARCOMBE, C. M.	35	22.06.43
F/Sgt	HARCOURT, J. G. W.	635	30.03.45
S/L	HARCOURT, V. R. G., DFC	139(Ja)	21.05.43
P/O	HARCUS, L. J.	7	03.06.42
ACW2	HARDCASTLE, R. D.	35	22.05.43
Sgt	HARDEE, E. T. D.	196	27.04.43
F/Lt	HARDING, A. C., DFC	7	18.11.43
Sgt	HARDING, A. C.	635	16.06.44
F/O	HARDING, F. W.	7	14.01.44
Sgt	HARDY, J.	7	20.10.43
F/O	HARDY, J. E. C.	608	06.12.44
P/O	HARDY, L. G.	405	12.09.44
F/O	HARDY, W. A. G.	405(Ca)	01.05.44
Sgt	HARE, J. A.	97	06.01.44
P/O	HARGRAVE, A.	7	19.08.44
Sgt	HARGREAVES, J. McG.	83	13.05.43
F/Sgt	HARLEY, W. T.	635	12.09.44
F/O	HARMAN, F. A.	405	24.08.43
F/Sgt	HARMAN, L. T., DFM	635	06.07.44
F/Sgt	HARMSWORTH-SMITH, F. R.	35	12.09.44
Sgt	HARPER, D. H.	83	30.03.43
F/Sgt	HARPER, J. F. P.	35	28.10.44
Sgt	HARPER, R. T.	156	31.03.44
Sgt	HARRIGAN, T. R.	405	29.12.44
P/O	HARRINGTON, A. G.	582	28.05.44
W/O2	HARRINGTON, J.	7	12.06.43
Sgt	HARRIS, A.	7	31.08.43
Sgt	HARRIS, A. R.	97	09.07.43
Sgt	HARRIS, F. W.	7	23.11.43
F/O	HARRIS, G. R.	83	03.01.44
F/Sgt	HARRIS, H.	582	16.06.44
Sgt	HARRIS, K. E.	35	22.03.44
Sgt	HARRIS, L. F. J.	7	15.04.43
F/Lt	HARRISON, C. M.	139	10.12.44
F/Sgt	HARRISON, D. E., DFM	7	15.02.44
F/O	HARRISON, F. P.	405(Ca)	24.05.43
LAC	HARRISON, J. J.	2763	10.03.45
P/O	HARRISON, J. W.	35	12.11.43
Sgt	HARRISON, K. C.	156	13.05.43
Sgt	HARRISON, R.	156	19.04.43
F/Sgt	HARSLEY, J. H. S.	83	26.11.43
P/O	HART, A. R.	97	31.01.44
Cpl	HART, D. A.	9007 SE	10.04.44
P/O	HART, F. W., DFM	156	05.03.43
F/Sgt	HART, R. E.	405(Ca)	14.05.43
Sgt	HART, W. J.	405(Ca)	21.02.43
Sgt	HARTLEY, J. L.	128	17.09.44
F/Sgt	HARTMAN, C. L.	7	23.11.43
F/Sgt	HARTMAN, L. C.	7	14.01.44
F/Sgt	HARTSHORN, A. H.	7	16.12.43
P/O	HARTSTEIN, P.	7	09.10.43
F/O	HARVEY, A. M.	35	24.05.43
F/Lt	HARVEY, C. V., DFC	156	23.11.43
P/O	HARVEY, D. E. D., DFM	97	10.05.44
Sgt	HARVEY, F. M.	635	08.03.45
Sgt	HARVEY, J. W.	7	23.11.43
P/O	HARWOOD, H., DFM	7	08.03.43
F/Sgt	HASLAM, E.	7	22.03.44
F/Sgt	HASLEGRAVE, M.	156	04.10.43
Sgt	HASTINGS, T. E.	7	13.03.43
W/O	HATCHARD, T. H.	7	04.09.43
Sgt	HATELEY, A. P.	405	24.11.43
F/Sgt	HATHAWAT, S. A.	83	13.05.43
F/Sgt	HATTON, G. W., DFM	635	05.03.45
F/Sgt	HATTON, S.	83	24.08.43
P/O	HATWELL, S. W.	156	27.09.43
F/Sgt	HAUGEN, W. M.	405(Ca)	18.08.43
Capt	HAUSVIK, S. J., DFC	35	28.10.44
Sgt	HAWGOOD, G.	7	23.11.43
W/O	HAWKER, E. J.	582	08.08.44
F/O	HAWKINS, J. D.	405	17.08.43
W/O1	HAWKINS, W., DFC	7	15.02.44
Sgt	HAWLEY, S. B.	405(Ca)	14.05.43
F/O	HAWTHORNE, A. A.	163	22.04.45
F/Sgt	HAY, F.	35	15.04.43
Sgt	HAYES, B. A.	83	26.02.43
F/O	HAYES, E.	405	19.03.45
F/O	HAYES, E. S., DFC	156	17.06.43
P/O	HAYES, J. D.	405	16.06.44
F/O	HAYES, R. G., DFC	105	05.11.43
F/Sgt	HAYHURST, J.	7	25.05.44
S/L	HAYTER, J. E. R., DFC	83	04.10.43
F/Sgt	HAYWARD, A. H.	156	03.01.44
W/O	HAYWOOD, R., CGM	7	14.01.44
F/O	HAZELL, A.	97	06.01.44
F/O	HAZELL, L. A.	35	15.02.44
F/Sgt	HAZELWOOD, K. R.	156	04.04.43
W/O	HAZLEHURST, A.	405(Ca)	31.01.44
Sgt	HEAD, A. E.	156	14.01.44
F/Sgt	HEADLEY, G. M.	156	02.01.44
F/O	HEALAS, H. E. H.	35	12.09.44
F/Lt	HEALEY, F. W., DFC	635	30.08.44
Sgt	HEALEY, H. R.	105	27.04.44
F/Sgt	HEALY, B. J.	35	18.11.43
Sgt	HEAP, D., DFM	156	05.03.43
F/O	HEARN, W. E.	635	06.12.44
F/Sgt	HEATH, A. D.	7	20.05.44
F/O	HEATLEY, W. G.	35	18.11.44
F/O	HEDGES, P. O.	1655 MTU	05.02.44
F/Sgt	HEDGES, R. E.	7	16.12.43
W/O	HEDGES, V. A. M., DFC	156	14.01.44
Sgt	HEDLEY, D. H.	7	11.06.44
F/Sgt	HEDLEY, W. H.	405	20.10.43

Rank	Name	Squadron	Date
F/O	HEELEY, F. R.	83	04.10.43
F/Sgt	HEFFERON, A. V.	83	06.09.43
S/L	HEGMAN, J. A., DFC, DSO	7	15.02.44
F/Lt	HEITMAN, A. W.	128	15.01.45
Sgt	HELLYER, C. C. O.	139(Ja)	20.08.43
S/L	HEMMINGS, G. C.	156	13.08.44
W/O	HEMSWORTH, E. W.	582	06.03.45
Sgt	HENDERSON, C. O.	405(Ca)	11.03.43
Sgt	HENDERSON, G.	97	20.12.43
F/Lt	HENDERSON, G. S.	635	13.08.44
P/O	HENDERSON, J.	83	26.02.43
P/O	HENDERSON, J. H.	83	26.02.43
P/O	HENDERSON, R., DFM	83	22.11.43
F/Sgt	HENDERSON, T. D.	35	20.02.44
P/O	HENDY, G. K.	635	07.01.45
S/L	HENEY, H. W. B., DSO	582	28.05.44
F/O	HENNESSY, J. W.	156	17.12.44
P/O	HENNESSY, T. A.	635	12.09.44
F/O	HENRY, J. W.	156	31.03.44
AC1	HENWOOD, H.	SHQ Gransden Lodge	20.04.44
Sgt	HEPWORTH, H. L.	156	31.03.44
P/O	HERBERT, G. R.	35	12.06.43
F/Sgt	HESLOP, N.	7	15.10.44
P/O	HEWERDINE, J. J.	156	12.07.43
F/Lt	HEWETT, R. J., DFM	7	20.05.44
Sgt	HEWITT, G. W.	7	04.12.43
F/Lt	HEWITT, J. H., DFC	582	15.06.44
P/O	HEWITT, K. W., DFM	582	23.12.44
P/O	HEWITT, S.	582	04.05.44
F/Sgt	HEWITT, W.	635	22.04.44
Sgt	HEWLETT, R. D.	635	25.04.44
W/O	HEWSON, J. F.	627	08.05.44
F/Lt	HEWSON, W. H.	83	27.01.44
F/Sgt	HEXTER, R. W.	405	24.07.42
P/O	HEYS, D. S.	7	31.03.44
F/Lt	HIBBERT, I. A., DFC	635	04.08.44
F/Sgt	HIBBERT, K.	582	24.07.44
F/O	HIBBERT, N. P., DFC	156	29.07.45
W/O	HICKLING, W. L. C., DFC	156	20.12.43
Sgt	HICKS, D. F.	97	31.01.44
F/Lt	HICKS, S. C.	627	06.01.44
F/Sgt	HIE, E.	35	21.01.44
P/O	HIGGINS, N. J.	83	09.05.44
F/Sgt	HIGGS, W. C.	405	24.11.43
F/Sgt	HIGHTON, C.	635	11.04.44
F/Sgt	HILL, E.	97	31.03.44
F/O	HILL, F. D.	582	23.09.44
F/Sgt	HILL, G. J.	97	10.05.44
Sgt	HILL, J. J.	156	24.12.43
F/O	HIL, T. H. A., DFM	156	13.08.44
P/O	HILL, T. W.	35	22.06.44
W/O1	HILL, W., DFM	97	22.11.43
Sgt	HILL, W. J.	156	02.03.44
F/Sgt	HILL, W. R.	635	06.01.45
Sgt	HILLIER, T.	83	26.11.43
W/O2	HILLMAN, G. T.	156	27.03.43
Sgt	HILLMAN, R. V.	156	03.01.44
W/O2	HILLS, W. J.	7	26.05.43
F/O	HILLS, W. J.	97	04.07.43
Sgt	HILTON, F.	7	21.01.44
F/Lt	HILTON, F., DFC	7	25.06.43
W/C	HILTON, R., DSO, DFC *	83	23.11.43
F/Sgt	HINDE, R.	97	22.03.44
F/Sgt	HINKS, B. C.	156	02.01.44
F/O	HINSCLIFFE, A., DFC	405	07.05.44
F/Sgt	HIRST, T. J.	7	31.03.44
P/O	HITCHEN, J. T.	83	03.01.44
F/Sgt	HOBBS, E. J.	97	22.12.44
F/Sgt	HOBBS, V. G.	582	23.12.44
P/O	HODGE, F. W.	405	22.06.43
Sgt	HODGE, R. W.	35	30.05.43
Sgt	HODGES, C. W.	156	27.09.43
Sgt	HODGES, R. H.	156	23.11.43
F/O	HODGSON, K.	582	29.10.44
P/O	HODGSON, W.	97	14.01.44
F/Lt	HODGSON, W. McK., DFC, AFM	109	27.12.44
P/O	HOGAN, L., DFM	105	29.09.43
Sgt	HOGG, J.	35	26.05.43
P/O	HOGG, R. M., DFM	97	04.10.43
F/Lt	HOGG, T. L., DFC	627	07.05.44
F/O	HOLBROOK, F., DFC	156	15.07.44
F/Lt	HOLBROW, S. C.	1655 MTU	21.05.44
P/O	HOLDEN, W.	7	05.05.43
F/Sgt	HOLDER, C. M.	405	04.12.43
F/Sgt	HOLDERNESS, J. A.	156	04.04.43
Sgt	HOLDING, D. C. H.	97	09.07.43
Sgt	HOLFORD, W. L.	83	27.04.44
P/O	HOLLAND, F.	405	11.03.43
P/O	HOLLAND, G. C.	405	04.12.43
P/O	HOLLAND, L. G., DFM	35	06.03.45
P/O	HOLLAND, R. S.	635	12.09.44
F/Sgt	HOLLEDGE, F. R.	635	13.08.44
F/Sgt	HOLLIDAY, D. A.	405	15.03.45
Sgt	HOLLIDAY, M. K.	405	16.06.43
Sgt	HOLLIDGE, H. K.	156	28.08.43
Sgt	HOLLINGSWORTH, C. H.	7	23.11.43
F/Sgt	HOLLIS, W. J.	156	25.02.44
P/O	HOLMAN, H.	156	28.07.43
F/Sgt	HOLMES, F. N.	582	04.05.44
Sgt	HOLMES, J.	405	28.05.43
F/Sgt	HOLMES, R.	635	22.04.44
Sgt	HOLMES, W. H.	7	14.01.44
W/O	HOLMWOOD, J. N.	635	25.03.44
Sgt	HOLT, L.	35	04.12.43
Sgt	HOMER, T. W. G.	156	30.12.44
F/O	HOMERSHAM, G. J.	97 Straits Settlement	30.07.43
F/O	HONE, E., DFC	156	14.01.44
Sgt	HONE, S. F.	97	20.10.43
F/O	HOOD, R. T., DFM	156	03.09.43
Sgt	HOOK, J. B. J.	7	05.05.43
P/O	HOOKWAY, A. F.	7	22.05.44
W/C	HOOKWAY, S. G., DFC	156	05.03.43
Sgt	HOOS, R.	35	30.05.43
P/O	HOOSON, J., DFM	35	29.12.43
Sgt	HOPCRAFT, E.	156	20.02.44
Sgt	HOPE, C. L.	97	17.12.43
F/Lt	HOPE, R. B., DFC	83	03.04.43
P/O	HOPE, T. W.	635	12.06.44
Sgt	HOPKINSON, S.	156	24.02.44
S/L	HOPTON, C. G., DFC	156	08.06.44
F/O	HORNBY, N. H.	692	12.10.44
Sgt	HORNE, L. A.	97	02.03.43
F/O	HORNE, W. J., DFC	105	01.05.43
F/Lt	HORNER, C. F., DFC	156	02.01.44
F/Sgt	HORNER, M. D.	97	29.06.43
F/O	HORSBURGH, G., DFM	7	08.08.44
F/Sgt	HORTON, G. J. T.	83	04.10.43
F/Sgt	HORTON, T.	7	23.04.44
F/Lt	HOSKING, L. D.	35	12.11.43
Sgt	HOSSACK, C. McK..	156	25.02.44
F/Lt	HOUGH, J., DFC	7	18.11.43
F/O	HOUGHTON, W.	163	11.04.45
Sgt	HOULDING, E. C.	405	14.01.44
F/Sgt	HOULDSWORTH, H. E., DFM	83	22.06.44
F/Sgt	HOUSTON, J. Y.	405	28.05.43
1/Lt	HOVERSTAD, G.	35	02.12.43
F/Lt	HOWARD, J. P. O., DFC	139	02.01.45
F/O	HOWDEN, A. MacK.	139	07.04.44
F/Sgt	HOWE, E. A.	7	20.02.44
Sgt	HOWE, H. W. F.	35	12.09.44
F/O	HOWE, S. G., DFC	35	12.06.43
F/Sgt	HOWELL, E. L. C.	635	16.06.45

Rank	Name	Squadron	Date	Rank	Name	Squadron	Date
Sgt	HOWELL, N. R.	7	05.01.45	F/O	JACKSON, W. W.	139	14.10.44
F/O	HOWELLS, G. E. W.	97	30.07.44	F/O	JACKSON-BAKER, T. W.	7	16.12.43
Sgt	HOWES, C.	83	20.02.44	F/Sgt	JACOBS, E. R.	83	20.01.44
F/Sgt	HOWES, H. G.	635	31.03.44	S/L	JAGGER, J. J., DFC	35	21.01.44
LAC	HOWLETT, O. S.	7	22.11.42	F/O	JAMES, B. A.	83	29.01.44
P/O	HOWSAM, H. E.	83	13.06.43	F/Sgt	JAMES, D. S.	35	06.01.44
Sgt	HOYLE, J. W.	635	25.04.44	Sgt	JAMES, L. C.	139(Ja)	20.10.43
Sgt	HOYLE, T.	156	03.09.43	Sgt	JAMES, T. S.	156	29.07.43
F/Sgt	HUBBARD, E. G.	97	17.12.43	F/O	JAMES, W. J.	83	02.01.44
W/O2	HUCKER, J. A. N.	405	09.10.43	F/O	JAMIESON, J.	156	17.04.45
Sgt	HUDSON, F. W.	692	26.08.44	F/O	JARDINE, W. B.	97	23.05.44
F/O	HUDSON, G. D., AFC	571	27.03.45	F/lt	JARVIE, R. B.	405	14.01.44
F/O	HUDSON, J. M.,	156	26.07.43	Sgt	JARVIS, F. J.	35	30.05.43
F/Sgt	HUDSON, R. J.	156	02.01.44	F/O	JARVIS, G. F.	139(Ja)	27.05.44
P/O	HUDSON, R. J.	156	24.06.43	F/O	JELLEY, C. F., DFC	635	06.01.45
F/Sgt	HUDSON, W. P., DFM	7	08.03.43	W/O	JENKINS, B. D.	7	05.01.45
P/O	HUFF, W. D.	405	16.06.44	F/O	JENKINS, M.	97	22.03.44
F/Sgt	HUGHES, C. D.	35	30.07.43	F/Sgt	JENKINS, R. M.	35	04.02.45
F/Sgt	HUGHES, F. A.	97	18.10.43	Sgt	JENKINS, W.	7	31.03.44
Sgt	HUGHES, H. W.	156	20.02.44	W/O	JENNINGS, P. J.	156	09.10.43
F/Sgt	HUGHES, L. F.	97	04.05.44	Sgt	JENNINGS, R. V.	7	15.04.43
F/O	HUGHES, P. A., DFM	582	12.12.44	F/Sgt	JENNINGS, R. W.	405(Ca)	24.05.43
Sgt	HUGHES, S. F.,	35	14.07.43	W/O2	JEPSON, A. A.	635	22.05.44
Sgt	HUGHES, W.	35PFF	29.06.43	F/Sgt	JERVIS, F. P., DFM	NTU	25.01.44
P/O	HUME, G. W.	692	13.05.44			Upwood	
F/Sgt	HUMPHREY, A. F.	7	25.05.44	Lt	JESPERSEN, F. V.	97	06.06.44
F/O	HUMPHREYS, D. G. W.	7	24.03.44	Sgt	JOEL, L. H.	156	31.03.45
F/Sgt	HUMPHREYS, H., DFM	7	12.06.43	F/O	JOHN, W. F., DFC	1409 Flt	14.11.43
AC2	HUMPHRIES, S. A.	Bourn	30.09.43	Capt	JOHNSEN, F.	156	31.03.44
Sgt	HUNT, G. J.	97	31.01.43	P/O	JOHNSON, A. A., DFM	97	18.11.43
Sgt	HUNT, K.	156	03.01.44	P/O	JOHNSON, A. D.	7	20.02.44
F/Lt	HUNT, R. B.	7	20.05.44	F/Lt	JOHNSON, A. E.	35	04.02.45
Sgt	HUNT, T. W.	7	05.05.43	Sgt	JOHNSON, C.	35	20.10.44
F/Lt	HUNT, W. J.	97	23.06.44	F/Lt	JOHNSON, D., DFC	582	06.06.44
F/Sgt	HUNTER, A. I. G.	635	10.04.44	Sgt	JOHNSON, F.	83	05.05.43
Sgt	HUNTER, E. W.	156	13.08.44	Sgt	JOHNSON, G.	156	23.11.43
P/O	HUNTER, M. R.	35	22.03.44	P/O	JOHNSON, G. A., DFM	97	02.01.44
F/Sgt	HUNTER, R. J.	83	03.01.44	F/Sgt	JOHNSON, G. C., DFM	156	14.01.44
F/Sgt	HURLEY, I. E.	35	25.07.44	F/O	JOHNSON, H. O., DFM	83	11.05.44
Sgt	HURSON, J. M.	83	23.06.43	Sgt	JOHNSON, J. E.,	7	28.04.44
Sgt	HURST, J.	7	16.12.43	F/O	JOHNSON, J. J. R.	405	21.07.44
P/O	HURST, J. R.	156	07.09.43	Sgt	JOHNSON, J. R.	35	24.05.43
Sgt	HUTCHINSON, W.	405(Ca)	03.08.43	Sgt	JOHNSON, K. L.	156	14.01.44
W/O	HUTSON, L. J.	156	03.02.45	F/Sgt	JOHNSON, L. J.	156	30.07.43
F/O	HUTTLESTONE, G. H.	7	20.03.45	P/O	JOHNSON, L. J.	156	02.12.43
Sgt	HUTTON, R.	7	22.09.43	Sgt	JOHNSON, M. A.	97	04.05.44
F/O	HUTTON, W. K.	83	21.01.44	F/O	JOHNSON, N. C.	83	30.03.43
F/Lt	HYDE, H. R.	83	29.01.44	Sgt	JOHNSON, W. H.	156	25.02.44
F/Lt	HYDE, L. V., DFC	97	31.03.44	F/Sgt	JOHNSTON, A. C.	156	13.05.43
F/O	HYNES, K. F.	109	19.10.44	P/O	JOHNSTON, D. C.	7	20.01.44
F/Sgt	IBALL, W. H.	635	16.06.44	F/Sgt	JOHNSTON, G. A.	7	15.03.44
F/O	ILLIUS, A. B. W.	156	24.08.43	Sgt	JOHNSTON, H. C.	7	05.01.45
F/Lt	INCE, C. D., DFC*	7	22.06.43	P/O	JOHNSTON, N.	405	03.06.44
Sgt	INGHAM, F. W.	7	23.04.44	S/L	JOHNSTON, P., DFC	35	30.05.43
F/Sgt	INGHAM, J. R.	582	04.05.44	Sgt	JOHNSTONE, H.	NTU	10.04.44
F/Sgt	INGLES, A. N.	156	25.02.44			Warboys	
P/O	INGLIS, R. E.	156	02.12.43	P/O	JOLLEY, H. F.	156	13.05.43
S/L	INGRAM, G. F. H., DFC	35	24.06.44	W/O	JOLLEY, K. A., DFC	635	31.03.44
F/O	INGREY, P. A.	7	08.08.44	F/Sgt	JOLLIFFE, C. B., DFM	7	20.10.43
Sgt	INNES, A.	97	02.03.43	Sgt	JOLLY, E. N.	405(Ca)	17.08.44
F/Lt	INNES, H. G., DFC	156	27.09.43	W/O	JOLLY, H. A. W., DFM	NTU	25.01.44
Sgt	INNES, R. McK.	9	18.11.43			Upwood	
P/O	IRELAND, N. A.	635	06.07.44	Sgt	JOLLY, J.	35	04.07.43
F/Sgt	IRVINE, D. R.	97	17.12.43	F/Lt	JOLLY, K. F.	1655 MTU	07.01.44
F/Lt	IRWIN, J. G., DFC	635	04.08.44	Sgt	JONES, A.	97	04.07.43
F/Lt	IRWIN, W. A., DFC	7	24.06.44	Sgt	JONES, C. R. W.	97	04.12.43
F/O	ISFELD, I. A.,	139	31.08.43	Sgt	JONES, D.	7	06.09.44
F/Sgt	JACKETT, W. G., DFM	35	11.08.43	P/O	JONES, D. G.	635	19.08.44
F/O	JACKSON, A. H.	7	09.04.43	Sgt	JONES, D. J.	35	22.06.43
Sgt	JACKSON, A. J.	156	08.04.43	Sgt	JONES, D. S.	35	25.07.44
F/O	JACKSON, F. R., DFM	109	22.10.43	F/Lt	JONES, F. C., DFC	7	15.02.44
P/O	JACKSON, H. N., DFC	156	15.02.44	W/O	JONES, F. P.	7	14.01.44
F/Sgt	JACKSON, L., DFM	35	28.10.44	P/O	JONES, G.	582	25.05.44

Rank	Name	Squadron	Date
Sgt	JONES, H.	156	25.06.43
LAC	JONES, H. B.	156	09.09.44
Sgt	JONES, H. W.	156	25.02.44
F/Lt	JONES, I. A.	1655 MTU	30.08.44
F/Sgt	JONES, J. A.	83	23.05.44
F/Sgt	JONES, J. E., DFM	35	02.04.44
F/Lt	JONES, L. C., DFC	97	10.05.44
P/O	JONES, L. G.	97	29.01.44
Sgt	JONES, L. J.	156	30.07.43
F/O	JONES, P. C.	15	08.05.44
P/O	JONES, R. B.	405	16.03.45
F/Sgt	JONES, R. J.	405	07.04.43
F/O	JONES, R. M.	1655 MTU	24.11.44
F/Lt	JONES, R. V.	35	20.02.44
F/Lt	JONES, W. A., DFC	109	06.03.45
Sgt	JONES, W. J.	97	31.01.44
P/O	JORDAN, J. W.	635	06.12.44
W/O2	JORDAN, W. F.	405(Ca)	05.04.43
Sgt	JOSLYN, K. S.	405	14.01.44
P/O	KAESMODEL, E. R.	405	29.12.44
Sgt	KARSMAN, R.	156	31.03.44
F/O	KAUCHARIK, J. A.	405	14.02.45
AC2	KAVANAGH, A. R.	Upwood	25.01.44
W/O2	KAVANAUGH, J. G. S.	405	23.11.43
P/O	KAVIZE, J. F.	156	29.01.45
S/L	KAY, D. H. S., DFC	109	19.10.44
P/O	KAY, S.	405	24.02.44
F/Lt	KAYLL, A. G. R.	156	27.04.44
F/O	KEARNEY, R.	156	24.03.44
F/Sgt	KEATING, R.	156	22.05.44
F/Sgt	KEAY, J. S.	83	03.04.43
F/O	KEENAN, J. I. J.	405	16.06.44
Sgt	KEETCH, R. A. W.	156	14.01.44
P/O	KELLEY, D. A.	405	03.06.44
F/Sgt	KELLEY, R. R.	156	02.03.44
Sgt	KELLY, D.	35	02.03.43
W/O	KELLY, D. R., DFM	83	22.06.44
P/O	KELLY, I. W.	156	31.03.45
F/Sgt	KELLY, T.	635	08.03.45
Sgt	KEMP, A.	97	29.03.43
W/O	KEMP, J. C.	35	09.05.44
F/Lt	KEMP, K. D.	405	17.08.44
Sgt	KEMPSON, E	7	09.10.43
Sgt	KENDALL, H. H.	97	25.02.44
F/Sgt	KENDRICK, A. C.	156	31.03.44
Sgt	KENNEDY, J. G.	35	30.05.43
F/Lt	KENNEDY, T. W.	156	01.06.44
F/Lt	KENNY, J. H., DFC	139(Ja)	07.08.44
F/O	KENT, D. H.	35	21.01.44
F/Sgt	KENT, H. M.	97	10.05.44
P/O	KENYON, A. T.	35	24.12.44
Sgt	KENYON, E.	156	01.03.44
F/Sgt	KERCKHOVE, R. A.	97	25.06.43
F/Sgt	KERR, P. G. L.	97	06.01.44
F/O	KERR, W. T.	109	21.12.44
Sgt	KERRIGAN, A. B.	156	17.06.43
W/O2	KETTLEY, C. J. V.	405(Ca)	25.07.43
F/Lt	KEYS, C. C., DFC	139	05.05.44
F/Lt	KIDD, C. A.	156	28.04.44
F/Sgt	KIDD, D. W.	PFF, NTU Warboys	11.03.45
F/O	KIDD, L.	7	08.08.44
F/Lt	KIDDER, G. A.	156	25.03.44
F/Sgt	KIELY, E. J.	35	20.10.44
F/Sgt	KIFF, A. E. S.	405(Ca)	09.02.45
F/Sgt	KIFT, R. S.	35	22.10.43
Sgt	KILCOYNE, T.	149	07.08.44
F/O	KILLE, R. H.	35	05.07.44
Sgt	KILLEN, J.	97	17.12.43
Sgt	KILLICK, D. E.	35	26.07.43
Sgt	KILVINGTON, J.	7	09.03.43
F/O	KIMMEL, S. G.	105	26.02.43
Sgt	KING, A. L.,	83	06.09.43
Sgt	KING, C. R.	156	03.01.44
Sgt	KING, C. V.	97	09.07.43
F/Sgt	KING, F. P.	156	23.11.43
Sgt	KING, H.	405(Ca)	10.03.43
F/O	KING, K. H., DFC	128	31.10.44
F/Lt	KING, L. F. D.	105	19.03.45
P/O	KING, L. R., DFM	405	24.08.43
F/Sgt	KING, M. H.	83	26.11.43
F/Sgt	KING, P. C.	156	14.01.44
W/O2	KINGHORN, H. H.	156	14.01.44
F/O	KINMAN, J.	582	12.12.44
W/O2	KINNEY, I. J.	635	05.04.45
W/O	KINSEY, W. E.	635	26.08.44
F/Sgt	KINSEY, W. N.	7	24.11.43
Sgt	KIRKCALDY, A.	405	19.03.45
F/O	KIRKLAND, H. N.	105	26.02.43
P/O	KIRKPATRICK, W. W.	405	11.03.43
F/O	KIRKWOOD, J., DFC	97	17.12.43
F/O	KITCHEN, A. E., DFC	109	28.11.44
W/O	KITTO, H., DFM	582	06.06.44
Sgt	KLEINHORN, M.	83	17.04.43
F/O	KNIGHT, B. E.	571	17.05.44
F/Sgt	KNIGHT, J.	97	22.06.44
F/Sgt	KNIGHT, K.	35	20.02.44
Sgt	KNIGHT, S. J.	35	11.04.43
F/Lt	KNIGHTS, J. K., DFC	405	14.02.45
F/Lt	KNOBLOCH, D. L.	35	27.08.44
P/O	KNOESEN, B. G.	97	30.07.43
W/O	KNOX, C. W., DFC	156	20.12.43
F/Lt	KNUPP, G. W.	405	09.05.44
Sgt	KOFOED, P. J. J.	7	20.05.44
F/Sgt	KRAEMER, J. R.	97	24.08.43
F/Sgt	KROHN, H. J.	35	22.06.43
F/Sgt	KRULICKI, L. J.	7	21.04.43
F/Sgt	KUCINSKY, J. W.	405(Ca)	25.06.43
P/O	KYLE, T. E. B.	7	24.03.44
F/O	LABARGE, B. H.	405	11.03.43
Sgt	LACINA, E. G.	405(Ca)	12.03.43
F/Lt	LAGESSE, M. J. M., DFC	128	10.01.45
Sgt	LAGNA, N.	7	26.05.43
F/Lt	LAING, L. N.	405	19.03.45
F/O	LAISHLEY, C. E.	405	26.09.44
P/O	LAMB, F. M.	97	04.07.43
Sgt	LAMB, L. E.	7	23.04.44
Sgt	LAMB, M. G.	582	16.09.44
F/Lt	LAMB, R. D.	582	28.05.44
S/L	LAMBERT, G. F., DFC	35	05.07.44
F/Sgt	LAMBERT, J.	7	22.03.44
F/O	LAMBERT, W. T., DFM	109	23.12.44
W/O	LAMONBY, J.	7	20.05.44
Sgt	LAMPEN, L. C.	105	11.04.43
F/O	LAMPIN, F. E.	156	14.01.44
Sgt	LANCASTER, E.	635	26.08.44
Sgt	LANE, E. A.	405	14.01.44
Sgt	LANE, R. M.	97	31.03.44
P/O	LANGFORD, D., DFC	156	24.06.44
P/O	LANGFORD, V. A. R.	83	20.02.44
F/O	LANGHAM, D. F., DFC	7	15.02.44
F/O	LANGWORTHY, W. D., DFC	1655 MTU	07.01.44
F/Sgt	LAPTHORNE, L. N.	156	03.01.44
W/O	LARKINS, A. R. P.	156	08.06.44
P/O	LARSON, R. H.	405	17.11.43
F/Sgt	LASCELLES, J. H., DFM	156	03.02.45
F/Sgt	LAURIE, L. G.	97	29.01.44
Sgt	LAVER, L. N. J.	97	14.01.44
F/O	LAVERICK, W., DFM	35	29.12.43
F/O	LAW, A. C.	405	10.07.43
F/O	LAW, N. C.	97	30.01.44
F/O	LAW, R. G.	7	08.08.44
F/Sgt	LAWLEY, R.	635	31.03.44
W/O	LAWRENCE, C. H., DFM	156	14.01.44
F/Sgt	LAWRENCE, A. G.	7	20.05.44

Rank	Name	Squadron	Date	Rank	Name	Squadron	Date
W/O2	LAWRENCE, A. K.	405	14.01.44	F/Lt	LIVELY, E.	7	24.06.44
Sgt	LAWRENCE, R. A.	97	17.12.43	P/O	LIVINGSTON, R. A., DFC	405	22.06.43
F/O	LAWRENCE, W. J.	405	23.11.43	F/Sgt	LLOYD, W. D. L.	83	20.02.44
F/Lt	LAWSON, C. D.	405	16.06.43	S/L	LOBB, H. C., DFC	635	26.08.44
F/O	LAWSON, G. S.	35	23.12.44	Sgt	LOBB, R.	156	28.07.43
W/C	LAWSON, K. J., DSO, DFC	405	02.01.45	F/Sgt	LOCK, L. G. K.	97	04.12.43
F/Sgt	LAWSON, R.	7	04.09.43	W/C	LOCKHART, W. G.,	7	28.04.44
F/O	LAWTON, E. E.	97	29.06.43		DSO, DFC		
F/Sgt	LAY, K. L. W.	156	11.06.43	F/O	LOCKWOOD, F. J., DFC	156	15.07.44
F/Lt	LAYLEY, R. G.	7	14.01.44	F/O	LOCKYER, C. C.	83	29.01.44
P/O	LAYTON-SMITH, M. S.	7	19.08.44	F/Lt	LODER, G. B., DFC	156	20.12.43
Sgt	LEADER, J. L.	156	27.07.43	F/O	LOFTUS, W. T., DFC	83	09.05.44
F/O	LEADER, R. A.	635	11.04.44	Sgt	LOGAN, J. A.	83	11.04.44
F/Sgt	LEAHY, A. F. G.	7	22.03.44	P/O	LOGAN, R. H.	109	29.05.43
P/O	LEATHERDALE, C. G.	156	31.03.44	F/Lt	LONG, R. W., DFC	405	16.09.44
S/L	LEATHERLAND, D.	97	21.04.44	P/O	LONG, S. H.	405	28.09.43
F/Sgt	LEAVESLEY, W. D.	405	16.09.44	F/Sgt	LONG-HARTLEY, P.	582	16.06.44
F/Sgt	LEBIHAN, G. E. J.	405	28.05.43	W/C	LONGFIELD, G. P.	105	26.02.43
Sgt	LECOMBER, J. E.	83	13.05.43	F/O	LONGLAND, G. A.	635	12.12.44
Sgt	LEDGER, R. V.	35	02.03.43	F/Sgt	LONSDALE, G. H.	83	08.02.45
F/O	LEE, E. V.	156	27.07.43	F/O	LOPEZ, R. H.	97	24.10.44
W/O1	LEE, J. L.	35	30.05.43	W/O	LORD, J.	405	22.04.45
P/O	LEE, R. J.	156	05.05.43	P/O	LORD, M.	7	27.03.43
Sgt	LEE, W.	635	22.04.44	W/O	LORD, R. T.	635	10.04.44
F/Sgt	LEEDER, V. V. R.	635	04.08.44	Sgt	LOVEGROVE, R. G.	582	04.05.44
Sgt	LEES, D. M.	83	11.04.44	Sgt	LOVELL, B. D. S.	7	22.10.43
Sgt	LEES, J.	7	21.04.43	P/O	LOVELL, D. G.	83	12.03.43
F/Lt	LEFROY, H. K., DFC	405	23.11.43	P/O	LOVELOCK, J. H.	405	20.10.43
F/O	LEGGE, K. C. S.	571	06.02.45	W/O	LOVIS, J. A. C., DFC	156	22.11.43
LAC	LEIGH, J.	Wyton	30.06.45	F/Sgt	LOWE, D. S.	156	17.12.44
Sgt	LEIGH, J. R.	83	05.05.43	W/O	LOWE, R.	635	06.07.44
F/O	LEIGH, R. E.	109	10.02.44	F/O	LOWTHER, J. C.	405	28.09.43
Sgt	LEISHMAN, J. J.	635	12.06.44	Sgt	LUCAS, D. G. J.	7	21.01.44
F/O	LEITCH, J. W., DFC	7	20.10.43	F/O	LUCKETT, B. M.	97	23.03.44
F/O	LEITHEAD, J. C.	692	18.03.44	Sgt	LUDGATE, J. O.	15	28.08.42
P/O	LEMIEUX, J. H. T. J.	405	22.06.43	F/O	LUFF, E.	156	05.03.43
P/O	LENNOX, J. W.	405	05.05.43	F/O	LUKER, H. W.	83	18.06.43
W/O	LEO, A. J. O.	35	20.08.44	Sgt	LUMLEY, J. G.	156	17.06.43
P/O	LEONARD, A. M.	7	26.11.43	F/Sgt	LUMSDEN, W., DFM	156	02.01.44
Sgt	LEONARD, J.	196	11.11.44	F/O	LUND, E. T.	7	20.05.44
P/O	LEONARD, R. H.	156	11.09.44	F/Sgt	LUNN, D.	692	01.01.45
W/O2	LEONE, N.	405	14.01.44	F/O	LUTHER, C. P.	7	16.12.43
F/Sgt	LEVEY, J.	635	08.03.45	P/O	LUTON, L. R. S., DFC	7	11.03.43
F/O	LEVIN, M. H. O., DFC	139(Ja)	07.08.44	F/Lt	LUTZ, A. M., DFC	156	07.09.43
F/O	LEWIS, A.	635	31.03.45	F/Lt	LUXFORD, F. E.	405(Ca)	03.04.43
Sgt	LEWIS, B. E.	97	29.06.43	F/Sgt	LUXTON, D. N.	7	25.03.44
F/O	LEWIS, F. E.	7	04.09.43	Sgt	LYALL, G.	582	23.04.44
F/O	LEWIS, G. W.	139	11.05.44	P/O	LYFORD, P. R., DFC	156	02.01.44
Sgt	LEWIS, H.	156	26.07.43	F/Sgt	LYNCH, A., DFM	83	11.03.43
Sgt	LEWIS, H. J.	97	08.10.43	P/O	LYNN, T., DFC, DFM	109	25.04.45
F/O	LEWIS, J. W.	582	15.03.45	F/Lt	LYON, C. A.	635	31.03.44
Sgt	LEWIS, L. A.	35	09.05.44	W/O	LYONS, J.	156	17.12.44
F/Sgt	LEWIS, R. C. L.	582	29.07.44	W/O	LYTHGOE, G. E.	582	08.09.44
F/Sgt	LEWIS, S. J. R.	635	11.04.44	Sgt	McADAM, J. P.	83	22.11.43
F/Sgt	LEWIS, V. C., DFM	83	24.08.43	F/Sgt	McALLISTER, J.	83	19.02.43
F/Sgt	LIDDLE, S. M.	7	29.01.44	Sgt	McALLISTER, J.	97	21.04.44
Sgt	LIDDLE, T. B.	7	31.03.44	P/O	McALPINE, K. G.	35	20.02.44
Sgt	LIDSTER, E.	83	22.06.43	W/O2	McALPINE, W. J.	405(Ca)	03.04.43
F/Sgt	LIGHTFOOT-SHANDLEY, E. L'E.	83	03.04.43	P/O	MacARTHUR, G. R.	582	20.07.44
				W/O1	McARTHUR, E. M., DFM	405	01.09.43
W/O1	LINDSAY, B. E.	7	04.09.43	W/O2	McARTHUR, L. N.	83	03.04.44
Sgt	LINDSAY, W.	635	31.03.44	W/O2	McAULAY, N. T.	35	22.06.43
Sgt	LINEHAM, W. A.	156	29.09.43	F/O	McCABE, T. M.	156	31.03.45
F/O	LINTON, A., DFC	35	20.10.44	Sgt	McCABREY, W.	405	28.01.45
Sgt	LISSNER, P. R.	35	04.07.43	Sgt	McCAFFERY, J. T. F.	156	22.05.44
Sgt	LISTER, G. P.	105	27.05.43	F/Sgt	McCALLUM, M. W.	635	12.12.44
F/Sgt	LISTER, H. A.	156	28.05.43	F/O	McCARTHY, A. G.	405(Ca)	21.07.44
W/O	LITTLE, A.	7	20.05.44	P/O	McCARTHY, C. A.	7	24.06.44
Sgt	LITTLE, D. H. W.	97	26.11.43	F/Lt	McCARTHY, P. G., DFC	7	19.08.44
F/O	LITTLE, G. J.	97	16.12.43	S/L	McCARTHY, R. W.	7	15.04.43
Sgt	LITTLE, J.	97	02.03.43	P/O	McCARTNEY, J.	83	28.02.43
W/O	LITTLE, J. F.	139	30.08.43	Sgt	McCASH, T. K.	83	29.01.44
F/Lt	LITTLE, S. W., DFC	582	25.05.44	Sgt	McCLEMENTS, H.	7	20.03.45

137

Rank	Name	Squadron	Date
F/Sgt	McCLEMONT. P. D.	166	08.10.45
S/L	McCLURE, D. A. J., DFC	83	12.03.43
Sgt	McCONNELL. S.	156	31.03.44
F/O	McCONNELL-JONES, A. C. H.	1655 MTU	22.07.44
F/O	McCORMICK, G. W.	105	27.02.43
F/Sgt	McCORMICK. W. H.	35	20.02.44
F/O	McCRACKEN. A. P.	405	25.07.43
P/O	McCREA. J. R.	405	23.04.44
P/O	McCREA. L. A.	405	03.06.44
W/O2	McCUBBIN. F. C.	35	02.12.43
F/Sgt	McCULLAGH. R. D.	83	30.03.43
F/Sgt	McCULLOCH. W.	35	07.03.44
F/Lt	MacDONALD. B. A.	1655 MU	11.08.43
F/O	MacDONALD. I. R.	7	16.12.43
P/O	MacDONALD. M., DFC	83	06.08.44
F/Sgt	MacDONALD. R. G.	405(Ca)	12.03.43
F/O	MacDONALD. R. H.	156	23.11.43
F/O	MacDONALD. W. H.	7	20.05.44
Sgt	McDONALD. D.	97	30.07.43
F/Lt	McDONALD. J. N., DFM	136	13.08.44
F/Lt	McDONALD. S. C.	405	04.05.44
P/O	MacDONNELL. J. H. D.	7	24.03.44
Sgt	McDONNELL. D.	156	30.01.44
Cpl	McDOWELL. M. W.	SHQ Wyton	26.11.43
F/O	McEGAN, E. F.	97	22.11.43
Sgt	McEWAN. D.	83	03.04.43
F/Lt	McFADDEN, A. S.	97	31.03.44
P/O	MacFARLANE, D. J.	405	29.12.44
Sgt	MacFARLANE, J.	83	12.03.43
F/Sgt	McGARVA, J. G.	83	27.04.44
P/O	McGEE, J	35	23.12.44
P/O	McGEEHAN, P. J. D., DFM	139	16.03.43
F/O	McGILL, J. A. D.	97	10.06.44
W/O	McGINLAY, J.	7	06.01.44
Sgt	McGINN, J. P.	582	23.04.44
F/Lt	McGLASHAN, A. N.	156	03.01.44
Sgt	McGLORY, S.	405(Ca)	24.05.43
Sgt	McGLYNN, A. B.	692	31.10.44
F/O	McGOWAN, T. C.	692	27.05.44
F/Sgt	McGRATH, T. W. N.	97	28.08.43
F/Lt	McGREAL, T., DFC	109	25.04.45
F/O	MacGREGOR, D. A.	35	22.01.44
W/O	McGREVY, D., DFM	7	08.08.44
W/O	McHAFFIE. D.	7	22.03.44
F/Lt	McHARDY, G. L. S., DFC	105	28.01.45
F/Sgt	McHUGH, E. T.	156	04.04.43
P/O	McINTOSH, W. P. MacD., DFM	35	24.08.43
F/O	McINTYRE, H. B.	405	09.02.45
F/O	McINTYRE, H. S.	405	18.08.43
F/O	McINTYRE, J. A.	405	04.05.44
F/O	McINTYRE, N. G.	97	16.12.43
LAC	McIVER, F. C.	2746 RAF Regt	18.07.44
F/Lt	McIVER, M., DFC	1655 CU	13.05.44
S/L	MACK, M. C. X., DFC	35	24.08.43
F/O	MacKAY, J. G.	83	17.06.43
F/O	McKAY, D. G.	405	16.01.45
W/O2	McKAY, G. C.	405(Ca)	17.08.43
W/O2	McKAY, H. R.	7	20.02.44
P/O	McKENDRY, D. C. J.	83	03.06.44
F/O	McKENNA, C. D.	109	08.04.43
P/O	McKENNA, G. C.	156	03.02.45
Sgt	McKENNA, J. H.	83	28.02.43
W/O	McKENNA, M. G.	156	28.04.45
Sgt	MacKENZIE, A.	156	27.03.43
P/O	MacKENZIE, C. D.	635	06.01.45
Sgt	MacKENZIE, D. B. G.	156	03.01.44
S/L	MacKENZIE, D. F., DFC	97	17.12.43
F/O	MacKENZIE, D. G.	1655 MTU	24.11.44
P/O	MacKENZIE, E. S.	156	13.05.43
Sgt	MacKENZIE, M. W.	405(Ca)	11.03.43
W/O2	McKENZIE, J. A. W.	35	04.12.43
Cpl	McKENZIE, J. W.	RAF Graveley	25.07.43
Sgt	McKERLAY, R.	83	29.01.44
Sgt	McKERRELL, R.	7	27.03.43
F/Lt	MACKIE, S. C. R.	35	20.12.43
Sgt	McKIERNAN, S. C.	35	03.08.43
F/Sgt	MACKINLEY, W. B.	156	04.10.43
S/L	McKINNA, R. A., DFC*	97	23.09.43
S/L	MACKINTOSH, J. C.	156	17.06.43
F/Lt	MacLACHLAN, A. R. A., DFC	156	07.09.43
P/O	McLACHLAN, J. T. D., DFC	7	15.02.44
Sgt	McLAREN, A. S.	35	23.05.44
P/O	McLAREN, W. G. K., DFC	7	15.02.44
F/Lt	MacLEAN, M. H. M., DFC	608	05.03.45
P/O	McLEAN, J.	608	06.11.44
Sgt	McLEAN, R. V.	405(Ca)	21.02.43
P/O	McLEISH, J. C., DFC	97	15.03.44
W/O2	McLELLAN, C. C.	405(Ca)	02.08.43
F/O	McLELLAN, N. M.	83	17.04.43
F/O	McLENNAN, B. A.	405	17.12.43
Sgt	MacLEOD, A. C.	35	22.06.43
F/Sgt	McMILLAN, R. R.	7	16.12.43
S/L	McMILLAN, J. P.	97	25.06.43
P/O	McNABNEY, S.	7	08.08.44
F/O	McNALLY, F. H. T.	35	27.08.44
Sgt	MacNAMARA, N.	582	17.01.45
P/O	McNICHOL, G. A.	83	17.04.43
P/O	McNULTY, N. M.	128	28.02.45
F/Lt	MACONACHIE, J. R. A.	128	28.02.45
W/O	MacPHEE, I. M.	629	22.03.45
F/Lt	MacPHERSON, A. N., DFM	83	24.08.43
F/O	MacPHERSON, B. E. C.	7	09.10.43
F/Sgt	MacPHERSON, E. D., DFM	83	20.01.44
F/Lt	MacQUEEN, A. F., DFC	83	12.03.43
Sgt	McQUEEN, H. J.	405(Ca)	03.04.43
F/O	McRAE, R. C.	405(Ca)	24.03.43
F/Lt	McSORLEY, B. F., DFC	MTU Upwood	25.01.44
F/Lt	McSWEENEY, C. B. T., DFC	156	04.10.43
Sgt	McWILLIAMS, F.	156	24.03.45
F/Lt	MADDOCKS, J.	571	14.01.45
Sgt	MADDOCKS, J. E.	83OTU	12.10.44
Sgt	MADELEY, L.	97	17.12.43
F/O	MAGSON, P. J. A.	405	24.08.43
F/O	MAHLER, L. H.	405	09.12.45
F/Sgt	MAHONEY, R. C.	582	29.10.44
F/Sgt	MAKING, L. J.	635	22.05.44
Sgt	MALLABER, J.	97	23.09.43
Sgt	MALPASS, J.	156	25.06.43
Sgt	MALTHOUSE, R. H. F.	635	10.04.44
W/O2	MALZEN, A. P.	Warboys	10.04.44
F/O	MANDER, G. W., DFC	1655 MTU	26.02.44
F/O	MANIFOLD, N.	156	29.07.43
P/O	MANK, M.	7	15.04.43
Sgt	MANLEY, F. J.	156	24.12.43
Sgt	MANLEY, J. D.	156	27.04.44
Sgt	MANN, R. P.	405	30.11.44
F/O	MANNING, F. S.	692	28.03.45
S/L	MANSBRIDGE, D. W., AFC	635	20.04.44
Sgt	MANSBRIDGE, R.	582	04.05.44
Sgt	MANSFIELD, J. A. A.	582	04.05.44
F/Sgt	MANSFIELD, J. J.	97	23.06.43
W/C	MANSFIELD, N. R., DFC	156	14.01.44
P/O	MANSON, D. H.	582	06.07.44
S/L	MANTON, R. J.	83	20.10.43
F/Lt	MANVELL, R. E., DFC, DFM	156	24.06.44
P/O	MAPLESON, D.	7	12.09.44

Rank	Name	Squadron	Date	Rank	Name	Squadron	Date
F/O	MAPPIN, H.	83	22.06.43	Sgt	MELBOURNE, L. E.	97	18.10.43
F/O	MARCHAND, C. J. F.	7	26.08.44	F/O	MELLOR, A. J.	582	11.11.44
F/Sgt	MARCHANT, J. E.	97	04.12.43	F/Lt	MELLSTROM, M. L., DFC	405	10.04.45
F/Sgt	MARCHANT, W. S.	405	16.06.44	F/Sgt	MENZIES, A.	405	24.08.43
F/Lt	MARGACH, D. S., DFC	582	29.07.44	Sgt	MERCES, A. C. G.	156	20.02.44
P/O	MARKS, D. J., DFM	97	30.07.43	F/Lt	MEREDITH, J. A. T., DFC	83	10.05.44
P/O	MARLOW, E. H.	156	31.03.45	Sgt	MERRILL, G.	35	02.12.43
F/Sgt	MARRIOTT, F. J.	35	22.03.44	F/Lt	MEYER, W. A., DFC	97	15.03.44
P/O	MARRIOTT, J. R.	405	27.04.43	F/O	MIDDLETON, A. J.	405(Ca)	10.08.43
F/O	MARRIOTT, K., DFM	7	20.02.44	F/Sgt	MIENERT, V.	405	17.12.43
F/O	MARSH, A. B., DFC	156	04.04.43	Sgt	MILES, L. J.	35	28.05.43
F/O	MARSH, F. J.	405	17.03.45	F/Lt	MILLAR, A.	156	11.09.44
Sgt	MARSH, J.	35	14.07.43	P/O	MILLAR, K. R. G.	83	26.11.43
F/Sgt	MARSH, P. A.	97	21.01.44	F/Sgt	MILLARD, A. E., DFM	83	20.01.44
W/O	MARSHALL, A. M.	7	18.10.43	Sgt	MILLARD, H. G.	83	09.05.44
Sgt	MARSHALL, B.	156	30.07.43	F/Sgt	MILLEN, B. B.	156	25.02.44
F/Sgt	MARSHALL, E.	7	15.02.44	P/O	MILLER, A. B.	405	16.01.45
F/O	MARSHALL, G. L.	139	14.09.43	F/O	MILLER, C. G.	83	12.06.43
Sgt	MARSHALL, H. A.	405	16.01.45	P/O	MILLER, F. J.	405	15.03.45
W/O2	MARSHALL, J. S.	7	21.04.43	F/Lt	MILLER, H. J.	7	29.01.44
Sgt	MARSHALL, L.	35	28.05.43	F/O	MILLER, J.	571	16.06.44
P/O	MARSON, J. A.	156	22.06.43	F/Sgt	MILLER, J. A.	405(Ja)	24.08.43
F/Sgt	MARTIN, F.	97	21.01.44	F/Sgt	MILLER, J. MacT.	35	25.07.44
Sgt	MARTIN, G. L.	156	20.12.43	Sgt	MILLER, L. G. R.	405	02.01.44
Sgt	MARTIN, H.	156	03.01.44	Sgt	MILLER, M. S.	405(Ca)	16.08.43
F/Sgt	MARTIN, H. E.	7	25.04.44	P/O	MILLER, R. B.	156	17.06.43
F/O	MARTIN, H. MacN.	83	11.04.44	F/Sgt	MILLER, S. I.	156	25.02.44
W/O1	MARTIN, J.	405(Ca)	24.05.43	W/O1	MILLIDGE, E. G.	7	18.11.43
F/Sgt	MARTIN, J. J.	83	29.01.44	P/O	MILLIDGE, N.	156	27.08.42
S/L	MARTIN, J. L., DFC *	7	28.04.44	F/Sgt	MILLIKEN, R. E.	405(Ca)	29.11.42
F/O	MARTIN, M. J.	405	09.02.45	Sgt	MILLS, C. A.	97	22.03.44
P/O	MARTIN, R. C.	7	16.06.44	F/Sgt	MILLS, D. A., DFM	156	02.01.44
F/O	MARTIN, R. L., DFC	156	31.03.45	F/O	MILLS, M. A.	35	05.01.45
F/Sgt	MARTIN, T.	83	21.10.43	F/Sgt	MILNE, D. H.	35	04.07.43
F/Lt	MARTIN, T. J.	139	12.09.44	F/Lt	MILNE, O. S., DFC	582	23.12.44
F/Sgt	MARTIN, W. F.	35	22.03.44	F/Sgt	MILNE, W. S.	405(Ca)	29.11.42
F/Sgt	MARTYN, J. R.	35	16.04.43	Sgt	MILOT, A. V. B.	405	16.10.42
F/O	MASKELL, H. T.	35	23.05.44	P/O	MILTON, F. C., DFM	83	17.04.43
F/Sgt	MASON, G. E., DFM	156	20.12.43	Sgt	MILTON, G. E.	156	28.07.43
F/O	MASON, H., DFM	83	27.04.44	Sgt	MINNS, G. R.	156	03.04.43
F/Sgt	MASON, N. R.	156	13.05.43	F/Sgt	MINNS, H.	7	05.04.45
Sgt	MASON, R. C.	156	28.08.43	F/Sgt	MINTJENS, W. J.	35	12.09.44
P/O	MASON, T. D. L.	7	15.10.44	F/Lt	MIRFIN, E.	83	27.04.44
Sgt	MASSEY, W. C.	156	14.09.42	P/O	MIROW, R. J.	571	13.04.45
P/O	MASSIE, R.	105	27.05.43	Sgt	MITCHELL, A. G. L.	405(Ca)	24.07.41
F/Lt	MASSY, M. I.	635	04.08.44	F/Lt	MITCHELL, C. G., DFC	35	08.03.45
F/Sgt	MATHER, J. J.	635	04.08.44	F/Sgt	MITCHELL, C. J.	582	23.09.44
F/O	MATHESON, A. A., DFM	692	11.07.44	F/O	MITCHELL, D. G.	15	24.08.43
P/O	MATHESON, K. D.	7	31.03.44	F/O	MITCHELL, E. R., DFM	156	23.11.43
F/Sgt	MATHISON, J. A.	35	29.11.44	F/Sgt	MITCHELL, H. G.	97	23.09.43
F/Lt	MATKIN, S. G., DFC	7	15.08.43	F/Lt	MITCHELL, J. M., DFC	405	07.05.44
Sgt	MATTHES, A. G.	7	06.01.44	F/Sgt	MITCHELL, K. A. L.	156	31.03.45
Sgt	MATTHEWS, C. P.	97	04.12.43	P/O	MITCHELL, P. E., DFC	109	05.04.44
F/Sgt	MATTHEWS, D. G.	7	03.05.44	Cpl	MITCHELL, W.	Graveley	25.07.43
F/Lt	MATTHEWS, T. W.	1655 MTU	26.03.44	Sgt	MITRA, B. K.	Upwood	25.01.44
F/O	MATTHEWS, V. R.	35	11.04.43	Lt	MOE, T. C.	139(Ja)	26.02.43
F/O	MAULE, J.	35	27.08.44	F/O	MOFFATT, J., DFC	156	21.02.44
Sgt	MAWSON, H.	582	12.12.44	Sgt	MOHUN, J. S.	635	08.03.45
F/Sgt	MAY, F. J.	7	24.06.44	Cpl	MOLE, J. A.	156	09.04.44
Sgt	MAY, S. F.	156	14.01.44	Sgt	MONAGHAN, A.	97	29.06.43
Sgt	MAY, W. B.	635	13.05.44	Sgt	MONAGHAN, E. S.	97	29.01.44
F/Sgt	MAYCOCK, J. R.	83	30.01.44	P/O	MONK, E. J.	156	17.06.43
F/Sgt	MAYHEW, D. J.	7	05.05.44	W/O1	MONTGOMERY, R. J., DFC	405	07.05.44
Sgt	MAYNARD, W. H.	7(P)	18.09.44	F/Lt	MOODIE, D. McN., DFC	97	18.10.43
Sgt	MAYS, J. C.	35	23.12.44	Sgt	MOODY, B.	405	05.05.43
Sgt	MAZIN, F. M.	35	22.06.43	F/O	MOONEY, L., DFM	156	30.02.45
F/Lt	MEADOWS, A. E.	139(Ja)	20.05.44	F/O	MOONEY, R. L., DFM	97	02.01.44
F/Sgt	MEARS, J. R.	7	21.02.45	Sgt	MOORE, D. M.	97	04.12.43
Sgt	MEDLOCK, H. E.	635	06.12.44	Sgt	MOORE, E. R.	35	14.07.43
F/O	MEE, J. M., DFC	7	25.03.44	F/Sgt	MOORE, G. E.	405	29.06.44
Sgt	MEEK, W. A.	7	26.11.43	F/Lt	MOORE, J. L., DFC	97	25.06.43
F/O	MEIKLEJOHN, R. B.	7	22.06.43	F/O	MOORE, L.	608	23.02.45
Sgt	MEIKLEJOHN, W. M.	7	13.03.43				

Rank	Name	Squadron	Date	Rank	Name	Squadron	Date
Sgt	MOORE. R.	405(Ca)	11.03.43	F/Lt	NAIRN. G. D. T.	692	01.01.45
P/O	MOORE. R. E., DFM	83	13.06.43	P/O	NAIRN. R. B.	405	26.08.44
F/Sgt	MOORE. R. G.	7	05.01.45	F/Sgt	NALLEN. C. P.	635	04.06.44
F/Sgt	MOORE. R. V.	635	04.04.45	P/O	NAPIER. J. McD.	7	25.04.44
Sgt	MOORE. W.	7	11.04.43	F/Sgt	NAPIER. W. A., DFM	83	27.04.44
P/O	MORASSI. A.	156	02.01.44	W/O2	NASH. C. A.	83	12.06.43
W/O2	MORGAN. C. E.	156	27.09.43	Sgt	NASH. I...	7	27.03.43
F/Sgt	MORGAN. F. H.	156	24.12.43	Sgt	NASH. R. H.	7	31.08.43
F/Sgt	MORGAN. J. H.	635	13.08.44	Sgt	NASON. R. A.	35	11.04.43
F/O	MORGAN. J. P.	692	15.01.45	F/O	NAYLOR. J. H.	35	27.03.43
P/O	MORONEY. W. P.	97	22.03.44	Sgt	NEAL. D. A.	156	14.01.44
P/O	MORRILL. W. A.	405	16.06.44	F/Sgt	NEALE. D.	7	13.03.43
Sgt	MORRIS. C. T. R.	156	03.01.44	Sgt	NEALE. J.	156	08.03.43
P/O	MORRIS. J. E.	139	27.05.43	F/Sgt	NEALE. R.	35	04.02.45
Sgt	MORRIS. J. G.	635	22.04.44	P/O	NEIGHBOUR. S. W. G.	156	24.02.44
Sgt	MORRIS. R.	405	15.03.45	F/Lt	NEIL. G. J. B.	7	22.11.43
F/O	MORRIS. R. C., DFC	139	16.03.43	F/Sgt	NELSON. R. S.	83	27.11.43
F/Lt	MORRISH. H. F., DFC	156	24.09.44	S/L	NESBITT. E. H. M.	7	22.11.43
P/O	MORRISON. A. D., DFC	635	24.12.44	W/O	NESBITT. H. E.	7	11.04.43
Sgt	MORRISON. B. R.	405	21.01.44	F/O	NESDEN. J.	156	28.08.43
F/O	MORRISON. G. A. J.	156	31.03.45	F/Lt	NEVILLE. J.	635	30.08.44
F/Sgt	MORRISON. N. R.	7	25.06.43	F/Sgt	NEWELL. A. J.	97	21.02.44
F/Lt	MORRISON. R. G., DFC	405	14.07.43	F/Sgt	NEWELL. A. V.	156	25.06.43
F/O	MORROW. W. C.	405(Ca)	29.07.44	Sgt	NEWMAN. J. L.	7	22.09.43
F/Sgt	MORTHAM. R. S.	97	23.11.43	F/Lt	NEWSHAM. G. S.	35	31.08.43
Sgt	MORTIMER. A. F. J.	156	14.09.42	F/O	NEWTON. A. J., DFM	97	04.05.44
Sgt	MORTIMER. A. W.	156	14.01.44	F/Lt	NEWTON. J. V.	7	14.01.44
F/Sgt	MORTLOCK. V. V.	7	25.03.44	F/O	NEWTON. R. A.	582	08.09.44
F/Lt	MORTON. A. S., AFC	35	25.07.44	Sgt	NEWTON. T.	405	30.01.44
Sgt	MORTON. E. R.	156	24.02.44	Sgt	NEWTON. W. A. L.	7	16.06.44
F/Sgt	MORTON. J. K.	7	06.01.44	Sgt	NICHOLAS. B. H.	97	25.03.44
AC2	MOSELEY. A. E.	819(D)	29.12.41	LAC	NICHOLAS. J. T.	83	26.11.43
F/O	MOSS. E. J. B.	405	24.11.43	F/Lt	NICHOLLS. G. A., DFC	139	03.04.45
Sgt	MOSS. M. H.	128	24.11.44	P/O	NICHOLS. A. W., BEM	405	22.06.43
Sgt	MOTTISHAW. H. E.	97	14.01.44	F/Sgt	NICHOLS. W. D., DFM	7	15.02.44
W/O	MOULD. G. A.	635	22.05.44	F/Sgt	NICOL. J. C.	97	14.01.44
Sgt	MOULDING. E. R. R.	635	31.03.44	F/Sgt	NICHOLSON. C	7	16.06.44
F/Sgt	MOUNT. J. P. R.	156	03.01.44	F/O	NICOLSON. I. H.	7	15.03.44
F/Sgt	MOUNTAIN. C. D.	635	07.01.45	P/O	NIXON. E. C., DFM	35	06.01.44
F/Lt	MOYES. P. J., DFC	156	08.06.44	F/Lt	NIXON. G. W.	582	16.09.44
W/O	MUCKART. G., DFC	97	21.04.44	Sgt	NIXON. J. W.	635	10.04.44
S/L	MUIR. A., DFC	156	21.02.44	F/Sgt	NIXON. R.	7	24.06.44
F/Sgt	MUIR. S. D.	7	16.06.44	P/O	NIXON. R. W., DFC	35	24.08.43
Sgt	MUIRHEAD. M. McK.	156	16.04.43	S/L	NIXON. T. R., DFC. DFM	7	20.02.44
Sgt	MULDOON. R. A.	35	22.06.43	P/O	NOAKES. L. F. G., DFC	7	23.04.44
F/Lt	MULLAN. G. P.	128	01.01.45	F/Sgt	NOBLE. P. E.	7	20.10.43
S/L	MULLER. M. M. V. L.	35	08.04.45	F/O	NOBLE. J. A.	156	24.09.44
F/O	MUMBY. J. L., DFC	692	20.02.44	W/O2	NOLAN. T. H.	405	03.01.44
F/Lt	MUNRO. J. C., DFC	97	22.11.43	P/O	NOLL. L. O.	7	22.09.43
F/Lt	MUNRO. L. E., DFC	156	31.03.45	F/O	NORDHEIMER. K. A.	405	17.08.44
F/Lt	MUNRO. L. W.	83	03.01.44	Sgt	NORDHOFF. C. F.	97	03.09.43
F/O	MUNSEY. R. H.	7	26.08.44	Sgt	NORMAN. H. J.	35	04.05.44
Sgt	MUNTON. G. C.	97	25.04.44	F/O	NORRINGTON. D., DFM	83	26.02.43
F/Sgt	MURDOCH. R. D.	97	15.02.44	P/O	NORRIS. J. T. W. G., DFM	582	16.09.44
Sgt	MURGATROYD. J.	35	12.09.44	Sgt	NORRIS. R.	7	22.09.43
W/O	MURPHY. J. A.	156	31.03.44	P/O	NORSWORTHY. R. K.	35	23.12.44
P/O	MURPHY. J. H. M.	128	29.11.44	Sgt	NORTON. L. V.	635	31.03.44
W/O	MURPHY. M. J.	83	26.11.43	F/O	NORTON. P. H.	97	30.03.43
P/O	MURRAY. C.	83	17.06.43	F/O	NOVAK. H. E.	405	16.01.45
Sgt	MURRAY. G.	582	15.03.45	Sgt	NUGUS. C.	Chelveston	27.05.42
Sgt	MURRAY. G. M.	156	17.06.43	F/Sgt	NUNDY. B.	582	23.12.44
F/Sgt	MURRAY. J.	156	02.01.44	F/O	NUNN. V. W. J.	83	27.11.43
Cpl	MURRAY. J. D. H.	35	02.01.45	W/O2	NUTIK. L.	7	01.05.43
F/Lt	MURRELL. S. L., DFC	405	22.06.43	F/Sgt	NUTTALL. S.	97	25.03.44
P/O	MUSGRAVE. P. A.	405	17.08.44	Sgt	OATS. R. H.	35	26.05.43
F/Sgt	MUSK. P. J., DFM	83	12.03.43	P/O	O'BRIEN. J. B.	156	20.12.43
Sgt	MUSSETT. D. R.	635	13.05.44	Sgt	O'BRIEN. B.	83	03.04.43
Sgt	MUTCH. G. C.	35	17.08.43	F/O	O'BRYAN. W. E. H.	571	19.03.45
P/O	MUTCH. R. D.	405	17.11.43	F/O	O'CONNELL. F. E.	35	05.07.44
F/Sgt	MYERS. J.	156	29.08.42	P/O	ODELL. J. G.	405	23.11.43
F/O	NAIFF. R. A.	692	15.10.44	F/Sgt	O'DONOHOE. F. J.	405(Ca)	21.02.43
Sgt	NAINBY. T.	35	06.05.44	F/O	O'HARA. J. W.	7	15.08.43
P/O	NAIRN. A. F.	83	02.01.44	P/O	O'HARE. F. E.	405	27.04.43

Rank	Name	Squadron	Date
W/O2	OKE, H. D.	7	15.04.43
P/O	OLDE, W. J.	109	19.03.43
W/O	OLDFIELD, S.	Warboys	11.03.45
Sgt	OLIVER, J. R.	7	27.03.43
P/O	OLIVER, W. R.	405	23.04.44
F/O	OLSON, D. B.	405	14.02.45
F/O	OLYOTT, W. T.	635	04.06.44
P/O	O'NEIL, G. M.	405	30.01.44
P/O	O'NEILL, C. J. E.	582	04.05.44
F/Sgt	O'NEILL, W. P. H.	156	31.03.44
F/Lt	ONLEY, R. C.	128	11.12.44
F/O	OPENSHAW, F.	139(Ja)	27.05.43
F/Sgt	ORAM, A. W.	582	25.05.44
F/O	ORAM, L. L.	Upwood	25.01.44
W/O	ORCHARD, D. H.	156	17.06.43
F/O	O'REILLY, F. W.	156	17.04.45
Sgt	ORGAN, J. L.	83	05.03.43
F/O	OSBORNE, J. C.	7	02.01.44
W/O	OSTERLOH, V. G.	83	27.01.44
F/Sgt	O'SULLIVAN, T. C.	7	09.10.43
F/Sgt	OSWALD, K A.	35	04.05.44
F/Sgt	OTT, J.	405	24.09.43
P/O	OTTER, J. C., DFC	156	18.11.43
Sgt	OTTEY, J. A.	156	22.06.43
F/Sgt	OWEN, F. C.	635	26.08.44
F/Sgt	OWEN, G.	582	23.12.44
F/Sgt	PAGE, F. R.	7	24.11.43
F/Sgt	PAGE, H. R.	97	23.09.43
P/O	PAINTER, K.	97	20.10.43
F/Sgt	PALLISTER, W. R.	35	10.08.43
W/O	PALMER, A. S., DFM	635	20.04.44
W/C	PALMER, C. W., DFC	405	26.09.44
F/O	PALMER, G.	156	14.01.44
Sgt	PALMER, P. J.	7	26.11.43
S/L	PALMER, R. A. M., VC, DFC *	109	23.12.44
F/O	PALMER, W. McL.	405	12.03.43
Sgt	PALMER, W. R.	405	30.01.44
F/Sgt	PANNIERS, E. D.	156	14.01.44
P/O	PAPWORTH, J. N., DFC	582	06.06.44
F/Sgt	PARFITT, W. R. C.	582	13.08.44
Sgt	PARGETER, T. A.	405(Ca)	18.08.43
F/Lt	PARISH, C. W., DFC	7	21.04.43
P/O	PARKER, A. S.	405	14.01.44
F/O	PARKER, B. A.	635	12.12.44
F/Sgt	PARKER, B. F. J.	405(Ca)	21.02.43
A/W/C	PARKES, S. M. P., DSO	97	26.08.44
F/Lt	PARKHURST, K. E.	405	15.03.45
W/O	PARR, F., DFM	156	03.02.45
F/Sgt	PARR, S.	582	16.06.44
S/L	PARROTT, E. H.	97	24.08.43
Sgt	PARROTT, S. G.	97	17.12.43
F/O	PARRY, H. W.	97	04.07.43
W/O2	PARSLEY, W. A.	97	21.01.44
F/O	PARSONS, W. E.	405	04.05.44
W/O	PARTOS, D. G., DFM	97	23.06.44
F/Sgt	PARTRIDGE, G. J.	405	17.11.43
P/O	PARTRIDGE, H. A.	83	05.03.43
Sgt	PASSEY, S. J.	405	03.08.43
F/O	PASSINGHAM, C., DFM	635	13.05.44
Sgt	PATERSON, G. I.	83	20.02.44
Sgt	PATERSON, J.	582	23.12.44
P/O	PATERSON, J. B.	7	15.08.43
P/O	PATRICK, M. M., DFC	156	23.11.43
P/O	PATTERSON, D. R.,DFC	635	24.12.44
Sgt	PATTISON, C.	35	27.03.43
Sgt	PAUL, J. H.	405	21.01.44
F/O	PAYNE, A. M.	109	05.03.45
F/Lt	PAYNE, H. L.	405	16.01.45
F/O	PAYNE, J. W.	7	22.10.43
Sgt	PEACHEY, N. A.	7	01.05.43
F/O	PEACOCK, W. G., DFC	405	26.09.44
F/O	PEAKE, C. E.	635	31.03.44

Rank	Name	Squadron	Date
F/O	PEAKER, G. E.	405	19.03.45
F/Lt	PEARCE, J. M.	1655 MTU	19.08.44
Sgt	PEARCE, N. A. J.	35	26.07.43
Sgt	PEARMAN, T. F.	83	06.09.43
F/Sgt	PEARSON, A. B.	83	02.01.44
F/Lt	PEARSON, I. McL., DFC	7	03.01.44
Sgt	PEARSON, K.,	156	07.09.43
F/O	PEARSON, R. A.	405	08.07.44
W/O	PEDRAZZINI, R.	635	13.08.44
F/Sgt	PEEK, S. J., DFC	97	17.12.43
Sgt	PEEL, J. A.	97	30.03.43
Sgt	PEERS, J.	97	25.02.44
Sgt	PEGG, L. F.	608	16.09.44
LAC	PEGG, R.	35	02.02.44
Sgt	PEGG, R. G.	83	03.04.43
Sgt	PENFOLD, A.	35	18.11.43
W/O	PENFOLD, D. J., DFM	97	17.12.43
F/Sgt	PENNELLS, R. H., DFM	83	26.11.43
Sgt	PENNER, A. H.	83	30.03.43
Sgt	PENNER, I. A.	405	27.04.43
F/Lt	PENNINGTON, A.	83	27.04.44
F/O	PENROSE, G. W., DFC	156	14.01.44
F/O	PENTELOW, P. J.	35	06.03.45
Sgt	PEPPER, J. H.	7	23.11.43
F/Sgt	PERCIVAL, W.	35	21.01.44
P/O	PERCY, G.	156	09.03.43
W/O2	PERDUE, V. T.	7	31.08.43
F/Lt	PERFECT, J., DFC	7	22.11.43
F/O	PERKINS, A. J.	35	18.08.43
F/O	PERKINS, R. P. D.	83	20.02.44
F/Sgt	PERRAULT, E. F.	405	19.03.45
Sgt	PERRETT, R. G.	35	30.07.43
W/O1	PERRY, K. O.	405(Ca)	23.08.43
F/Sgt	PETERS, N. E.	635	31.02.45
F/Sgt	PETERSON, R. F.	405	14.01.44
P/O	PETHARD, W. T.	635	07.01.45
F/Lt	PETRIDES, B. O., DFM	156	21.02.44
F/Lt	PETRIE, J. R., DFC	7	16.12.43
F/Lt	PEXTON, H. C., DFC	35	30.07.43
F/O	PEZARO, J. B. G.	83	25.04.44
Sgt	PHELAN, F.	156	22.11.43
Sgt	PHILLIPS, A. J.	7	05.05.43
Sgt	PHILLIPS, D. H.	582	24.07.44
F/Sgt	PHILLIPS, F. D. T.	35	20.10.44
F/O	PHILLIPS, I. D.	105	12.12.43
F/Sgt	PHILLIPS, J.	571	14.01.45
Sgt	PHILLIPS, J. I.	97	23.05.44
F/O	PHILLIPS, J. M.	405	29.12.44
F/Sgt	PHILLIPS, R.	7	15.10.44
P/O	PHILLIPS, R. J.	405	11.06.44
F/Lt	PHILPS, J. A.	156	30.07.43
Sgt	PHIPPS, W.	35	12.11.43
F/Sgt	PICKERING, C. W.	405(Ca)	10.08.43
Sgt	PICKERING, W. E.	7	21.02.45
P/O	PICKLES, R.	635	30.08.44
Sgt	PICKUP, H.	35	03.08.43
F/O	PIDGEON, A. H. J.	35	07.03.45
P/O	PIKE, R. C., DFM	97	15.03.44
F/O	PILE, K. L., DFM	PFF, NTU, Warboys	11.03.45
F/Sgt	PILLINGER, L. C.	156	24.02.44
Sgt	PIMM, J. E. W.	83	28.08.43
F/Sgt	PIMM, S. A.	635	30.03.45
F/Sgt	PITCON, R. C.	635	26.08.44
Sgt	PITT, S. T.	405(Ca)	03.08.43
F/Sgt	PLANT, H.	83	13.05.43
F/O	PLATANA, D. D., DFC	156	15.07.44
Sgt	PLATT, V. S.	35	30.05.43
W/O2	PLAUNT, D. C.	97	12.03.43
F/Sgt	PLEYDELL, H. J	97	29.01.44
F/Sgt	PLIMMER, A. L., DFM	582	12.12.44
F/Sgt	PLUMB, C. F.	83	20.01.44
Sgt	POCKNELL, E. C.	7	21.10.43

Rank	Name	Squadron	Date
P/O	POCOCK, R. L.	582	29.10.44
W/O2	PODOLSKY, A.	83	17.04.43
F/Sgt	POGONOWSKI, J. E.	35	15.02.44
W/O	POINTER, E. G., DFM	7	25.06.43
F/O	POLGLASE, D.	105	11.04.43
F/O	POMEROY, E. C.	405	29.07.44
P/O	PONTING, F. L. J.	156	17.04.45
P/O	POOL, D. L. A.	7	30.07.43
Sgt	POOLE, S.	156	27.03.43
F/Lt	POPE, A. C., DFC	156	31.03.45
F/Sgt	POPE, G. A.	35	05.01.45
Sgt	PORRITT, A.	97	25.02.44
P/O	PORTCH, A. L. S.	156	04.04.43
F/Lt	PORTEOUS, W. F. W., DSO, F. M *	7	20.05.44
W/O	PORTER, A. H.	35	19.04.45
W/C	PORTER, E. F.	156	25.02.44
W/O	PORTWAY, J. C.	608	08.06.45
P/O	POTHIER, B. F., DFC	405	07.05.44
Sgt	POTTS, D. E.	83	06.09.43
F/O	POTTS, K., DFC	35	05.01.45
F/Lt	POULTON, N. T. R., DFM	156	16.12.43
F/O	POUNDER, G.	139	11.04.43
Sgt	POUT, P. E.	156	03.01.44
F/Sgt	POWELL, J.	97	17.12.43
F/Lt	POWELL, L. J., DFC	156	16.12.43
F/Sgt	POWELL, R. J.	7	29.06.44
Sgt	POWELL, T.	83	11.04.44
F/Sgt	POYNTON, A. F.	35	20.02.44
Sgt	PRANKETT, R.	156	20.02.44
F/Sgt	PRATT, E. W. R.	582	20.07.44
P/O	PRATT, J. T., DFC	97	17.12.43
F/Sgt	PRENDERGAST, J.	83	22.11.43
LAC	PRESTON, A. C.	NTU, Upwood	26.01.44
P/O	PRICE, A.	7	20.05.44
P/O	PRICE, A. D., DFC	7	12.09.44
P/O	PRICE, J. H.	83	06.09.43
Sgt	PRICE, T.	35	26.07.43
Sgt	PRIOR, D. C.	35	11.09.44
F/Sgt	PRITCHARD, H.	635	04.06.44
Sgt	PRITCHARD, R. G.	35	24.05.43
F/Sgt	PRITCHARD, T. J., DFM	156	13.05.43
F/Sgt	PRUDHOE, J. K.	83	04.10.43
Sgt	PUGH, T. G. G.	97	23.09.43
F/Sgt	PULLEE, L. W.	7	11.06.44
P/O	PULLIN, B. A., DFC	582	13.08.44
F/O	PURKIS, C. S.	635	12.06.44
P/O	PURMAL, V. R.	156	03.01.44
F/O	PUSHOR, D. E.	7	30.07.43
P/O	PUTT, M. E.	97	31.03.44
F/O	PUVER, J.	635	31.03.44
F/Lt	PYE, T. J.	156	13.08.44
Sgt	PYKE, N.	405	21.01.44
F/O	PYRAH, A.	7	30.07.43
F/O	QUICK, A. W. F.	1655 MTU	05.11.43
F/Sgt	QUINN, R. A.	405	17.01.45
F/Sgt	RABINER, J.	692	31.03.45
Sgt	RACE, G. A.	156	30.01.44
F/O	RADCLIFFE, E. E.	582	24.07.44
Sgt	RAE, G. P.	156	24.03.44
F/Sgt	RAE, J. MacC.	405	28.01.45
P/O	RAGGETT, P. R.	35	18.08.43
W/O2	RAIKE, J.	405	16.09.44
W/O	RAINE, A. T.	635	19.08.44
Sgt	RALPH, G. J. P.	582	06.03.45
F/Lt	RALPH, J. C., DFM	156	03.01.44
G/Cpt	RAMPLING, K. J., DFC, DSO	7	22.03.44
F/Lt	RAMSAY, D., DFC	405	28.04.44
F/O	RAMSAY, G. L.	582	06.06.44
F/Lt	RANALOW, P. B. O.	35	08.04.45
F/O	RAND, K. P.	97	06.01.44
P/O	RANKIN, J.	405	04.07.43
F/O	RANSOM, G. I.	83	20.01.44
F/O	RAPER, W.	156	02.01.44
F/Sgt	RAPERE, N. J.	35	21.01.44
Sgt	RATCLIFF, R. E.	156	12.06.43
P/O	RATCLIFFE, J. R. F.	405	03.08.43
Sgt	RATHBONE, J. D.	620	26.07.43
S/L	RAW, A. W., DFC, AFC	156	11.09.44
F/O	RAWLINS, K. W.	139	13.08.43
F/Sgt	RAWLINSON, N. A.	582	25.05.44
F/Sgt	RAY, F. H.	156	29.09.43
S/L	RAYBOULD, A. W., DSO, DFM	582	06.06.44
F/Sgt	RAYNER, W.	7	03.01.44
F/O	REA, G. M.	1655 MTU	21.05.44
F/Sgt	READ, G. S.	405(Ca)	28.09.43
F/Sgt	READ, R. A.	97	19.03.44
F/Sgt	REDFEARN, I. C., DFM	35	06.01.44
W/O	REDFERN, A. T.	635	06.07.44
F/Sgt	REDFERN, J. G.	156	02.12.43
F/Sgt	REDFORD, G. H., DFM	35	18.11.44
Sgt	REDHEAD, J.	405	02.01.44
F/O	REDPATH, J. N. R.	405	20.10.43
F/Sgt	REDSTONE, P. G. E.	405	24.02.44
F/O	REDWOOD, C. H. G.	7	22.06.43
Sgt	REED, J. C. L.	156	21.02.44
F/O	REEDER, A. J.	35	05.01.45
F/O	REEDER, S. W.	608	12.10.44
Sgt	REES, T. E.	156	24.12.43
Sgt	REEVE, C. H.	156	17.12.43
F/Lt	REEVES, C. W., DFC	156	11.09.44
F/O	REEVES, R. L.	156	20.02.44
Sgt	REID, C. C.	83	17.12.43
P/O	REID, J. A.	83	24.08.43
F/O	REID, M. J.	83	20.02.44
W/O	REID, T.	635	04.04.45
F/Lt	REIF, A. W.	582	23.12.44
Sgt	REILLY, A.	97	05.05.43
F/O	REILLY, R. L.	105	28.03.43
F/O	REMBER, R. A.	582	24.07.44
F/O	REMBRIDGE, L. G.	97	04.07.43
F/Sgt	REMILLARD, J. L. R.	156	17.12.44
P/O	RENAUD, J. G. M.	405	03.06.44
P/O	RENDELL, K. L.	571	06.10.44
Sgt	RENDTORFF, D. E. A.	7	26.03.43
Sgt	RENSHAW, A. S.	83	13.05.43
P/O	RETTER, A. J.	405	16.06.44
F/O	REYNOLDS, B. F.	105	12.12.43
F/Sgt	REYNOLDS, B. S.	156	25.02.44
F/Sgt	REYNOLDS, J. C.	97	29.01.44
Sgt	REYNOLDS, W. G.	35	14.04.45
W/O2	RHOADES, E. A.	7	23.04.44
Sgt	RHODES, D. C.	35	09.05.44
Sgt	RICHARDS, D. J.	35	13.05.43
P/O	RICHARDS, I. L.	83	21.10.43
Sgt	RICHARDS, J. H.	97	11.08.43
P/O	RICHARDS, J. N.	7	14.01.44
Sgt	RICHARDS, K.	156	25.06.43
F/Lt	RICHARDS, S. J.	156	13.08.44
P/O	RICHARDSON, D. A.	35	02.12.43
Sgt	RICHARDSON, L.	620	24.08.43
Sgt	RICHARDSON, R.	83	22.01.44
F/Sgt	RICHER, J. G. P. E.	35	22.06.43
S/L	RICHES, W. C., DFC *	635	06.07.44
F/Sgt	RICHMOND, J.	156	02.12.43
F/Lt	RICHMOND, R.	156	24.03.44
F/Lt	RICKINSON, L. A., DFC	83	13.05.43
P/O	RIDD, J. H.	83	03.04.43
Sgt	RIDDLE, H. P.	7	15.03.44
Sgt	RIDDLE, R. A. K.	156	27.04.44
F/Sgt	RIDINGS, D. G.	156	05.05.43
F/Sgt	RIDLEY, G.	97	30.01.44
P/O	RIDLEY, J. K., DFM	83	19.02.43
F/O	RIGBY, J.	635	25.04.44

Rank	Name	Squadron	Date	Rank	Name	Squadron	Date
P/O	RIGBY, K. G.	405	03.08.43	W/O2	ROSS, H. R.	156	03.09.43
F/Sgt	RILEY, E. B.	156	24.06.44	F/Sgt	ROSS, J. H. C.	635	13.08.44
F/Sgt	RILEY, J. C.	35	18.11.43	F/Sgt	ROSS, W.	7	26.08.44
Sgt	RILEY, R. G.	156	09.03.43	F/Lt	ROSS, W. G., DFC, DFM	83	20.01.44
Sgt	RIMMER, D. F.	97	21.04.44	F/O	ROSSER, J. R.	35	12.09.44
F/Sgt	RINGE, W. A.	83	26.02.43	Sgt	ROUGHLEY, J.	83	18.06.43
P/O	RITCHIE, E. W., DFC	156	20.12.43	F/Lt	ROUND, F. D., DFM	35	05.07.44
F/O	RITCHIE, J. L.	582	04.05.44	F/Lt	ROUTEN, D. A., DFM	7	27.09.43
Sgt	RITCHIE, K. V.	635	26.08.44	F/Sgt	ROUTLEDGE, F. W. T., DFM	83	03.04.43
P/O	RIVERS, E. T.	7	15.10.44	Sgt	ROWBOTHAM, D.	405(Ca)	03.08.43
F/Sgt	RIXON, A.	156	04.04.43	P/O	ROWE, E. D.	405	22.06.43
F/Sgt	ROBERTS, A. E., DFM	97	15.03.44	Sgt	ROWE, H. D.	156	16.04.43
P/O	ROBERTS, C. E.	405	16.06.44	Sgt	ROWLANDS, A. R.	97	10.05.44
F/Sgt	ROBERTS, E. E. E.	156	22.05.44	F/Lt	ROWLANDS, D. H., DFC	97	31.03.44
F/Sgt	ROBERTS, F. D.	405	07.04.43	Sgt	ROWLANDS, E. J.	635	22.05.44
F/Lt	ROBERTS, F. J., DFC	97	21.01.44	W/O2	ROY, J. T. R. J.	7	15.04.43
Sgt	ROBERTS, G. V.	7	02.01.44	Sgt	ROYALL, G.	1655 MTU	27.06.44
F/Sgt	ROBERTS, G. W.	1409 Flt	27.03.44	Sgt	RUDGE, R. A. J.	83	20.02.44
Sgt	ROBERTS, J.	97	06.01.44	Sgt	RUGG, G. W.	156	24.02.44
F/Lt	ROBERTS, L., DFC	35	28.10.44	P/O	RULE, J. E.	156	30.01.44
F/Lt	ROBERTS, R., DFC	156	18.11.43	F/Sgt	RUMBLES, M. B.	635	22.05.44
Sgt	ROBERTS, W.	582	29.10.44	F/Sgt	RUSSELL, A.	97	17.12.43
F/Lt	ROBERTS, W. A.	405	30.01.44	F/Lt	RUSSELL, C. O., DFC	35	07.03.45
F/Sgt	ROBERTS, W. J.	156	24.09.44	F/Lt	RUSSELL, G., DFC	105	23.12.44
F/Sgt	ROBERTSHAW, T.	635	07.01.45	Sgt	RUSSELL, R. G. S.	35	04.05.44
F/Sgt	ROBERTSON, D. L.	156	03.04.43	Sgt	RUSSELL, S. E. A.	35	05.05.43
AC1	ROBERTSON, F. J.	2746AA	27.07.43	P/O	RUST, M. E.	83	23.06.43
F/O	ROBERTSON, G. A.	7	21.02.45	F/Lt	RUTLEDGE, A. W.	1655 MTU	16.09.44
F/Lt	ROBERTSON, I. J.	7	21.01.44	F/Sgt	RUTTER, D. M.	83	22.11.43
F/Lt	ROBERTSON, J., DFM	Warboys	11.03.45	Sgt	RYAN, S. J.	156	22.11.43
F/Lt	ROBERTSON, O. B., DFC	97	28.08.43	Sgt	RYDER, D. H.	97	10.05.44
F/O	ROBERTSON, W. A.	156	02.01.44	Sgt	RYDER, R. G.	7	15.03.44
Sgt	ROBERTSON, W. D.	35	22.06.43	P/O	RYDER, T. J.	7	11.04.43
W/O	ROBINSON, A. W.	405	03.01.44	S/L	RYLE, G., DFC	7	28.04.44
G/Cpt	ROBINSON, B. V., DSO, DFC *, AFC	35	24.08.43	F/Sgt	RYNSKY, J. B.	405	22.12.44
F/Sgt	ROBINSON, B. L., DFM	35	06.01.44	F/Sgt	SABINE, D. S.	1409 Flt	27.03.44
P/O	ROBINSON, C.	83	24.08.43	F/Sgt	SADLER, R.	635	04.06.44
F/Sgt	ROBINSON, C. L.	7	16.12.43	F/Sgt	SAGE, G. F.	7	21.02.45
F/Sgt	ROBINSON, E.	7	04.09.43	Sgt	SAGE, G. C.	156	20.12.43
F/Lt	ROBINSON, H. G. M., DFC	156	15.07.44	F/O	SAIDLER, J. D.	7	02.05.44
F/Sgt	ROBINSON, J. W.	35	12.09.44	F/O	St JOHN, J. H. R. S.	35PFF	22.06.43
F/Sgt	ROBINSON, N. O.	156	19.04.43	F/O	St LOUIS, B. A.	405	28.09.43
P/O	ROBINSON, P. S. M.	635	19.08.44	P/O	St PIERRE, A. L. J.	405	09.02.45
F/Sgt	ROBINSON, R. L.	40?	22.06.43	F/O	SALABA, A. J.	405	02.01.44
S/L	ROBINSON, S., DFM	83	26.02.43	S/L	SALE, D. J., DSO *, DFC	35	20.03.44
Sgt	ROBINSON, S. E.	635	30.03.45	F/O	SALOMAA, E. A.	582	06.07.44
F/O	ROBINSON, T. B.	35	08.04.45	F/Lt	SALT, F. C.	156	03.02.45
P/O	ROBINSON, W. E.	156	02.12.43	P/O	SALTZBERRY, R. A.	405	23.04.44
Sgt	ROBSON, A.	582	16.09.44	F/O	SALVONI, R. T., DFC	35	14.01.45
F/O	ROBSON, C. A.	Warboys	11.03.45	F/Lt	SAMUEL, J. F., DFC	156	16.12.43
F/Lt	ROBSON, J. H., DFC	139	15.01.45	Sgt	SANDER, W. J.	635	25.03.44
F/Sgt	ROBSON, R. W.	582	15.03.45	F/Lt	SANDERSON, E. A.	405	14.01.44
Sgt	ROBSON, S.	97	25.03.44	F/Lt	SANDERSON, E.	97	29.06.43
F/O	ROBSON, T. A., DFC	35	20.12.43	F/O	SANFORD, R.	635	06.07.44
F/O	ROBSON, W. B.	83	29.01.44	F/Sgt	SANKEY, T. N., DFM	35	02.03.43
Sgt	ROCHE, G. P.	156	21.02.44	F/Lt	SARGENT, E. W., DFC	83	27.01.44
Sgt	ROCK, D. H.	83	05.05.43	S/L	SAUNDERS, A. D., DFC	156	20.02.44
F/Sgt	RODD, J. A.	139	30.08.43	F/Sgt	SAUNDERS, H. M.	405	17.12.43
F/Sgt	RODGERS, L.	83	17.04.43	Sgt	SAUNDERS, R. C.	139(Ja)	03.04.43
F/O	ROE, R. S.	7	20.05.44	W/O	SAUNDERS, W. T.	97	04.10.43
W/O	ROE, V. A., DFM, CGM	35	06.03.45	F/Sgt	SAVAGE, E. R.	405	28.01.45
F/Sgt	ROOKES, A. L.	156	07.08.44	F/O	SAVAGE, J. F.	35	24.03.44
F/O	ROSBOTTOM, J. H.	692	13.09.44	S/L	SAVAGE, J. R.	7	25.06.43
P/O	ROSE, C. A.	156	31.03.44	F/Lt	SAWYER, R. C.	35	13.05.43
F/Sgt	ROSE, W.	35	22.03.44	F/Lt	SAYER, A. J.	7	15.02.44
P/O	ROSE, W. H., DFC	156	23.11.43	F/Sgt	SAYWELL, E. W.	35	14.07.43
Sgt	ROSENBERG, E. D.	635	11.04.44	Sgt	SCAMMELL, K. F.	7	20.02.44
F/Sgt	ROSS, D.	156	28.05.43	F/Sgt	SCARFF, D. G. B.	83	22.06.44
Sgt	ROSS, F. J.	136(Ja)	20.08.43	F/Sgt	SCHILDKNECHT, A. A.	83	19.02.43
P/O	ROSS, F. R.	582	28.05.44	W/O2	SCHNEIDER, G. R.	405	17.12.43
F/O	ROSS, H.	571	01.01.45	S/L	SCHNEIDER, M. S. F.	405	09.10.43
F/Sgt	ROSS, H. J.	35	30.05.43	Sgt	SCHOLEY, J. W.	97	19.03.44

143

Rank	Name	Squadron	Date
F/O	SCHULTZ, A. B.	405	30.01.44
P/O	SCHWARTZ, M. E.	405	24.02.44
W/O	SCHWERDFERGER, G. A.	582	04.05.44
F/O	SCOTLAND, E. D.	571	22.10.44
Sgt	SCOTT, A. S.	156	27.07.43
P/O	SCOTT, A. C.	7	12.09.44
F/Sgt	SCOTT, I. McD.	97	17.12.43
Sgt	SCOTT, J. S.	156	03.01.44
F/Sgt	SCOTT, L. A.	7	23.04.44
P/O	SCOTT, N. L. W.	405	07.01.45
P/O	SCOTT, P. J. MacI.	405	23.11.43
Sgt	SCOTT, P. L. W.	7	21.02.45
Sgt	SCOTT, R. M.	35	22.06.43
F/O	SCOTT, S. O.	35	06.03.45
F/O	SCOTT, W. V.	7	16.12.43
Sgt	SEARLE, L. W.	7	21.10.43
F/Lt	SEARLES, S. O., DFC	139	24.03.45
F/Sgt	SEDDON, R.	156	13.08.44
F/Sgt	SEFRY, C. J.	7	16.12.43
F/Sgt	SEFTON, N. B.	7	15.02.44
Sgt	SELBY, M. J.	7	04.10.43
F/Lt	SELMAN, C. L., DFC	7	08.03.43
P/O	SERVISS, D. T.	405	04.05.44
F/Lt	SEWARD, F. P.	97	29.06.43
F/Lt	SEYMOUR, A.	7	22.11.43
Sgt	SHACKLADY, A.	156	22.06.43
F/Lt	SHACKMAN, L., AFC	692	31.10.44
F/O	SHAGENA, C. J.	405	21.02.43
F/O	SHANAHAN, M. O'M.	156	03.09.43
W/C	SHAND, W. P., DFC	139	21.04.43
F/Sgt	SHANE, F. J. W.	7	29.07.44
F/O	SHARLAND, R. G., DFC	156	28.04.44
Sgt	SHARP, R. G.	7	29.01.44
Sgt	SHARPE, J. H.	1409 Flt	03.12.43
F/Sgt	SHARPE, R. A. W.	7	13.03.43
Sgt	SHARPLES, J. W.	405(Ca)	11.06.44
F/Sgt	SHAW, C., DFM	635	24.12.44
Sgt	SHAW, J. McD.	405(Ca)	29.06.44
F/Sgt	SHAW, J. G.	156	20.01.45
AC2	SHAW, M.	Graveley	25.11.43
F/Lt	SHAW, N. H.	635	12.12.44
F/Sgt	SHAW, T. R., DFM	97	15.03.44
P/O	SHEIL, E. G.	7	13.08.43
Sgt	SHELMERDINE, T. P.	83	28.08.43
P/O	SHEPHERD, J. E.	405	04.05.44
F/Sgt	SHEPHERD, J. G.	156	27.03.43
Sgt	SHEPPARD, H. E.	156	17.06.43
F/O	SHEPPARD, W. F.	405	17.12.43
Sgt	SHIELDS, C. R.	35	24.05.43
Sgt	SHIELDS, F. W.	7	28.04.44
F/Sgt	SHEILDS, G. L. B.	Warboys	10.04.44
W/O	SHIRLEY, F. G. C. G.	635	26.08.44
F/O	SHIRLEY, W. L.	582	23.09.44
F/O	SHNIER, C.	97	30.07.43
F/Lt	SHOCKLEY, H. G.	405	12.03.43
F/O	SHOOTER, F. A. M., DFM	83	28.02.43
Sgt	SHORTER, E. A.	156	30.01.44
Sgt	SICKLEMORE, H. H. G.	156	13.07.43
F/Lt	SILK, A. J. W., DFM	97	22.11.43
P/O	SILVERMAN, D. M. C., DFM	156	18.11.43
P/O	SILVERWOOD, H., DFM	582	29.08.44
F/Sgt	SILVESTER, C. H.	83	28.08.43
F/Sgt	SIMMONDS, F. H.	7	20.10.43
Sgt	SIMMONS, T. C. E.	35	26.05.43
Sgt	SIMPSON, A.	35	22.03.44
S/L	SIMPSON, E. R., DFM	83	26.02.43
P/O	SIMPSON, G.	35	29.11.44
F/O	SIMPSON, H. J.	156	05.09.43
F/Sgt	SIMPSON, J. T.	7	27.09.43
F/Sgt	SIMPSON, R. N.	97	23.05.44
Sgt	SIMPSON, W.	156	07.09.43
F/Sgt	SINCLAIR, D.	35	20.02.44
F/Lt	SINCLAIR, W.	405	09.05.44
F/Lt	SINDALL, H. R.	635	06.01.45
F/Sgt	SINDEN, R. W.	97	26.11.43
F/O	SINFIELD, D. F., DFC	156	21.02.45
F/O	SINGLETON, M. D.	35	18.11.44
W/O	SKINNER, C. J.	97	14.01.44
Sgt	SKUTT, H.	635	16.06.44
F/Lt	SLADE, L. C. B., DFC	83	24.08.43
P/O	SLADE, S. J.	405	28.09.43
F/Lt	SLATTER, J. E.	1655 MTU	05.02.44
Sgt	SLATTERY, E. K.	582	04.05.44
W/O2	SLEETH, S.	405	27.04.43
Sgt	SLOAN, J. J.	156	30.01.41
F/Sgt	SLOMAN, G. S.	35	02.03.43
F/Lt	SLOPER, J. L., DFC	Warboys	10.04.44
Cpl	SLOSS, F. N.	83	18.06.43
F/Lt	SMAILL, W. B., DFC	7	27.08.44
F/Lt	SMALLEY, R. M., DFC	83	27.11.43
W/O2	SMALLEY, R. W.	582	24.07.44
Sgt	SMALLRIDGE, M. G.	7	09.10.43
F/O	SMART, A. F. G.	7	20.05.44
P/O	SMART, A. B., DFM	83	13.06.43
Sgt	SMART, P. J.	156	02.12.43
F/O	SMEATON, A. B.	83	27.11.43
Sgt	SMEDLEY, J. E.	405	31.01.44
2/Lt	SMEDSAAS, O.	139	26.02.43
P/O	SMITH, A. J.	97	12.03.43
Sgt	SMITH, A. L.	35	18.11.43
F/Lt	SMITH, B. F., DFC	156	30.07.43
F/Lt	SMITH, B. H.	608	16.09.44
F/Sgt	SMITH, D. F.	405	14.01.44
F/O	SMITH, D. R.	97	25.02.44
F/O	SMITH, D. G.	405	17.03.45
F/Sgt	SMITH, D. E.	156	17.04.45
F/Sgt	SMITH, D. I. T.	582	23.09.44
W/O	SMITH, E. G., DFM	582	06.07.44
F/O	SMITH, E. W.	156	14.01.44
F/Sgt	SMITH, E. G.	405	16.06.44
Sgt	SMITH, E. L.	635	12.09.44
P/O	SMITH, F., DFM	156	17.04.43
F/Lt	SMITH, F. C.	HQ 8 (PFF)	17.12.43
F/Sgt	SMITH, F. K.	35	24.03.44
P/O	SMITH, G.	97	26.11.43
F/Sgt	SMITH, G. E.	97	02.01.44
F/Lt	SMITH, G. J.	405	01.05.44
S/L	SMITH, G. M.	109	06.03.45
Sgt	SMITH, G. W.	7	23.11.43
P/O	SMITH, G. A.	405	28.01.45
F/O	SMITH, H.	7	31.08.43
F/Sgt	SMITH, H. F.	83	22.01.44
Sgt	SMITH, J.	35	18.11.43
F/Lt	SMITH, J. B., DFC	97	10.05.44
Sgt	SMITH, J. D.	635	04.08.44
F/Lt	SMITH, J. T., DFC	156	22.11.43
F/Sgt	SMITH, K. L.	97	29.06.43
F/Lt	SMITH, K. S.	35	06.03.45
P/O	SMITH, N. L. L.	405	16.01.45
Sgt	SMITH, N. L.	97	11.07.42
Sgt	SMITH, N. R.	97	14.01.44
Sgt	SMITH, R. C.	35	27.03.43
W/O	SMITH, R. B., DFC	7	20.12.43
F/Lt	SMITH, R. B., DFC	105	09.04.44
Sgt	SMITH, R. E.	7	23.04.44
F/O	SMITH, R. S., DFC	156	16.12.43
Sgt	SMITH, R. V. D.	7	04.12.43
Sgt	SMITH, R. P.	405	19.03.45
F/Sgt	SMITH, R. S.	7	15.03.44
Sgt	SMITH, S. G.	156	22.05.44
F/O	SMITH, S. K.	156	29.09.43
F/Sgt	SMITH, T. W.	97	29.01.44

Rank	Name	Squadron	Date	Rank	Name	Squadron	Date
Sgt	SMITH, T. R. M.	35	04.07.43	P/O	STEVENSON, L., DFC	97	23.09.43
F/Sgt	SMITH, W., DFC	582	15.06.44	F/Sgt	STEVENSON, S. B., DFM	97	14.01.44
F/Sgt	SMITH, W. H.	156	15.02.44	F/Lt	STEWART, A. MacK.	PFF, NTU	11.03.45
F/Lt	SMITH, W. J., DFC	156	30.07.43			Warboys	
Sgt	SMITH, W. McK.	35	22.03.44	F/O	STEWART, A. W., DFM	156	03.09.43
Sgt	SMITH, W. P.	156	23.06.43	F/Sgt	STEWART, C., DFM	7	11.03.43
P/O	SMYTHE, N. B.	196	26.06.43	F/O	STEWART, C. F., DFM	582	29.08.44
F/Sgt	SNELLING, D. C. G.	156	03.01.44	F/Lt	STEWART, D. C.	635	13.05.44
Sgt	SNOWBALL, T.	635	04.06.44	F/Sgt	STEWART, E.	35	12.06.43
Sgt	SOAN, H. R. C.	571	22.10.44	Sgt	STEWART, H.	97	25.04.44
F/Sgt	SOBEL, H.	7	01.05.43	F/Lt	STEWART, H. W. L., DFC	156	23.11.43
P/O	SOLOMON, E.	35	03.08.43	Sgt	STEWART, J. C.	156	13.05.43
F/Lt	SOUAILLARD, J. J. H. O.	405	14.01.44	F/Lt	STEWART, J. K., DFC	35	23.05.44
Sgt	SOUTAR, R. A.	128	04.11.44	F/O	STEWART, J. J	7	09.04.43
Sgt	SOWERSBY, E. S.	83	25.04.44	Sgt	STEWART, R. C.	97	17.12.43
Sgt	SPANTON, D. R.	7	25.06.43	S/L	STEWART, R. G. F., DFC	156	02.01.44
F/Lt	SPARLING, L. G.	405	07.01.45	F/O	STILES, E. B.	83	03.01.44
P/O	SPEARMAN, G. D.	405	07.05.44	Sgt	STILL, G. T.	83	30.03.43
Sgt	SPENCE, D. L.	83	22.09.43	P/O	STILL, W.	635	24.03.44
Sgt	SPENCE, W. J.	35	30.07.43	F/Lt	STIMPSON, M. C., DFC	156	15.02.44
F/Sgt	SPENCER, C. G.	7	25.04.44	P/O	STINSON, H. V.	35	02.12.43
W/O	SPENCER, F. J.	139(Ja)	31.10.43	Sgt	STOCKS, T., DFM	156	22.11.43
F/O	SPENCER, H.	83	22.06.44	P/O	STOKES, G. J. H.	156	22.11.43
F/Lt	SPENCER, J. B. P.	83	31.07.44	F/O	STONE, E. J., DFC	35	29.12.43
W/O	SPENCER, K.	7	05.05.44	P/O	STONE, G. B.	156	13.08.44
Sgt	SPENCER, T. R.	7	09.10.43	Sgt	STONE, J. R.	83	13.05.43
F/Lt	SPEYER, L. G.	405	21.01.44	Sgt	STONE, J.	97	16.12.43
F/Lt	SPINLEY, M., DFM	156	03.02.45	P/O	STONE, T. A.	405	09.02.45
F/O	SPLATT, L. W.	405	07.01.45	P/O	STONELLEY, M. J. E., DFM	156	18.11.43
P/O	SPOONER, R.	35	30.07.43	F/Lt	STONEMAN, R. V.	7	12.09.44
P/O	SPRACK, C. F. J., DFM	83	13.06.43	Sgt	STONEMAN, W. G.	NTU	25.01.44
Sgt	SPREADBURY, G.	156	30.12.44			Upwood	
F/O	SQUIBB, W. A. F.	582	23.04.44	Sgt	STONESTREET, A. N.	139(Ja)	27.05.43
F/Sgt	SQUIRE, L. A.	7	04.09.43	Sgt	STOPFORD, N. G.	156	08.04.43
P/O	SQUIRES, R. L.	405	07.05.44	W/O1	STORBAKKEN, R. A.	83	27.04.44
W/O	STACEY, S. T., DFC	83	26.11.43	F/Sgt	STORDY, J. L.	405	27.04.44
W/O	STAFFORD, G. C., DFM	156	04.04.43	F/O	STRANG, C. R.	692	27.06.44
F/Lt	STAFFORD, H. M.	156	03.09.43	Sgt	STRANG, G. L.	405	16.12.43
F/O	STAIN, R. R., DFM	156	24.12.43	Sgt	STRANG, J. C. B.	139	31.08.43
Sgt	STALLY, E. C.	83	23.06.43	F/Sgt	STRANGE, R. C.	156	14.01.44
F/O	STAMERS, D. H.	405	16.12.43	F/Sgt	STREET, D. E.	7	13.03.43
F/Sgt	STAMP, T. E.	97	18.10.43	Sgt	STREET, J. W.	35	27.08.44
F/Sgt	STANBRIDGE, A. A.	635	25.03.44	W/O2	STRONG, R. D.	156	08.03.43
Sgt	STANDRING, W.	97	30.03.43	F/Lt	STROUT, A. C.	582	29.08.44
F/Lt	STANILAND, B. J.	156	02.12.43	P/O	STROUTS, F. S., DFC	109	26.03.44
F/O	STANISLAUS, A. F. P.	97	06.01.44	F/Sgt	STUART, R. A.	405	07.04.43
F/Lt	STANNARD, C. R.	156	14.01.44	Sgt	STURGEON, J. A.	582	23.04.44
W/O	STANNERS, R.	156	20.02.44	Sgt	STURROCK, J. A. McK	692	15.01.45
Sgt	STANTON, A. L.	7	24.11.43	F/O	SUGAR, G. R.	83	13.06.43
P/O	STAPLES, M. J.	156	30.07.43	F/Sgt	SULLIVAN, A. V.	692	22.03.45
F/O	STAPLETON, J. W.	582	06.07.44	F/Sgt	SULLIVAN, J. T., DFM	97	04.10.43
F/Lt	STARIE, B. J., DFC	97	15.03.44	F/O	SULLIVAN, J. P.	156	21.12.42
F/Sgt	STEEDMAN, W. K	7	22.05.44	F/Lt	SULLIVAN, M. A., DFC	156	20.12.43
Sgt	STEELE, K.	156	24.09.44	F/Lt	SUMNER, A. H. J., DFC	35	17.08.43
F/Sgt	STEGMAN, L. A.	163	11.04.45	Sgt	SUNLEY, A.	35	10.08.43
F/Sgt	STENHOUSE, H.	7	26.08.44	Sgt	SURGEY, W.	83	11.04.44
P/O	STENHOUSE, W. E.	7	22.09.43	F/Sgt	SUTCLIFFE, A., DFM	35	23.12.44
Sgt	STEPHEN, E. S.	608	08.06.45	F/Sgt	SUTHERLAND, R. J.	692	17.12.44
P/O	STEPHEN, W. J., DFM	97	25.06.43	F/Lt	SUTHERLAND, W. S. D.	139	27.05.43
S/L	STEPHENS, H. B., DFC	109	06.05.44	P/O	SUTHERST, J.	7	31.08.43
Sgt	STEPHENS, J. T.	156	17.04.43	Sgt	SUTTON, A. J.	7	22.06.43
P/O	STEPHENS, T. G., DFM	156	22.11.43	Sgt	SUTTON, E. J.	156	03.01.44
Sgt	STEPHENS, W.	97	09.07.43	F/Lt	SUTTON, H. R., DFC	139	27.05.43
F/O	STEPNEY, C. G.	35	18.11.43	Sgt	SUTTON, T. H.	35	31.08.43
F/Lt	STERNS, W. M., DFC	156	20.02.44	Sgt	SUTTON, W. R	83	20.02.44
F/Lt	STEVEN, W. J.	97	14.01.44	F/Lt	SWAIN, C. D.	105	31.03.44
F/Sgt	STEVENS, D. E. J.	582	29.08.44	F/Sgt	SWAIN, D. A. A.	35	26.11.43
Sgt	STEVENS, E. G. A.	156	16.04.42	F/O	SWALE, K., DFC	139	15.01.45
F/O	STEVENS, F.	139	07.04.44	Maj	SWALES, E., VC DFC	582	23.02.45
Sgt	STEVENS, J.	7	31.03.44	F/Lt	SWARBRICK, J., DFC	109	20.07.44
Sgt	STEVENS, R. R.	405	21.01.44	F/Lt	SWEENEY, J.	105	22.10.43
P/O	STEVENS, W. G.	105	27.04.44	F/O	SWEETMAN, O. C.	608	09.10.44
F/O	STEVENSON, J.	139	07.08.44	Sgt	SWIFT, C. R.	156	08.03.43

Rank	Name	Squadron	Date
F/Sgt	SWINNEY, A.	156	27.09.43
F/Lt	SWINNEY, C. R., DFC	156	14.01.44
P/O	SYLVAH, C. M.	405	09.05.44
F/Sgt	TAIT, H. S.	97	19.03.44
F/O	TALBOT, E., DFC	692	05.06.44
F/Sgt	TALBOT, L. M.	35	10.04.44
Sgt	TALBY, C.	635	25.03.44
P/O	TANDY, R.	156	25.02.44
F/Sgt	TANKARD, V. G.	83	17.12.43
Sgt	TANNER, C. E.	83	28.02.43
Sgt	TANNER, P. V.	83	22.06.43
Sgt	TANNOCK, A.	35	30.05.43
Sgt	TANSLEY, M. L.	608	06.11.44
W/C	TATNALL, J. B., OBE	7	15.02.44
F/Lt	TAYLOR, A. C. M. G.	35	05.07.44
S/L	TAYLOR, A. E., DFM	7	02.01.44
Sgt	TAYLOR, A. M.	35	30.05.43
Sgt	TAYLOR, A. W. R.	97	12.03.43
F/Sgt	TAYLOR, G. S.	83	04.10.43
F/Sgt	TAYLOR, G. D.	582	29.07.44
F/O	TAYLOR, H. F. McP., DFC, CGM	1409 Flt	05.12.43
F/Sgt	TAYLOR, J. A. C.	405(Ca)	05.04.43
F/Sgt	TAYLOR, J. J.	83	30.01.44
Sgt	TAYLOR, J. E.	7	20.03.45
P/O	TAYLOR, J. W.	156	20.02.44
F/O	TAYLOR, J. G.	405	09.10.43
Sgt	TAYLOR, K. W.	156	04.04.43
F/O	TAYLOR, M. J.	1655 MTU	26.02.44
F/Lt	TAYLOR, N., DFM	139	14.10.44
W/O1	TAYLOR, N. H. A.	405(Ca)	12.06.43
F/O	TAYLOR, P. A.	156	13.08.44
P/O	TAYLOR, R., DFC	97	31.03.44
F/Sgt	TAYLOR, R. A.	83	18.06.43
F/Sgt	TAYLOR, R. L.	83	20.10.43
F/Lt	TAYLOR, R. C. C.	7	15.08.43
Sgt	TEBBUT, G. N.	83	25.04.44
F/O	TEMPLE, H. L.	35	10.08.43
W/O	TENNANT, P. A.	7	20.03.45
F/O	TERPENING, R. P., DFC	582	28.04.45
P/O	TERRY, F. A.	7	11.04.43
F/Lt	TETLEY, W. A., DFC	35	30.05.43
F/O	THACKWAY, E.	97	17.12.43
F/Lt	THATCHER, W.	405	14.01.44
F/Lt	THEOBALD, W. M., DFC	7	12.01.44
F/Sgt	THOMAS, A.	35	24.12.44
W/O	THOMAS, A. E.	156	23.04.44
Sgt	THOMAS, A. H.	35	27.03.44
F/O	THOMAS, D. O.	83	12.06.43
F/Lt	THOMAS, D. L. C., DFC	7	14.01.44
Sgt	THOMAS, D. A.	405(Ca)	03.08.43
P/O	THOMAS, G. E.	1655 MTU	13.09.44
F/Sgt	THOMAS, J. A.	83	03.01.44
F/Lt	THOMAS, P. A., DFC	582	23.12.44
W/O	THOMAS, R. K.	156	02.12.43
Sgt	THOMAS, U.	156	27.03.43
F/Lt	THOMAS, W., DFC	692	20.02.44
W/O	THOMPSON, D., DFC	35	20.10.44
F/Lt	THOMPSON, E. M., DFC	156	18.11.43
Sgt	THOMPSON, F.	97	25.03.44
F/Lt	THOMPSON, F. D. J., DFC *	7	11.03.43
Sgt	THOMPSON, G.	7	25.06.43
P/O	THOMPSON, J. B.	156	09.03.43
Sgt	THOMPSON, L. W.	156	24.08.43
F/O	THOMPSON, O. W., DFM	105	01.05.43
Sgt	THOMPSON, R.	7	22.05.44
F/Sgt	THOMSON, A. J.	35	12.11.43
Sgt	THOMSON, T.	405(Ca)	17.11.43
F/Sgt	THORINGTON, F.	156	02.01.44
Sgt	THORNE, A. E. J.	35	27.08.44
F/Sgt	THORNE, E. J.	139(Ja)	15.07.43
F/Sgt	THORNE, R. G.	7	09.03.43
F/Sgt	THORNHILL, M. A.	405(Ca)	11.06.44
Sgt	THOROGOOD, S.	7	31.08.43
P/O	THORPE, J. H., DFC	35	29.11.44
Sgt	THROSBY, W. J.	83	11.04.44
Sgt	THURECHT, N. R.	156	03.04.43
S/L	THWAITES, M. E., DFC	7	11.03.43
F/Lt	TILBURY, E. A.	83	13.06.43
W/O	TILL, A. T.	635	21.08.44
Sgt	TILLAM, J. L.	635	25.03.44
Sgt	TIMMINS, L.	7	20.05.44
F/Sgt	TINDLE, G. W.	7	23.11.43
F/Sgt	TINMAN, W. R.	156	02.12.43
F/O	TITE, J., DFC	405	22.12.44
F/Lt	TODD, C.	7	05.05.44
Sgt	TODD, R.	608	05.03.45
F/O	TOLLEY, D. E.	83	27.04.44
Sgt	TOLSON, R.	7	11.04.43
F/O	TOMCZAK, M. E.	405(Ca)	26.07.43
F/Sgt	TOMLINSON, A.	97	25.06.43
P/O	TOMLINSON, F. M.	7	10.03.43
Sgt	TOMLINSON, L. R.	83	03.04.43
LAC	TOMLINSON, S.	Graveley	13.06.45
F/Lt	TOMPKINS, F. A. G., DFC	7	22.01.43
S/L	TONG, R. F. L., DFC	128	10.01.45
Sgt	TONGUE, C. W. L.	405	24.02.44
F/Sgt	TONGUE, J.	97	28.03.43
P/O	TONKYN, J. W.	405(Ca)	23.04.44
F/O	TOOMER, R.	35	12.09.44
F/O	TOPPINGS, I. J.	156	31.03.44
F/Lt	TOUGH, D. P.	105	19.03.45
P/O	TOUPIN, L. L. V.	7	09.03.43
F/O	TOWNSEND, E. A.	405(Ca)	29.07.44
Sgt	TRANTER, A. R.	35	04.05.44
Sgt	TRAVERS, W. S.	83	20.01.44
F/Sgt	TRAYLOR, G. W.	35	20.02.44
Sgt	TRAYNOR, F. M.	35	30.05.43
F/Sgt	TRAYNOR, P.	83	03.01.44
F/Lt	TREBY, T.	139	24.03.45
F/Sgt	TREE, J. R.	83	29.01.44
P/O	TREMBLAY, P. Y. C.	156	19.02.43
F/Lt	TRENCH, J. P., DSO	7	08.03.43
F/Sgt	TREVIS, S. C.	582	12.12.44
F/Lt	TREVOR-ROPER, R. D., DFC, DFM	97	31.03.44
Sgt	TRIGWELL, R. S.	156	03.04.43
F/Lt	TRILSBECK, T.	156	16.12.43
F/O	TRIPPE, T. D.	405	28.09.43
F/Lt	TROPMAN, F. W. G., DFC	35	22.02.45
P/O	TROTT, B. A.	156	14.01.44
Sgt	TRUMAN, W. C.	582	25.05.44
Sgt	TRUSCOTT, H.	156	22.11.43
F/O	TUCK, A. T., DFC	35	27.09.43
F/Sgt	TUCK, F. C. V.	635	04.08.44
F/O	TUCK, G. W.	128	24.11.44
Sgt	TUCKER, A. A.	7	16.12.43
F/Sgt	TUCKER, B. G., DFM	83	23.11.43
P/O	TUCKER, R. C.	35	24.08.43
LAC	TUCKWELL, W. H.	105	25.02.44
Sgt	TULLOCH, J.	635	26.08.44
F/Sgt	TUNBRIDGE, D. O.	97	19.03.44
Sgt	TUPMAN, D. H.	635	11.04.44
F/O	TURK, R. D.	156	05.03.43
F/Sgt	TURNBULL, W.	35	29.11.44
Sgt	TURNER, B. W.	405	21.02.43
Sgt	TURNER, F. W.	83	22.06.43
F/Sgt	TURNER, N. W.	97	04.12.43
F/O	TURNER, W. B.	405	28.01.43
P/O	TURP, K. C.	83	28.08.43
F/Sgt	TUTILL, J. W.	156	30.12.44
Sgt	TUTT, B. F.	97	26.11.43
P/O	TUTT, N. J.	582	16.01.44
F/Sgt	TWEEDIE, J.	156	17.06.43
Sgt	TWEEDIE, J.	582	24.07.44
F/Sgt	TWELL, N.	7	27.08.44

Rank	Name	Squadron	Date
Sgt	TYE, J.	97	20.01.44
P/O	TYLER, G.	7	16.12.43
F/O	TYLER, J. V.	97	22.11.43
F/Lt	TYNEDALE, L. V.	582	29.08.44
Sgt	UNDERHILL, C. R.	7	16.12.43
F/Sgt	UNDERWOOD, J. N.	97	27.11.43
F/Sgt	UNDERWOOD, R., DFM	156	02.01.44
F/O	UNDERWOOD, W. H. T., DFC	582	15.03.45
S/L	UNDRELL, G. A. R., DFC	156	11.09.44
Sgt	UNWIN, P. H.	97	30.07.43
Sgt	UNWIN, R.	97	02.03.43
F/Sgt	URCH, F.	156	24.01.44
Sgt	UREN, E. F.	405	17.11.43
Sgt	URQUHART, A. V.	635	13.08.44
F/Sgt	URWIN, R. M.	7	11.03.43
F/Lt	USHER, K., DFC	635	05.03.45
P/O	UZELMAN, P.	582	23.12.44
F/Lt	VALE, E. S.	692	27.03.45
F/Sgt	VALENCIA, R. H.	156	13.08.44
P/O	VALENTINE, E. F.	156	20.05.42
F/Sgt	VALENTINE, H. M.	139	13.08.43
F/Lt	VAN AMSTERDAM, A. A. J., DFC	139	27.03.45
P/O	VANCE, E. R.	7	21.04.43
F/Lt	VAN RAALTE, H. S.	97	23.06.44
Sgt	VARDY, G.	7	04.09.43
Sgt	VAUGHAN, W. J.	97	11.08.43
Sgt	VAULKHARD, J. J.	156	19.04.43
F/Sgt	VENN, F. M.	156	05.05.43
F/Lt	VENNING, D. L., DFC	635	05.03.45
S/L	VERDON-ROE, L., DFC	156	13.05.43
P/O	VERE-HODGE, H. M. J.	97	12.09.44
P/O	VERI, D.	405	07.01.45
Sgt	VESSEY, W. C.	635	12.06.44
F/Sgt	VIAU, J. A. J. L.	97	12.03.43
P/O	VICKERS, G., DFC	156	02.01.44
F/Sgt	VICKERS, H. S.	83	11.04.44
Sgt	VICKERS, P. V. De V.	83	20.01.44
F/O	VICKERY, J. L.	35	08.04.45
Sgt	VINCENT, N. D. J.	97	29.01.44
S/L	VINCENT, P. R., DFC	156	27.09.43
Sgt	VINE, G. D.	7	02.05.44
Sgt	VINER, F. A.	156	20.12.43
F/O	VINEY, F. H.	405	16.08.43
F/Sgt	VINICOMBE, S. S.	35	09.03.43
F/Lt	VIRTUE, J. D.	405	21.07.44
P/O	VIVIAN, J. K.	405	16.06.44
Sgt	VIVOUR, B. B.	156	31.03.44
P/O	VOLANTE, S. J., DFM	156	04.04.43
Sgt	WADDELL, J. J.	405	14.01.44
Sgt	WADDING, P.	7	15.04.43
Sgt	WADE, A. W.	83	25.04.44
F/O	WADE, E., BEM	105	23.11.43
Sgt	WADE, G.	7	15.04.43
F/Lt	WADHAM, B. S. H., DFC	7	05.04.45
F/O	WADSWORTH, P.	156	28.04.44
P/O	WAIN, J. H., DFC	7	02.05.44
F/Sgt	WAITE, A.	83	29.01.44
S/L	WAKEFIELD, M. G.	7	24.06.44
Sgt	WAKEMAN, W. E.	156	26.07.43
P/O	WAKLEY, C. A.	97	20.01.44
Sgt	WALDER, F. J.	156	27.03.43
W/O	WALDRON, W.	582	29.07.44
F/Lt	WALKER, A. W.	635	24.12.44
Sgt	WALKER, A.	7	15.04.43
F/O	WALKER, J.	109	08.04.43
P/O	WALKER, J.	156	22.11.43
Sgt	WALKER, J. A.	156	13.07.43
Sgt	WALKER, J. W.	405(Ca)	30.01.44
F/O	WALKER, R. E.	83	21.01.44
F/O	WALL, C. D.	83	03.01.44
Sgt	WALL, W. A.	83	02.01.44
F/Sgt	WALLACE, D. L.	156	28.05.43
F/O	WALLACE, E. P., DFC	128	04.11.44
Sgt	WALLACE, G.	7	31.08.43
Sgt	WALLACE, L. R.	405(Ca)	07.04.43
F/Sgt	WALLACE, S.	7	02.05.44
Sgt	WALLER, A.	156	03.01.44
Sgt	WALLER, C.	156	27.04.44
F/Sgt	WALLER, W. G.	97	22.11.43
F/O	WALLINGFORD, K. D.	635	06.12.44
P/O	WALLIS, B. F.	582	23.04.44
P/O	WALLIS, H. A., DFC	7	25.04.43
P/O	WALLIS, R. J.	156	27.03.43
P/O	WALSH, T. J. P., DFC	7	18.11.43
Sgt	WALSH, W. J.	7	06.01.44
F/O	WALTERS, J. W., DFC	7	20.05.44
Sgt	WALTERS, V.	7	09.04.43
Sgt	WALTERS, W. D. R.	35	30.07.43
Sgt	WARD, F. F.	35	14.07.43
F/O	WARD, H. T.	97	11.05.44
F/Sgt	WARD, J. T.	7	24.06.44
Sgt	WARD, K. A.	156	24.03.44
W/O2	WARD, R. H.	156	08.03.43
P/O	WARDROP, W.	83	24.08.43
Sgt	WARES, A. J. D.	635	08.03.45
F/O	WARFIELD, N. J., DFM	156	24.12.43
F/O	WARNER, S. G. A.	692	28.08.44
F/O	WARNER, E. F., DFM	156	07.05.44
Sgt	WARREN, H. E.	156	28.08.43
F/Lt	WARREN, J. W., DFC	35	20.02.44
P/O	WARREN, L. E.	83	12.03.43
Sgt	WARRENGER, S. J.	NTU Warboys	10.04.44
F/Sgt	WARWICK, N.	156	11.09.44
F/Sgt	WARWICK, R. G.	7	02.01.44
F/Sgt	WASPE, E. J.	635	16.06.44
F/Lt	WATERBURY, O. R., DFC	83	12.03.43
F/O	WATERHOUSE, V., DFC	156	02.01.44
W/O	WATERMAN, W. M.	7	16.12.43
Sgt	WATKINS, A. E.	83	22.01.44
F/Lt	WATKINS, K. B.	156	03.09.43
F/Sgt	WATKINS, W. H.	156	17.12.43
F/Lt	WATLING, G. A.	97	29.01.44
F/O	WATSON, D.	156	29.01.45
F/Sgt	WATSON, D. M.	7	21.10.43
F/O	WATSON, F. T., DFM	105	02.01.45
S/L	WATSON, F., DFC	35	06.03.45
F/Sgt	WATSON, H. M.	7	21.02.45
F/Sgt	WATSON, J. H.	635	07.01.45
Sgt	WATSON, J. M.	7	24.06.44
Sgt	WATSON, J. A.	156	17.12.43
P/O	WATSON, J. G., DFM	582	28.04.45
F/Sgt	WATSON, L. A.	7	04.09.43
P/O	WATSON, T.	97	26.11.43
W/O	WATSON, W. A.	7	16.12.43
F/Lt	WATT, J. S., DSO, DFC	7	22.06.43
F/Sgt	WATTERS, L. H.	156	27.04.43
F/O	WATTS, A. J. S.	83	11.04.44
F/Lt	WATTS, H. W. D., DFC	635	06.07.44
F/Sgt	WATTS, J. E.	7	16.06.44
Sgt	WATTS, L. G. W.	35	21.01.44
F/O	WATTS, P. A.	156	20.12.43
F/Sgt	WATTS, R. G.	156	22.05.44
P/O	WATTS, R. P.	83	03.01.44
Sgt	WATTS, R. E.	405	02.01.44
F/Sgt	WATTS, S. G.	35	18.11.44
F/Sgt	WATTS, S. L. C.	35	02.03.43
W/C	WATTS, S. D., DSO, DFC	692	11.07.44
F/Lt	WAUGH, A. W.	692	11.03.45
F/Sgt	WAUGH, D. H.	156	27.04.43
F/Lt	WAUGH, K. R.	97	25.04.44
F/Lt	WAY, W. H. L. S., DFC	35	06.01.44
F/O	WEARE, D. A., DFC	109	21.12.44
F/O	WEATHERALL, R. L., DFM	7	20.05.44

147

Rank	Name	Squadron	Date	Rank	Name	Squadron	Date
F/O	WEATHERILL, D. A., DFC	35	24.06.44	W/O	WHITEHOUSE, A., DFC	83	27.04.44
Sgt	WEATHERILL, E. S.	7	21.01.44	W/O	WHITEHOUSE, B. E. R., DFC	7	21.01.44
P/O	WEAVER, A. J.	635	06.07.44				
P/O	WEAVER, G. M.	405	04.05.44	F/O	WHITFORD, A. P., DFC	83	09.05.44
F/Sgt	WEBB, B. W.	582	25.05.44	Sgt	WHITING, W. H.	97	30.03.43
Sgt	WEBB, C. F.	156	28.08.43	ACW1	WHITLOCK, J. E.	8Gp	21.01.42
P/O	WEBB, C. W.	97	11.08.43	F/Sgt	WHITTAKER, F. W.	35	14.07.43
F/Lt	WEBB, F. C., DFM	83	04.10.43	F/Lt	WHITTLESTONE, F. S., DFC	7	29.01.44
F/Sgt	WEBB, F. S.	582	28.05.44				
Sgt	WEBB, F. H.	7	30.07.43	Sgt	WHYBROW, L. G.	582	24.07.44
F/Lt	WEBB, H. J. L.	635	31.03.44	Sgt	WHYBROW, R.	635	06.01.45
F/Sgt	WEBB, J. C. K.	35	22.03.44	F/O	WHYTE, W. E.	128	07.03.45
P/O	WEBB, J. W.	35	23.12.44	F/O	WICKENS, H. A.	405	16.06.44
F/Lt	WEBB, L. S., DFC	97	04.10.43	F/O	WICKENS, R. C.	97	25.04.44
F/Sgt	WEBB, R. A.	7	25.03.44	F/Sgt	WICKERSHAM, A. J.	35	26.11.43
Sgt	WEBB, R.	35	30.07.43	W/O	WICKS, R. R.	156	02.12.43
F/Lt	WEBB, S. D.	608	10.11.44	F/Sgt	WICKSON, G. C.	83	22.06.43
Sgt	WEBB, W. A.	156	23.04.44	Sgt	WIGGETT, C. E.	83	22.06.43
F/Lt	WEBSTER, H., DFC	35	24.08.43	P/O	WIGGINS, A. A.	635	07.01.45
Sgt	WEBSTER, J.	35	25.07.44	Sgt	WIGHTMAN, K.	7	16.12.43
P/O	WEBSTER, J. F.	156	14.01.44	F/O	WIGLEY, G. A.	97	17.12.43
F/O	WEBSTER, R. C.	35	08.04.45	F/Sgt	WILBY, G. A.	156	24.06.44
Sgt	WEBSTER, V.	35	18.08.43	Sgt	WILCOX, F. W.	83	18.06.43
F/O	WEIGHT, R. E.	97	29.03.43	LAC	WILD, R. H.	35	29.03.45
S/L	WEIGHTMAN, J. B., DFC	582(Att)	20.07.44	P/O	WILKES, R. E., DFM	35	15.04.43
Sgt	WEIR, A. P.	635	31.03.45	F/Sgt	WILKES, W. L. L.	97	28.08.43
F/O	WEIR, G. R. E.	608	06.12.44	Sgt	WILKIE, D. L., DFM	156	04.10.43
P/O	WELCH, H. W.	156	19.02.43	F/Sgt	WILKINS, C. L. Y.	7	14.01.44
Sgt	WELLER, A. H.	35	16.03.44	F/O	WILKINS, H.	582	16.09.44
F/O	WELLER, R. M., DFC	35	07.03.45	P/O	WILKINS, T. E.	83	30.01.44
F/O	WELLER, R. J., DFM	97	31.03.44	F/O	WILKINSON, S.	139	13.05.43
F/Sgt	WELLINGTON, D.	7	27.03.43	F/O	WILKINSON, W., DFC	156	18.11.43
Sgt	WELLS, P. E.	156	02.12.43	Sgt	WILLER, G. O.	582	15.03.45
Sgt	WELLS, R. H.	35	02.12.43	Sgt	WILLETT, F. J.	156	22.06.43
F/Lt	WELLS, W. B.	83	17.04.43	Sgt	WILLIAMS, D. E.	97	23.06.43
F/Lt	WELLSTEAD, L. C. R., DFC, DFM	128	01.01.45	F/Lt	WILLIAMS, D. L., DFC	83	27.04.44
				F/Lt	WILLIAMS, D. G., DFC	139	02.01.45
W/O	WENDES, R. J.	109	16.11.44	F/O	WILLIAMS, D. K., DFC	109	05.07.44
P/O	WENDON, W. M.	156	13.05.43	P/O	WILLIAMS, E. H.	35	22.03.44
F/Lt	WERNHAM, J. C.	405	30.03.44	F/Sgt	WILLIAMS, F. A.	97	22.11.43
Sgt	WEST, A. D.	7	23.11.43	F/Sgt	WILLIAMS, G. V., DFC	35	29.11.44
Sgt	WEST, A. R. E.	97	29.01.44	W/O2	WILLIAMS, G. I.	97	31.01.44
Sgt	WEST, B. S. J.	405	02.01.44	F/Sgt	WILLIAMS, G., DFM	635	05.03.45
F/Lt	WEST, F. T.	83	20.01.44	F/Sgt	WILLIAMS, J. K. S.	7	15.02.44
F/Lt	WESTON, A. W.	97	10.05.44	Sgt	WILLIAMS, J. P.	156	31.03.45
F/Sgt	WESTON, C. J.	7	16.06.44	W/O	WILLIAMS, J. T.	7	02.01.44
F/Lt	WHARMBY, R. B.	7	14.01.44	Sgt	WILLIAMS, L.	35	24.12.44
F/Sgt	WHARTON, S.	635	04.06.44	Sgt	WILLIAMS, M. N.	156	22.11.43
Sgt	WHATLEY, R. J.	97	29.03.43	F/O	WILLIAMS, R. C., DFC	35	29.12.43
Sgt	WHATMORE, A.	7	15.08.43	Sgt	WILLIAMS, S.	83	23.06.43
P/O	WHEATLEY, R. F.	635	19.08.44	Sgt	WILLIAMS, T. L.	97	12.03.43
F/O	WHEATLEY, R.	35	15.04.43	F/O	WILLIAMS, W. T.	582	16.06.44
Sgt	WHEELER, G.	83	20.02.44	Sgt	WILLIAMSON, H. R.	83	13.05.43
P/O	WHEWAY, R. J.	7	03.01.44	Sgt	WILLIS, E. F. J.	35	30.07.43
F/Lt	WHIFFEN, G. K.	105	05.07.44	F/Lt	WILMER, J.	1655 MTU	22.07.44
F/O	WHIPP, L. P.	105	19.10.44	Sgt	WILMOTT, R. W.	7	29.01.44
F/Sgt	WHITE, E. K.	405(Ca)	25.07.43	F/Sgt	WILMSHURST, L. T.	7	03.01.44
Sgt	WHITE, F. E.	7	21.10.43	F/O	WILSHER, F. H.	405	29.12.44
Sgt	WHITE, J.	35PFF	22.06.43	F/Lt	WILSON, C. T., DFC	97	29.01.44
F/Sgt	WHITE, J.	35	11.09.44	S/L	WILSON, C. H., DFC	7	31.03.44
W/O2	WHITE, J. D.	405(Ca)	03.04.43	F/Sgt	WILSON, D.	7	26.11.43
W/C	WHITE, J. H., DFC	156	18.11.43	Sgt	WILSON, D. D.	582	29.10.44
Sgt	WHITE, L.	35	23.12.44	Sgt	WILSON, D. S.	7	21.10.43
Sgt	WHITE, L. W. J.	156	30.12.44	Sgt	WILSON, D. C.	7	13.03.43
F/Lt	WHITE, M. J. A.	35	17.08.43	Sgt	WILSON, E.	156	17.04.45
P/O	WHITE, M. E., DFM	156	08.03.43	F/Sgt	WILSON, G.	156	03.09.43
Sgt	WHITE, S.	156	08.04.43	S/L	WILSON, G. H., DSO, DFC	139	25.06.44
W/O	WHITE, W. C., DFM	635	20.04.44	F/O	WILSON, G. S.	405	28.05.43
F/Sgt	WHITEAR, L. H.	7	14.01.44	F/Lt	WILSON, G., DSO, DFC, DFM	7	06.09.44
P/O	WHITEBEARD, R. E.	156	24.02.44	P/O	WILSON, H. L., DFM	582	15.06.44
Sgt	WHITEFIELD, L. W.	156	25.02.44	Sgt	WILSON, H. J.	83	11.04.44
F/Sgt	WHITEHEAD, A.	635	31.03.44	F/Sgt	WILSON, J. L.	7	12.06.43
F/Sgt	WHITEHEAD, H. P.	635	16.06.44	P/O	WILSON, K. C.	405	21.01.44

Rank	Name	Squadron	Date
P/O	WILSON. K. C.	405	21.01.44
Sgt	WILSON. P. C.	635	25.04.44
Sgt	WILSON. R.	7	09.04.43
F/Sgt	WILSON. R. MacL.	635	30.03.45
F/O	WILSON. T. F	635	10.04.44
Sgt	WILSON. W. M.	7	06.01.44
F/Sgt	WILSON. W. M.	7	22.11.43
Sgt	WILSON. W. P.	7	16.12.43
F/Sgt	WINLOW. D.	156	07.08.44
Sgt	WINTER. C. A.	35	24.12.44
F/Sgt	WINTER. J. S.	35	23.12.44
F/Sgt	WINTERBON. J. T.	156	23.06.43
Sgt	WINTERBURN. N. P.	156	29.09.43
F/O	WISBY. B. J.	156	17.12.44
F/Lt	WISHART. R. P.	97	30.01.44
P/O	WITT. E. M.	405	14.07.43
F/Sgt	WITTY. W. T.	582	29.10.44
S/L	WOLFE. D. L.. DFC	405	14.07.43
F/O	WOLFSON. I.	139	01.07.44
Sgt	WOLSTENCROFT. K.	35	04.07.43
P/O	WOLSTENHOLME. C. H.. DFM	7	27.09.43
F/Sgt	WOMAR. D. H. P.	635	30.08.44
Sgt	WOOD. A. J.	405(Ca)	25.07.43
F/Sgt	WOOD. A. H.	35	05.07.44
F/Lt	WOOD. D. T.. DFC	156	08.06.44
F/Sgt	WOOD. D. W.	7	20.05.44
F/Sgt	WOOD. D. S.	35	18.08.43
W/O	WOOD. G. R. N.	156	31.03.44
F/O	WOOD. J. K.	128	04.02.45
F/Sgt	WOOD. J. R.	156	29.01.45
F/Sgt	WOOD. J. B.	83	03.01.44
F/O	WOOD. K. R.	405	20.10.43
Sgt	WOOD. K.	156	02.12.43
W/O	WOOD. K. A.	156	02.12.43
Sgt	WOOD. N. H.	156	05.05.43
Sgt	WOOD. W. C. L.	7	04.09.43
F/Lt	WOOD. W. G.	105	22.10.43
P/O	WOODBURN. J. M.	156	25.02.44
F/Sgt	WOODCOCK. G.. DFM	7	27.09.43
F/Sgt	WOODCOCK. N.	83	18.06.43
F/Sgt	WOODCOCK. P.	156	17.06.43
F/O	WOODSEND. H. W.	156	27.07.43
F/Sgt	WOODWARD. N.	97	25.02.44
Sgt	WOODWARD. T. J.	156	04.04.43
F/O	WOODWARD. W.	7	29.06.44
Sgt	WOODWARD. W.	97	29.01.44
F/Sgt	WOOLF. G.	97	02.01.44
F/Sgt	WOOLISCROFT. A. K.	7	27.08.44
F/Sgt	WOOLNOUGH. W. O.	156	17.04.43
P/O	WOOLSTENHULME. H.	156	31.03.45
Sgt	WOOLVEN. F. E.	156	03.01.44
F/O	WOOLVEN. G. L.	139	12.06.44
F/Sgt	WORSDALE. J.. DFM	97	02.01.44
Sgt	WORSNOP. F. A.	83	13.05.43
F/O	WORT. H. E.	405	15.03.45
F/O	WORTH. I.	97	21.02.44
P/O	WORTHINGTON. R. F.	156	25.06.43
P/O	WRAGGE. G.	7	01.05.43
W/O	WRIGHT. B. C. N.	139(Ja)	31.10.43
F/Sgt	WRIGHT. C. H. L.. DFM	7	15.02.44
F/O	WRIGHT. G. H.	97	23.05.44
F/Lt	WRIGHT. J. H.. DFC	35	20.12.43
P/O	WRIGHT. J. R.	156	17.06.43
F/O	WRIGHT. J. E.	138	04.03.44
F/O	WRIGHT. J. H.. DFC	156	15.02.44
Sgt	WRIGHT. R. H.	35	18.11.43
F/O	WRIGHT. R. J.	405(Ca)	05.04.43
F/O	WRIGHT. R. J.	139(Ja)	27.05.44
S/L	WRIGHT. R. B.	156	24.08.43
W/O	WRIGHT. R.	35	20.02.44
F/Sgt	WRIGHT. S. J.	582	12.12.44
F/O	WYBORN. J. H.	7	22.03.44
P/O	WYN-EVANS. J. D.	7	25.04.44
P/O	WYNN. J. A.	35	29.11.44
F/Sgt	WYNN. R. G.	156	13.05.43
F/Sgt	WYNNE. R. I.	156	20.12.43
Sgt	YALLOP. R. F. A.	35	24.12.44
F/Lt	YANOVITCH. I. T.	635	06.01.45
Sgt	YEATES. G. H.	35	27.03.43
Sgt	YORK. R. I.	405	16.09.44
Sgt	YORK. W. I.	97	25.03.44
Sgt	YOUENS. L. W.	692	23.08.44
P/O	YOUNG. A. A.	1655 MTU	19.08.44
F/Sgt	YOUNG. G.. DFM	97	21.01.44
F/O	YOUNG. G. A.	635	04.06.44
Sgt	YOUNG. J. W.	35	16.04.43
Sgt	YOUNG. W. H.	7	05.05.44
F/Sgt	YOUNGER. R. G.	156	08.04.43
Sgt	ZIMMER. R.	405	02.01.44

---

* Denotes bar to decoration

Appendix I
British Pathfinder Operations as at March 1944

Issued by Luftwaffenfuhrungsstab Ic/Fremde Luftwaffen West

PREFACE

The success of a large-scale night raid by the RAF is in increasing measure dependent on the conscientious flying of the Pathfinder crews. The frictionless functioning of the attack is only possible when the turning points on the inward and outward courses, as well as the target itself, are properly marked. Lately, these attacks have been compressed into about 4 minutes for each wave averaging 120-150 aircraft.

Dense and high-reaching clouds, which hide the sky markers over the target, and exceptionally strong winds which blow the markers away quickly, represent an unpredictable barrier to Pathfinder operations and can often appreciably decrease the efficiency of an attack.

Another reason for the failure of a raid may lie in the partial failure of the first Pathfinders, the 'Initial Markers', to arrive, since experience has shown that succeeding Pathfinders, in spite of being equipped with H_2S and blind marking equipment, have allowed themselves to be influenced, to a certain extent, by the Initial Markers.

A: DEVELOPMENT

1.   The concentrated large-scale RAF raid on Cologne on 30/31 May 1942, during a full-moon night and with an alleged strength of more than 900 aircraft, was the first attempt to imitate the 'Focal Point' raids initiated by the German Air Force during this strategic air war against the British Isles during the years 1940 and 1941.

The lessons taught by this first large-scale raid, the increasingly high losses and the fact that the Hyperbola (Gee) navigation system could only be used in certain conditions, forced the AOC-in-C of Bomber Command to develop new systems of attack.

Using the German system of 'Illuminators' and 'Fire Raisers' as a model, the use of Pathfinders was developed towards the middle of August 1942, in order to bring on to the target all the aircraft, some with inexperienced, others with only medium-trained crews, and to allow the dropping of the bombs without loss of time.

2.   Air Vice-Marshal BENNET, at present still in command of these special units, was appointed Chief of the Pathfinder formations.

   This 35-year-old Australian — known as one of the most resourceful officers of the RAF — had distinguished himself as long ago as 1938 by a record long-range flight to South Africa in a four-engined seaplane which was launched in the air from a Sunderland flying boat (composite aircraft). In 1940, BENNET established the Transatlantic Ferry Command with aircraft of the Hudson type. As an example of his personal operational capabilities, an attack may be cited which he made on the German Fleet base at Trondheim.

   BENNET's appointment as Commander of the Pathfinder Formations is also based on the fact that he has written two standard books on astro-navigation.

3.   The use of Pathfinders in the first large-scale raids was comparatively primitive. Several particularly experienced crews were sent out first as Fire Raisers ahead of the Main Bomber Force and, in order to facilitate and ensure the location of the target, moonlit nights were especially favoured.

   Shortly after the formation of these Pathfinder groups, however, the principle of raids during moonlit nights was dropped and raids in dark cloudless periods began to take place.

   BENNET strove to render the raids independent of the weather and at the same time to make it easier for the less experienced crews to locate the target.

4.   At first there were only four bomber squadrons, equipped with Stirlings, Halifaxes, Lancasters and Wellingtons, and in January 1943 these units were organised into No 8 Bomber Group, the Pathfinder Group.

   The grouping of the Pathfinders into a Bomber Group of their own made it possible to standardise the equipment and the training, to put new ideas into operation and immediately to evaluate all experiences.

   During the course of 1943, the number of Pathfinder squadrons was increased to meet the increased demands, and among others, several Mosquito squadrons were detailed to the Pathfinder Group.

B: ORGANISATION AND EQUIPMENT
I: Organisation and Aircraft Types

1.   Eighth Bomber Group at present consists of: Five Lancaster squadrons, one Halifax squadron, four Mosquito squadrons (including two special bomber squadrons with 'Bumerang' [Oboe] equipment) and one Mosquito Met Flight.

   For further information concerning the organisation of these units, see 'Blue Book Series', Book 1: *The British Heavy Bomber Squadrons*.

2.   In addition to the normal navigational aids (see also 'Blue Book Series', Book 7: *British Navigation Systems*) the aircraft carry the following special equipment:

(a)   Four-engined aircraft (Lancaster and Halifax): Rotterdam (H_2S) for location of target and bombing without ground visibility;
hyperbola navigation instrument (Gee);
Identification Friend-Foe (IFF);
acoustic night-fighter warning instrument 'Monica';
visual night-fighter warning instrument (cathode ray oscilloscope) 'Fish Pond';
provision for bomb-release in the cabin as well as in the navigation room.

(b)   Twin-engined aircraft (Mosquito):
hyperbola navigation instrument (Gee);
special equipment according to mission, for example 'Bumerang' (Oboe);
the existence of Mosquitos equipped with H_2S have not as yet been definitely established. According to latest information available, this special equipment does not yet seem to have been installed in the Mosquito.

II: Personnel

1.   The crews are no longer composed mainly of volunteers as was formerly the case. Owing to the great demand and the heavy losses, crews are either posted to Pathfinder units immediately after completing their training, or are transferred from ordinary bomber squadrons. As in the past, however, special promotion and the Golden Eagle badge are big inducements to the crews.

At first Pathfinder crews had to commit themselves to 60 operational flights, but due to this high number there were insufficient volunteers, and the figure was decreased to 45.

After transfer to a Pathfinder squadron, a certain probationary period is undergone. The crews are not appointed Pathfinders and awarded the Golden Eagle until they have proved themselves capable of fulfilling the equipments by flying several operations (about 14) over Germany. Before the award of the Golden Eagle each member of the crew has to pass a special examination to show that he is fully capable of performing two functions on board, for example gunner and mechanic, or mechanic and bomb-aimer, etc.

2.   There is a special Pathfinder school (NTU Upwood Special School). All new crews, however, are sent on a special navigational course lasting 8-14 days at a Navigation Training Unit, where particularly experienced instructors, who have already completed their pathfinder tours, train the crews in the operation of the special equipment and put the final polish on their already good navigational training.

New Pathfinder crews fly training flights over Great Britain. These are usually made southwest from the Cambridge area, course then being set for the Isle of Man. On the return flight a large city, such as Birmingham or Manchester is approached, dummy bombing using H_2S is carried out, and target photographs are brought back to the home base. Flights of this kind are flown to a strict time schedule, just as in the case of a large-scale raid on Germany or the Occupied Western Territories, and are taken into consideration in the assessment of the crews as Pathfinders. If, on several occasions the schedule is not adhered to, the crew is transferred to an ordinary bomber squadron.

C: PATHFINDER OPERATIONS
I: General
The operational tactics of the Pathfinders have been under constant development ever since the earliest days, and even now cannot be considered as firmly established or completed. New methods of target location and marking, as well as extensive deceptive and diversionary measures against the German defences are evident in almost every operation.

Whereas the attacks of the British heavy bombers during the years 1942-43 lasted over an hour, the duration of the attack has been progressively shortened so that today, a raid of 800-900 aircraft is compressed into 20 minutes at the most. (According to captured enemy information, the plan for the raid on Berlin on 15/16 February 1944 called for about 900 aircraft in five waves of 4 minutes each.)

In spite of the increased danger of collision or of dropping bombs on other aircraft which must be taken into account, the aim has been achieved of allowing the German defences, the Commands as well as the defence weapons themselves, only a fraction of the time available to them during raids in the past.

The realisation of these aims was made possible by the conscientious work of the Pathfinder group and by the high training standard (especially regarding navigation) of the crews.

The markers over the approach and withdrawal courses serve as navigational aids for all aircraft and above all they help them to keep to the exact schedule of times and positions along the briefed course. Over the target, the markers of the Pathfinders enable all aircraft to bomb accurately without loss of time.

II: Markers
Up to date, the following markers have been identified:
TARGET MARKERS
(a) *Ground Markers:* also called cascade bombs, are red, green and yellow. Weather conditions govern the setting of the barometric fuse, whereby the Ground Marker container is detonated at a height varying from 800 to 5,000 metres, thereby releasing 60 flares which fall burning and burn out on the ground.

Ground markers are mainly dropped in the target area, but they are also sometimes used as Route Markers. Ground Markers are also dropped in 10/10ths cloud in order to illuminate the cloud base from below. When the clouds are thin, the crew can see the glare without difficulty. The average duration of burning of a Ground Marker is 3-4 minutes.

(b) *Sky Markers:* parachute flares, of which several are usually placed simultaneously. As a rule, the flares used are red ones from which, at regular intervals, quick-burning green flares ('dripping green stars') drop out.

Besides these, green Sky Markers with red stars and, although comparatively seldom, green Sky Markers with yellow stars are also used.

The bomb-aimers are for the most part briefed to drop their bombs into the middle of a group of Sky Markers. This corrects the opinion held until now that two sky markers are set, one to indicate the point of bomb release and the other to indicate the target.

(c) *White and Yellowish Flares:* used chiefly to illuminate the target. They are also sometimes used as dummy markers.

During raids in the autumn of 1943, the enemy attempted to mark a target approach corridor by setting numerous flares. It may be assumed that he dropped this system because of the heavy losses inflicted by German single-engined night-fighters in the target area.

ROUTE MARKERS
(a) *As Track Markers:* or Indicators, Sky Markers are used in 10/10ths cloud.
(b) *Ground Markers:* (Spotfires) are red, green or yellow; red and yellow are mainly used. A ground marker does not split up into different traces, but burns with a single bright light for from 3-8 minutes.

NEW KINDS OF MARKERS *(as yet not clearly identified)*
The enemy has often tried to introduce new kinds of markers with varying lighting effects:
(a) Among others, a quick-falling flare bomb was observed lately. After it hit the ground, a 90-metre high column of sparks was observed, which slowly descended in many colours. Confirmation, however, is not yet available.
(b) To designate the beginning and the end of the attack, a large reddish-yellow 'Fireball' has often been observed. Red flares fall from the Fireball and at low heights these again split up into green stars. The light intensity of these bombs is unusually high.
(c) The so-called red 'Multi-Flashes' are apparently used as Route Markers. They have been observed sparkling to the ground at intervals of 2-3 seconds.
(d) The enemy seem to have stopped using enormous 1,800kg-size flare bombs. The reasons for this could not be determined.

III: Execution of Pathfinder Operations
DIVIDING OF THE PATHFINDER CREWS
(a) At present, Pathfinder crews are divided into the following categories: Blind Markers, Blind Backers-up, Visual Backers-up, Visual Markers, Supporters — Pathfinder Main Force.

About 15% of the bombers used for a large-scale operation are Pathfinders. For example, out of a total strength of 900 aircraft, 120 would be Pathfinders, of which about 20 to 25 would be Blind Markers, 30 to 45 would be Blind and Visual Backers-up and 60 to 70 would be Pathfinder Main Force.

(b) *Blind Markers:* It is the duty of the Blind Markers to locate the target using H₂S and to set Ground or Sky Markers, or both, according to weather conditions, at zero hour minus 2 to 5 minutes.

The Blind Marker crews alone are responsible for the success or the failure of the raid. They are more strictly bound to the time schedule than all the other aircraft taking part in the raid. They are not allowed to drop their markers if the schedule is deviated from by more than one or two minutes, or if the instruments fail, or fail to indicate accurately. In such cases the Blind Marker aircraft automatically becomes part of the Pathfinder Main Force and must drop its HE bomb load exactly at zero hour.

With smaller targets, it is the duty of the Blind Markers to set flares over the target area, in order to illuminate it.

Another duty of good Blind Marker crews during the initial stages of the attack is not only to set new markers, but also to re-centre the attack. Experience has shown that the first aircraft of the Main Force drop their bombs near the Markers but that succeeding aircraft tend to drop them short of the target area during the progress of the attack. It is the duty of the Blind Markers detailed for this purpose to bring the bombing back to the original target by resetting the Markers past the first aiming point in the direction of withdrawal.

For several months past, the Blind Markers have had a further duty. In several operations it was repeatedly shown that errors in the navigation of the Main Force occurred owing to inaccurate wind forecasts. Experienced Pathfinders were therefore instructed to transmit their established wind calculations to England by W/T. Each Group picks up these reports and transmits them every half-hour to the airborne bombers.

(c) *Blind Backers-up:* The duties of the Blind Backers-up are similar to those of the Blind Markers, except that they fly in the bomber stream. Thus, they drop their Markers during the attack, also in accordance with a strict previously laid-down time schedule. Blind Backers-up are used to set Ground Markers and, above all, Sky Markers, which are always renewed by means of the H₂S and never visually.

(d) *Visual Backers-up:* In order to give new Pathfinder crews a chance to gain experience for future operations as Visual or Blind Markers, they are allowed to set new Markers visually; these, however, are always of a different colour. Theoretically, these Markers should be on, or very near to the original Markers, but as in practice this is very seldom the case, the impression given is that of the target being framed by markers. The bomb-aimers of the succeeding bombers are therefore briefed to release their bombs in the centre of the markers dropped by the Backers-up.

(e) *Visual Markers:* An attack on a small or pin-point target (definite industrial installations, dockyards, etc) necessitates still more accurate marking than is possible by the Blind Markers. The Visual Markers, therefore, locate the target visually from medium heights, sometimes from as low as 1,500 metres, and then release their Ground Markers on the centre of the target, in order to concentrate the attack of the high-flying bombers. The Visual Markers are aided by the illumination of the target area aided by several Blind Markers (Newhaven attack).

(f) *Supporters:* New crews who come from training units or other squadrons and who are to be trained as Pathfinders, fly their first operations in the Pathfinder Main Force. They carry only mines or HE bombs, arrive exactly at zero hour and try, at the first concentric bombing, to create the conditions necessary to allow the incendiary bombs of the succeeding waves to take full effect.

ROUTE MARKERS

Route markers are set by good Blind Marker crews and are renewed during the approach of the Bomber Stream by further good Blind Marker crews. Ground Markers (Spotfires) are sometimes set visually, and sometimes by instruments, but Sky Markers used as Track Markers or Indicators are set only by means of H_2S.

The routes of approach and withdrawal are generally identified by three Markers set at especially prominent points or turning points. The colours of these markers for any single night raid are usually the same: either red, green, yellow or white. It has often been observed that the Route Markers do not always lie exactly on course. They are set somewhat to one side so that the approaching bombers are not unnecessarily exposed to the danger of German night-fighters.

TARGET MARKERS

The Target Markers used will differ according to weather conditions. More Sky or Ground Markers are set, according to the visibility and cloud conditions prevailing. Up to date, the following methods of attack and target marking have been recognised:

(a) The 'Paramata' attack under a clear sky and with good visibility. Ground Markers are used only.

(b) The 'Wanganui' attack with 8-10/10ths cloud cover. Sky Markers only.

(c) The 'Musical Paramata' attack with 5-8/10ths cloud cover. Mainly Ground Markers, but some Sky Markers.

(d) The 'Newhaven' attack, in which the target area is illuminated by means of parachute flares, coupled with several Ground Markers.

(e) The 'Musical Wanganui' attack with 8-10/10ths cloud cover. Mainly Sky Markers, but some Ground Markers. This system of target marking has been used to a great extent lately during bad-weather operations.

DROPPING THE MARKERS

The setting of the Pathfinder Markers requires a great deal of experience. For this reason, training flights with Markers of all kinds are often carried out over Great Britain, serving for practical experiments with flares as well as for training purposes.

When the target area is already illuminated by previously dropped flares, the Ground Markers are released visually by means of the ordinary bomb-sight.

156

In cases where 10/10ths cloud or dark conditions are found over the target area, H_2S is used for dropping all Markers.

A great deal of experience is required for the setting of Blind Markers. Close co-operation between the navigator and the H_2S operator (see 'Blue Book Series', Book 7: *British Navigations Systems* for the difference between the two), who sit side by side in the navigation room, is the first essential for the precise setting of Markers by means of H_2S. Above all, drift must be calculated before the Markers are set, so that the Main attacking force only has to navigate on the Markers themselves.

NAVIGATION

The basis for all Pathfinder navigation is dead reckoning, and all other systems are only aids to check and supplement this. H_2S equipment is valueless without dead reckoning because the ground is not shown on the cathode ray tube screen as it is on a map.

To facilitate the location of the target, an auxiliary target, which experience shows to give a clear picture on the cathode ray tube, is given during the briefing. This auxiliary target should be as close to the actual target as possible, in order to eliminate all source of error. Cities, large lakes, or sometimes even the coastline features are used as auxiliary targets.

The course and the time of flight from the auxiliary target to the actual target are calculated in advance, taking the wind into consideration. The H_2S operator then knows that the main target will appear on the screen a given number of seconds after the auxiliary target has been identified.

MOSQUITO PATHFINDER OPERATIONS

The Mosquito aircraft have special duties as Pathfinders, concerning which the following information is available:

(a) *Setting ordinary Markers:* 15 to 20 minutes before the beginning of the actual attack, in conjunction with other Lancaster Pathfinders, over an auxiliary target.

(b) *Setting dummy Markers:* along the coast and at other places to indicate a false course and a false target.

(c) *Dropping so-called 'Fighter Flares':* these are imitations of the white and yellow flares dropped by German flare-carrying aircraft, to attract and divert German night-fighters.

   These dummy Markers are often 3-5 minutes flight from the target, or are sometimes placed at points off the approach and withdrawal courses, although always in some sort of relationship to these.

(d) *Dropping 'Window' from great heights:* this is so timed, after taking wind conditions into consideration, that a cloud of Window will be over the target when the first four-engined Pathfinders get there. This is made necessary by the fact that the target must be approached in straight and level flight, without evasive action, in order to get a good H_2S picture. It is supposed to eliminate to a great extent aimed fire by the Flak.

(e) *Release of single HE bombs:* 20 to 30 minutes after the main attack and observation of the results of the main attack.

(f) *Identification of pin-point targets:* for succeeding Mosquito waves by setting Ground Markers with the aid of 'Bumerang' (Oboe). The succeeding Mosquitos then drop their bombs visually on the marked target.

D: CONCLUSIONS

1.   Strong criticism from amongst their own units was at first levelled against the British Pathfinder operations, but they were able to prevail because of the successes achieved during the years 1943/44.

2.   The original assumption that the majority of bomber crews whould be less careful in their navigation once they became used to the help of the Pathfinders, and that therefore the total efficiency and success of raids would diminish, has hitherto not been confirmed.
     The navigational training and equipment of the ordinary British bomber crews has also been improved.

3.   The operational tactics of the Pathfinders cannot be considered as complete even today. There are, in particular, continual changes of all markers and marking systems.

4.   The trend of development will be towards making possible on one and the same night two or more large raids on the present scale, each with the usual Pathfinder accompaniment.

Distribution:
Units of the Rdl and Obdl
Luftflotten down to operational Gruppen
Flakabteilungen and Ln Regiments.

(*Source:* No 61008 Secret Ic/Foreign Air Forces; A/Evaluation West)

Appendix II
Hamish — A Testimonial

Squadron Leader Mahaddie, OC of 'A' Flight, 7th Squadron (Oakington) has been all his adult life in the RAF, having risen from Nuts & Bolts at Halton, via Cranwell as Flight Mechanic to his present position. He has been flying for more than eight years and is an excellent pilot with 13 more ops yet to do on his second Tour. Wing Commander Sellish selected him to put 'A' Flight Pathfinders on the top line. He has made that Flight what it is — and it is a damned fine outfit. Mahaddie is the living embodiment of the Halton idea, the repository of its tradition and a credit to any air force in the world. He has an absolutely exceptional capacity to select and foster talent, that is to say he's a born trainer and educationist both on the Station and off it. He has wide and various operational experience and could, I feel confident, do magnificently in Bomber Command in a job to do with Training. (He tends to think in terms of training — instinctively sharing Wellington's view that 'habit is 10 times nature'.) While the deuse of a man for thoroughness in detail, he is neither a machinet, a pedant nor a fanciful theorist but a shrewd and pawky Scot from Edinburgh with lots of humour and an altogether uncommon allowance of tact (both natural and acquired). He works like the devil: the RAF is his grand passion and takes precedence of all else, including his married life which is a happy one. He is an absolutely square-shooter with strong opinions, soberly but firmly expressed. Among them is one very strongly held to the effect that Commissions — other than purely ground jobs — should be granted in the field and only in the field. (This view is founded on much experience and, I take it, particularly on his latest experience with 'A' Flight, of which as it was handed him, he only kept one crew which somewhat shook the Wing Commander but I think he has been justified by the very fine results.)

I venture to suggest, Sir, that it would be to the benefit of the service were you personally to see this officer, so genuine an article and a man of such experience of the actual men and machinery of ops, and let him speak his mind.

He knows I am going to see you and that I hold him in high esteem. He knows, too, that I know a good deal about him for I have been at pains to draw him out as the representative of the Halton idea and tradition. But I don't think he knows that it is his capacity as Trainer — I have been in my time an educationist — that especially interests me, this sort of capacity being in my experience rare and Training as much a vocation as a posts! His interest in my seeing you is chiefly this business of Commissions and his persuasion that the 'High Ups' don't realise how much resentment the present system creates in operational establishments. He should, I do most strongly urge, be heard on this and any other topic which closely concerns personnel — from Nuts & Bolts to Squadron Leaders — on operational stations in Bomber Command.

At present he is 'stood down' for all but exceptional ops but is by way of fighting to get his 13 more ops done. His attitude to becoming a casualty is the old-fashioned fatalistic (bullet with my name on it) one, but should he 'buy it' — and we've lost some much experienced men since August — the RAF will lose something that has taken years in the making and that cannot easily be replaced. I haven't met anyone in the RAF who has the Halton tradition so strongly diffused throughout his whole life and conduct.

(Letter to Chief of the Air Staff, attributed to Robert Nicholls, 1942.)

Bibliography

Andrew E. Adam; *Beechwoods & Bayonets*; Barracuda Books
Gordon Anthony; *Air Aces*; Holm & Van Thal Ltd
C. Babington-Smith; *Evidence in Camera*; Chatto & Windus
P. R. Banks; *I Kept No Diary*; Airlife
Elmer Bendiner; *The Fall of Fortresses*; Souvenir Press
AVM D. C. T. Bennett; *Pathfinder*; Goodall
Chaz Bowyer; *For Valour*; William Kimber
Alan Bramson; *Master Airman*; Airlife
Alan Bramson; *The Funny Side of Flying*; Blandford Press
Anthony Brown; *A Bodyguard of Lies*; W. H. Allen & Co
Gp Capt L. Cheshire, VC, DSO, DFC; *No Passing Glory*; Andrew Boyle
Winston S. Churchill; *Memoirs of the World War*, Vol II; Bonanza Books
Aileen Clayton; *The Enemy is Listening*; Hutchinson
Alan W. Cooper; *Beyond the Dams to the Tirpitz*; William Kimber
Len Deighton; *Bomber*; Jonathan Cape
Alexander Frater; *Beyond the Blue Horizon*; Penguin
Philip Gibb; *The New Elizabethans*; Hutchinson
Guy Gibson, VC; *Enemy Coast Ahead*; Michael Joseph Ltd
J. D. G. Gilman, and John Clive; *KG 200*; Pan Books
E. B. Haslam; *Cranwell*; HMSO
Sir Philip de la Fert Joubert; *The Third Service;* Thames & Hudson
David Kahn; *Hitler's Spies*; Hodder & Stoughton
Wg Cdr C. T. Kimber; *Son of Halton*; Thorley Publications
C. E. Kingsford-Smith & C. T. P. Ulm; *The Great Trans-Pacific Flight*;
    Hutchinson
T. E. Lawrence; *The Mint*; Jonathan Cape
Laddie Lucas; *Out of the Blue*; Hutchinson
Laddie Lucas; *Flying Colours*; Hutchinson
Charles Messenger; *Bomber Harris*; Arms & Armour Press
Martin Middlebrook; *The Berlin Raids*; Viking
Martin Middlebrook and Chris Everitt; *The Bomber Command War Diaries*;
    Viking
Wilbur H. Morrison; *Fortress Without a Roof*; W. H. Allen
Gordon Musgrove; *Operation Gomorrah*; Jane's

Gordon Musgrove; *Pathfinder Force*; MacDonald & Jane's
Robert S. Nielsen; *With the Stars Above*; Published Privately
Murray Peden; *A Thousand Must Fall*; Canada's Wings
John S. Peskett; *Strange Intelligence*; Hale
Ursula Powys-Lybbe; *The Eye of Intelligence*; William Kimber
Dr Alfred Price; *German Bombers of World War II*; Hylton Lacy Publications
Dr Alfred Price; *Instrument of Darkness*; MacDonald & Jane's
Denis Richards; *Portal of Hungerford*; Heinemann
Sir Robert Saundby; *Air Bombardment*; Chatto & Windus
Dudley Saward; *Victory Denied*; Buchan & Enright
Dudley Saward; *Bomber Harris*; Cassell, Buchan & Enright
Dudley Saward; *Bomber's Eye*; Cassell & Castle
Air Cdre John Searby; *The Everlasting Arms*; William Kimber
Ron Smith, DFM; *Rear Gunner Pathfinder*; Goodall
William Stevenson; *A Man Called Intrepid*; Book Club Associates
John Terraine; *The Right of the Line*; Hodder & Stroughton
Kenneth Wakefield; *The First Pathfinders*; William Kimber
Sir Charles Webster, and N. Frankland; *The Strategic Air Offensive Against Germany 1939-45* Vols 1-4; HMSO
F. W. Winterbotham; *Secret & Personal*; William Kimber

Index